FOR PEDESTRIANS ONLY

FOR PEDESTRIANS ONLY

PLANNING, DESIGN, AND MANAGEMENT OF TRAFFIC-FREE ZONES

**BY ROBERTO BRAMBILLA
AND GIANNI LONGO**

WITH A FOREWORD BY BERNARD RUDOFSKY

WHITNEY LIBRARY OF DESIGN
an imprint of
Watson-Guptill Publications / New York

To the memory of Duccio Turin

Copyright © 1977 by Whitney Library of Design

First published 1977 in the United States by Whitney Library of Design
an imprint of Watson-Guptill Publications,
a division of Billboard Publications, Inc.
1515 Broadway, New York, N.Y. 10036

Library of Congress Cataloging in Publication Data
Brambilla, Roberto, 1939–
  For pedestrians only.
  Bibliography: p.
  Includes index.
  1. Pedestrian facilities design. I. Longo, Gianni,
1947–   joint author. II. Title.
TE279.5.B68   711'.551   76-55752
ISBN 0-8230-7174-X

Manufactured in U.S.A.

First Printing, 1977

Contents

Foreword

The authors, best known for their previous endeavors to make Americans aware of what causes the plight of cities, here and abroad, now have drawn on their experience to provide a guide for planners, town fathers, and imperfectly enlightened citizens in general on how to give back that no-man's-land, the urban street, to those no-account people, pedestrians. Mindful of the undertaking's vastness, they confined themselves to the pith of the matter: to purge city centers of cars.

This they do with exemplary tact. Once past the generalizations, they present a meticulously researched study of pedestrianization in which text, pictures, and statistics cover the entire procedure on how to attend to malformed or ailing downtowns, from diagnosis over surgery to post-operative treatment. Twenty case histories from the United States, Canada, and Europe are adduced to raise the reader's level of ordinary consciousness.

The complexity of the subject may not be immediately apparent. Technical and financial problems pall before psychological ones since making pedestrian streets come to life requires everybody's participation. Alas, the nation has been devoted to sedentariness too long. Urban and surburban children grow up unaware that human legs once were commonly used for locomotion; "I would run away from home if I knew how to drive," says the tot in a *New Yorker* cartoon. At best, Americans rush. The stroller, in their eyes, equals a bum.

To induce the urbanite to leave his home with its batteries of entertainment machines, the new walking street must needs offer—well—entertainment. According to the author's blueprint, it holds out the promise of playlots, playgrounds, and programmed happenings while people loath to walk can be sure to find benches. All of which adds up to that American specialty, the mall. The pedestrian mall is what this book is about, says the introduction.

By definition, a mall is an umbrageous promenade, usually the constituent part of a park, favored by fashionable society. L'Enfant's Washington Mall, conceived more or less along these lines, was a flop. Although most respectable European cities have their mile-long labyrinthine walkways, they do not seem to be malleable. A Paris mall or a Rome mall would be patently absurd. Latin American cities are in a category of their own. They always banned wheeled traffic in downtown districts during business hours as a matter of course and, let it be noted, without wasting time on debates or polls, without the outlay of a penny.

Clearly, the 70 North American malls discussed here signal a very nearly native trend. Their success speaks volumes. The main task for the towns now is to elevate the pedestrian street from a design concept to a social institution. The newly created legroom might even encourage the nation to take the necessary steps toward an urban utopia—a Declaration of Rights of the Pedestrian.

Bernard Rudofsky

Acknowl-edgments

This book is the result of a public information program on planning, design, and management of traffic-free zones carried out by the Institute for Environmental Action, in association with Columbia University Center for Advanced Research in Urban and Environmental Affairs.

The project was initially sponsored by the Graham Foundation for Advanced Studies in the Fine Arts, the Rockefeller Family Fund, and the National Endowment for the Arts.

We want to express our gratitude to James S. Polshek, the Dean of the Graduate School of Architecture and Planning at Columbia University, for his encouragement and advice during the development of the entire project. We also acknowledge the contributions of Carter H. Manney, Jr., Harold Snedcof, and Robert McNulty for their trust in our commitment, their confidence in the project, and their willingness to help spread support for it.

The inauguration of the Madison Avenue Mall in midtown Manhattan was scheduled for 1973. It was to be the longest pedestrian street in North America. Our first task was to produce a public education program and an exhibit in support of the project. During this phase we received the encouragement and endorsement of Lewis Mumford, Jane Jacobs, Bernard Rudofsky, William H. Whyte, Saul Steinberg, Niccolo Tucci, and Renato Bazzoni. We are deeply indebted to them and to Jaquelin T. Robertson, Don C. Miles, Brian Richards, Ray Bradbury, and Thomas R. Reid III. Their contribution to our program is documented in *More Streets for People*, published in 1973 by the Italian Art & Landscape Foundation.

When the Madison Mall was defeated, our exhibit was postponed until October 1974. By this time we had received further support from the Kaplan Fund, Columbia University, and the Guggenheim Foundation.

The North American tour of the exhibit "More Streets for People" proved to be a most valuable vehicle for collecting information about pedestrian projects throughout the United States and Canada and for establishing contacts with municipal authorities, architects, and planners advocating the creation of pedestrian streets in their cities. Joe Silver, Claude Shostel, Frank Gilmore, Joseph Canizaro, Marjorie Lyman, Arthur M. Skolnik, and Nancy Sussman worked on this stage of the project.

The availability of all this information induced us to write about it. Robert McNulty took the initiative to involve both HUD (the U.S. Department of Housing and Urban Development) and CEQ (the President's Council on Environmental Quality) into an interagency agreement to produce four publications for the U.S. Government Printing Office. Charles Gueli, Marylin Klein, and Merril Ware enthusiastically supported this undertaking.

The year of the United Nations Conference on Human Settlements, 1976, coincided with the last phase of our program. Thanks to Enrique Peñalosa, Secretary General of the Habitat Conference, and the late Duccio Turin, the Deputy Director of UNEP (the United Nations Environment Program), dedicated the 1976 World Environment Day to traffic-free zones and sponsored a special demonstration program coordinated by the Institute for Environmental Action. As part of this program, 136 cities throughout the world agreed to ban automobile traffic from selected downtown streets on June 5, 1976—World Environment Day—and to monitor the results of the experiments.

The German Marshall Fund of the United States sponsored the production of a handbook addressing municipal authorities of UN member countries attending the Habitat Conference in Vancouver, Canada. We owe the successful completion of this handbook to Benjamin H. Read, Peter Weitz, and Kenneth Orsky.

The formulation, management, and promotion of such an extensive program could not have been accomplished without the help of the principal collaborators and members of the staff of the Institute for Environmental Action. In particular we want to thank Virginia Dzurinko for handling the administration of the project and creatively contributing to its editing and promotion; Ingrid Bengis, Robert Coombs, and Margot Villecco for the editing; Igor Jozsa for the coordination of urban design aspects; Robert Cook, Glenn Goldmann, Rita Khurana, Alessandra Latour, and Don C. Miles for their collaboration in the research and organization of the information; Kenneth Halpern and Lars Lerup for their constructive criticism. We also thank Susan Braybrooke, Susan Davis, and James Craig of the Whitney Library of Design for their help in making *For Pedestrians Only* a reality. Thank you all again.

Introduction

In recent years, there has been a barrage of predictions about the imminent death of the cities. Critics and disaster buffs have cataloged in minute detail the symptoms of every possible urban disease, and today there is little doubt that cities are in serious trouble. Yet, despite constant fiscal and social problems, the cities have not died, though the turmoil which has plagued them continues to exist and many of their fundamental problems remain unsolved.

Perhaps this is part of the fascination of urban pedestrian malls; they represent a positive response to some urban problems and, what is more, even sound like fun. They conjure up fantasies of outdoor cafes with parasols, play areas filled with laughing children, bustling shop activities, and an oasis of trees, grass, flowers, and fountains in the middle of the urban morass.

The reality of the pedestrian mall, however, is quite different, and the reality is what this book is about. Pedestrian malls are not urban idylls created in an artist's eye, but practical solutions to some urgent urban problems—solutions which are created in the offices of architects, lawyers, government officials, traffic planners, merchant associations, and community groups, among others. A mall can be successful only insofar as it can cope with the problems facing it, which include deteriorating economic and physical situations, a declining quality of life, pollution, congestion, and the flight of the middle class. In addition to alleviating these problems, a pedestrian mall can bring new life and liveliness to the downtown area, so that people will come to the mall for what it offers, not because there are only unsatisfactory alternatives.

A pedestrian mall is an instrument for action, especially in relation to urban economics, environmental quality, and social well-being. In the area of economics (which is often the primary reason for a mall's creation), pedestrianization will hopefully improve the business of local merchants and the livelihood of local residents by drawing people, not only from the city proper, but from surrounding regions, into the downtown area. In many cities, real estate values have appreciated and the tax base has increased several fold following the implementation of a pedestrian zone.

WHAT IS A TRAFFIC-FREE ZONE?

The term "traffic-free zone" has been applied to a wide range of urban spaces, such as parks, plazas, and promenades, to name a few. Recently, however, the expression has been used to define a more specific concept, indicating *urban areas where private motor vehicles have been banned and priority has been given to pedestrian movements and public transportation.* There are various types of traffic-free zones that fit this definition. The following are analyzed in this book:

Pedestrian districts are created by eliminating vehicular traffic over a portion of a city—considered as a unit for architectural, historic, or commercial reasons. European cities have often adopted this type of traffic-free zoning because it suits the physical conditions of historic central areas.

Pedestrian Streets are isolated, individual streets from which traffic has been eliminated. Emergency vehicles, however, have access, and service and delivery trucks are allowed during restricted hours. The term "pedestrian street" is synonymous with *pedestrian mall*. "Mall" is widely used in North America to describe areas where all vehicular traffic has been banned from a central street.

The pedestrian mall concept emerged in new commercial shopping centers that were developed in American suburbs after World War II. Urban pedestrian malls are an attempt to create favorable innercity shopping conditions analogous to those offered by suburban shopping malls.

In most pedestrian streets or malls, the entire roadway is filled to grade between curbs. Pedestrian-oriented amenities are introduced to encourage pedestrian movement. An emergency lane is always incorporated into the design, allowing access for policy vehicles, ambulances, and fire trucks.

Transitways are pedestrian precincts that restrict, but do not totally ban, vehicles. Some transitways are also called malls. Private cars are usually prohibited; but buses, trams, and taxis are often allowed, subject to pedestrian priorities. Motor routes are narrowed to one or two lanes of roadway at the maximum, while the rest of the street and sidewalk area is repaved and furnished for the pedestrians.

Semimalls are very similar to transitways in their design. However, private traffic is not prohibited. Access may be limited, and severe speed limits are normally imposed on through-traffic. Semimalls are sometimes an interim step toward a larger traffic ban. They may also be considered as partial improvements for the pedestrian environment, with goals similar to those of mini-parks, small urban plazas, or pedestrian concourses.

Enclosed malls are city streets that have been totally enclosed and climatized. They offer physical conditions similar to those of suburban shopping centers. Their design is very complex and the cost is almost prohibitive, placing them out of the reach of smaller cities. However, enclosed malls have particular application in colder climates.

Reducing the number of motor vehicles in central districts has the potential for improving the city's environmental quality. Creating traffic-free zones will hopefully lead to reduced street levels of noise and air pollution, the preservation of historic districts, and restoration of architectural landmarks. At the same time, such zoning provides incentives for building owners and operators to improve the physical appearance of their stores, homes, and offices. This in turn can stimulate the upgrading of city services. Even the safety in downtown areas increases, since pedestrian zones eliminate dangerous confrontations between cars and people.

The social impact of a mall can be tremendous, drawing all ages and social strata, tourists and residents alike, into these areas, where they spend longer and more leisurely periods of time. As a result of the generous availability of public space, pedestrian-oriented amenities can be introduced and a wide range of special activities promoted.

But the mere notion of a pedestrian zone cannot perform any of the benefits just described. It takes a project that is designed and maintained with each of these purposes in mind throughout the entire implementation process and for as long as the pedestrian zone continues.

Many pedestrian malls have been built as an omnibus solution to all of a city's problems, and in such cases they have usually failed. Unless a traffic-free zone is conceived in the context of an overall effort to solve a city's problems, it cannot succeed for long. Furthermore, the project must be designed at a time and for a place where it can function as designed. Some malls have simply been built too late; if stores and people have already deserted the downtown, adding cars to the list is unlikely to turn the tide.

These are some of the problems which those who support a mall must consider. Is the timing right? Is a pedestrian street the answer to the nature and scope of particular problems? Is it possible to generate the necessary monetary, administrative, and popular support? To answer these questions, it is necessary to know what an urban mall is and how it works.

Pedestrian zones are both physical and institutional entities, both of which must be understood and developed. The physical aspects of a mall are usually thought of in terms of visible characteristics: so many blocks long, with this kind of paving, and those kinds of chairs. Actually, some important physical components are invisible. In fact, the greatest costs of a mall are usually the things we never see, such as rebuilt or relocated underground utilities.

What we do see is a repaired and reproportioned street without cars, or with limited vehicular access. Sidewalks may have disappeared altogether, merging into what was formerly the street. Often the space is brightened with patterns of different colors and materials. The storefronts may have been renovated, sometimes with stylistic unity in signage or advertising. Sometimes, the whole pedestrian district will have a theme, such as the one in New London, which stresses a nautical atmosphere appropriate to this maritime community.

A pedestrian mall often features special amenities for relaxation, entertainment, or broader and more intimate communication. The space may be landscaped with trees, flowers, and water. Fountains can be a focus of activity for children as well as adults. Street lighting is usually proportioned to pedestrian scale, with variations for dramatic effect. Amphitheater or speaker platforms are often included in a mall's design to encourage use of the street as a public place. Benches and tables provide places for socializing.

Whether or not these amenities work as planned, however, depends on both their design and administration. In Springfield, Illinois, for example, there is a playground area protected from the street by a waist-high concrete wall; inside there is a variety of playground equipment, but there are no children. They and their parents are afraid to enter a space where no one can see in or out.

The location of physical amenities will also determine their use. Benches that are set apart into conversational circles will draw people who are interested in other people. A bench near a playground will attract parents and others who want to watch children play.

Nonphysical factors also give a mall identity. The operation of public space, such as whether or not street vendors are allowed, sitting and strolling encouraged, fund raising per-

mitted, will affect who frequents a pedestrian zone and why.

Of itself, a mall represents a series of policy decisions about zoning, building, health and safety codes, traffic regulations, taxes and assessments, and other maintenance and operation practices. These policy decisions have historically varied from country to country, city to city, though there are common elements which highlight the evolution of the pedestrian strollway as both a pleasure and a growing necessity.

In European cities, pedestrian streets were first introduced in the late 1940s. Following the destruction of World War II, city administrators and planners had the chance to carry out extensive renovation of inner-city areas as part of reconstruction programs. Most planners opted for the accommodation of the city center to increased traffic and new construction. Streets were widened and entire blocks demolished. As a result, the character of many historic city cores was lost.

At the same time, however, some highly revolutionary traffic-free experiments were being conducted. Rotterdam's Lijnbaan and Stockholm's Torg adopted policies which separated not only types of traffic, but urban functions, in an approach which anticipated the change in planning that was to come later.

At that time, however, it was impossible to predict the explosion of private motor traffic which became characteristic of European cities. Within a short time, it became apparent that even the most drastic measures taken by planners to modernize core areas were not sufficient to contend with the sheer volume of cars which appeared during the postwar boom. The radial pattern of European cities exaggerated the difficult conditions until congestion simply became intolerable. Deliveries were delayed, efficiency was impaired, environmental conditions declined, and the safety of pedestrians was threatened.

By the late 1950s, these conditions had reached alarming proportions. It was clear that private cars had to be restricted in historic cores if these areas were to survive. Traffic restriction became a widely adopted policy; the trend gained momentum, and by 1975, nearly every major city had banned cars from significant portions of its historic district and retail areas.

In North America, the idea of traffic-free zones did not take firm hold until the early 1960s. People had been steadily deserting cities for the suburbs, and after World War II this exodus picked up as the number of cars and highways increased. The car took people away from high taxes, crime, pollution, racial unrest, and income disparities. In the suburbs, land was cheap, population density lower, and life styles more homogeneous.

City cores suffered a great loss of vitality. Streets became congested with commuter cars during the day. At night, these same streets were deserted and intimidating. Pollution, accidents, and crime increased as a result. Cities were losing not only high and middle-income residents, not jobs, customers, and tax revenues.

The U.S. government tried to balance urban decline with the 1954 Urban Renewal Program. However, this program fell far short of its goals since "renewal" was primarily manifested by demolition of highly integrated and vital neighborhoods to make way for civic and corporate structures. The Urban Renewal Program also brought with it more urban expressways, which made it easier to leave the city, and even more people were lost.

Suburban shopping centers also struck a blow at city vitality by offering convenient alternatives to downtown shopping. Ironically, the design of these centers, which maximized the benefits of traffic-free environments, became the basis for downtown revitalization.

Beginning in the early 1960s, urban advocates such as Lewis Mumford, Bernard Rudofsky, Jane Jacobs, and William H. Whyte, as well as architects such as Victor Gruen, began emphasizing the potential of street life in cities. They pointed to European pedestrian experiments as the model for a new approach to renewal.

The studies of leading sociologists, such as Herbert Gans and Nathan Glazer, also pointed out the failure of early urban renewal attempts. They offered a new perspective on city revitalization based on the relationship between physical and social change.

The combination of professional recommendations and widespread dissatisfaction on the part of downtown businessmen and residents led to a rearrangement of urban priorities. City planners and administrators shifted their focus, and the general public changed its attitude toward the potential of the city.

By the mid-1960, following the example of well-publicized projects, such as Kalamazoo, Michigan; Miami Beach, Florida; and Pomona, California, the process of banning cars from central commercial streets was well on its way. Planners focused on new legislation, methods of financing, and public involvment, thinking to rebuild the image of "Main Street" as a center of trade, society, and politics.

And as American cities were beginning to realize the potential of traffic-free zoning, the suburban dream was starting to crumble. Increased environmental awareness, the shortage and skyrocketing prices of fossil fuels, and the general concern about energy tarnished the shiny image of suburban living. Furthermore, many of the social problems that had driven people from the cities had followed them, but the richness of urban life had failed to take root in suburban soil.

As a result, people took a new look at cities and recognized not only their physical and economic assets, but their human potential. Building restoration and conversion, neighborhood rehabilitation, public transportation, and revitalization of public open spaces became key issues. Today, this new approach is beginning to alter the image of American urban life.

Planning policies are now being tailored to suit human needs. City streets are being redesigned for pedestrians, empty lots and alleys are being recycled into mini-parks and playgrounds, and sidewalks are being widened. Developers are being encouraged to provide pedestrian amenities, such as plazas, arcades, fountains, and street furniture, as part of their construction.

Whether or not this trend will continue and lead to a renaissance of urban centers depends, in part, on government policies. But it also depends on the willingness of citizens to take action on behalf of themselves. This can happen only through increased awareness of the complex interrelations of urban issues and an understanding of the resources and opportunities for self-help and advocacy planning that are available to all urban dwellers.

"This city is going to hell! That used to be a parking lot."

B. B. Tobey; © 1975, the New Yorker Magazine, Inc.

Why Pedestrian Zoning: An Appraisal of Basic Goals

The decision to create a pedestrian zone requires an understanding of the reasons why similar projects have been undertaken and a familiarity with the various approaches to establishing and maintaining traffic-free streets. The goals of traffic-free zoning may vary from situation to situation, but the intentions, problems, and aspirations behind them are all interconnected. For the purposes of this book, we have grouped them under four major headings: Traffic Management, Economic Revitalization, Environmental Improvements, and Social Benefits.

Stuttgart, Germany.

1

Traffic Management

It is only within the past 20 years that pedestrianization has been used as a means for controlling traffic in crowded city centers, which typically have a high density of vehicles and a wide range of activities. In the central business districts of large American cities, in smaller towns threatened with the development of suburban shopping facilities, as well as in the historic cores of European cities, the creation of traffic-free streets represents the opening up of new territory.

IMPROVING MOBILITY IN CENTRAL BUSINESS DISTRICTS

As a functional reality, a pedestrian mall simply discourages the use of private vehicles. The continuity and development of a mall's success, however, depend on its being part of an overall traffic plan, which is capable of solving the technical and human problems of transporting workers, shoppers, and residents from one place to another with a maximum of comfort and ease through the use of low-cost, efficient, and attractive public transportation, while at the same time providing for goods delivery. In addition, it must confront the potential problems created by increased traffic on surrounding streets.

The most popular argument against traffic-free zones is that the elimination of cars from certain streets merely forces them onto adjacent streets, which then become more congested. The threat of such a situation was successfully used against the proposed closing of Madison Avenue in New York City.

Experience, however, seems to negate this theory. A recent study on the effects of reducing traffic in selected areas summarizes its findings as follows: "The amount of motor vehicle travel in any area is, in part, dependent on the amount of available space. . . ." This simply means that if there is less space for cars there will be fewer cars. The same report indicates that "rather than building to a standstill, congestion will reach a maximum point where the average speed in a central business district decreases to eight miles per hour. Beyond this point, traffic disappears. People turn to other kinds of transportation. Therefore, reducing the amount of vehicular space will not create a monumental traffic jam. It will simply reduce the amount of vehicular traffic."[1]

A wide variety of strategies have been adopted to permit deliveries to stores which face pedestrian areas. Rear servicing has been the most successful method. However, this has not always been possible, especially in European cities where the layout of historic districts does not provide the necessary parallel streets.

In cases where rear service has proved impractical, deliveries within a pedestrian area have been permitted on a restricted basis. In Norwich, England, for example, goods are carried in hand trucks. In Venice, Europe's largest pedestrian city, goods have been hand delivered for centuries.

Complaints from larger retail establishments—such as furniture stores for whom size and volume are important factors and banks which are unable to remove their valuables at the usual hours and have had to rearrange their schedules—have not yet been met with adequate solutions. Although a central delivery system would seem to be the most practical, it has turned out to be prohibitively expensive, and no alternative system has been found.

There has been more success for shoppers for whom ease of movement, particularly in extended areas, is essential. In Europe, where people are accustomed to walking, very few people-moving systems have been adopted. Mini-buses used on pedestrian streets in Leeds, England, were removed after a short period of time because their discomfort to shoppers far outweighed their other advantages.

People-movers have been employed more frequently in the United States. For example, Pomona, Fresno, and Sacramento, in California, have introduced colorful, electrically powered vehicles for shoppers' convenience. In Lake Charles, Louisiana, the city decided to operate a tractor-hauled wagon to pick up shoppers on the mall and carry them to an adjacent parking lot.

Transitways are a compromise between a completely traffic-free district and the need for a shoppers' transportation system on the mall. Recently, this kind of pedestrian street has become increasingly popular in North America, because federal and state funds are more readily available for transitways than they are for traffic-banned areas. Nicollett Mall in Minneapolis is a successful example. Only buses are allowed on the street.

Even so, shoppers and merchants still complain about noise and fumes.

Discouraging Use of Private Vehicles The impact of pedestrian streets on downtown conditions has been strengthened in a number of cities by taking additional measures to discourage people from driving into the central area. Reducing the number of parking spaces, increasing parking rates, and instituting time restrictions for parking have all proved very effective strategies. A large residential population in an urban center creates the problem of providing parking for residents, while discouraging parking by commuters. This situation occurs more frequently in Europe than in the United States.

Reducing parking facilities, however, does not eliminate through traffic. A standard solution to this problem has been the creation of traffic diversion routes. Almost all large cities are surrounded by major arteries which allow different degrees of access to the central area. Primarily in Europe, inner rings have been created to allow for circulation around pedestrian zones, and one-way loops have been constructed to accommodate service and deliveries to the area. In a number of cities, a combination of peripheral parking, improved public transportation, and a ring road was adopted. Shoppers and commuters coming into the city by car use a mini-bus shuttle between parking areas and downtown. Chicago, among other cities, has experimented with such a system.

Encouraging Use of Public Transportation Improved public transportation is fundamental to the success of a pedestrian zone. Trains, buses, and subways have always been necessary for people who do not own cars. Once traffic restrictions are initiated in an urban center, however, public transportation provides the easiest access for everyone to shopping and business areas. The most common measures for increasing the capacity and appeal of public transport have been creating additional bus stops, increasing the frequency of service, introducing reserved lanes for public transit, and extending routes. Some cities have introduced express buses that provide nonstop service from peripheral areas.

ANNUAL GROWTH RATE OF POPULATION AND PRIVATE AUTOMOBILES IN SELECTED CITIES: 1960–1970

Setting goals for the implementation of a traffic ban requires the recognition of existing trends in car ownership. During the past 10 years, private automobile ownership in large cities has increased far more rapidly than the population. The number of private cars has risen an average of 10 percent a year, with even higher peaks in developing countries. Data obtained from World Bank Sector Policy Paper, *Urban Transport* (Washington: World Bank, May 1975).

Kuopio, Finland.

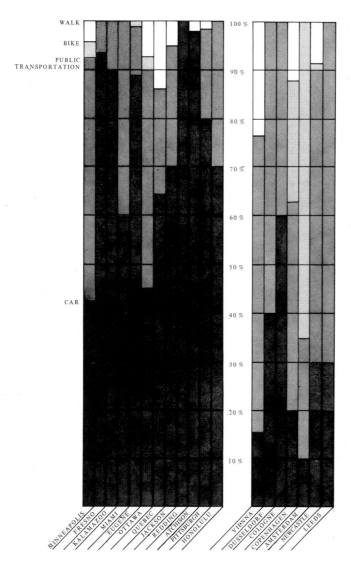

A comparative analysis of transportation modes used in journeys to work shows that accessibility to American and Canadian downtowns depends almost totally on cars. This explains the emphasis on providing better access to and parking facilities in North American city centers.

Great efforts have also been made to construct new subway systems and to improve those already in existence. However, only large cities can rely on subways, since their cost is much higher than that of surface transit. Many passengers must be carried per hour to make the system economically feasible.

Yet another alternative in the area of public transportation has been the development of "para-transit" systems, such as car pools and subscription car and bus services. Para-transit, which is now operational in many cities, also includes demand-response services, such as shared taxis and dial-a-ride service.

Para-transit has gained popularity because of its adaptibility to specific traffic-control objectives and because it affords a change from poor conventional public transportation systems. Furthermore, these systems have proved particularly useful to the elderly and the handicapped. Para-transit is inexpensive and can be quickly organized. The flexibility of the systems allows for gradual implementation which can parallel other improvements in public transportation.

Dial-a-ride is a basic form of para-transit, incorporating features of both bus and taxi travel. Vehicles are dispatched in response to telephone requests. The bus or taxi carries a person to the requested destination, while at the same time picks up and delivers other passengers who have called. The number of stops depends on the type of service, time of day, and other passengers who have called.

In the United States, the costs of para-transit systems have been subsidized. Danville, Illinois, has used federal funds to provide a "subscription" transportation service for 750 senior citizens and the handicapped.[2]

Combining para-transit measures with existing conventional transport systems increases mobility and, at the same time, decreases the use of private automobiles.

IMPROVING ACCESS TO CENTRAL BUSINESS DISTRICT

In a number of North American cities, pedestrian streets have been created to provide better accessibility to downtown stores and offices. Therefore, emphasis has been on reorganizing traffic patterns, rather than reducing the number of automobiles.

Smaller American cities rely on cars to bring people downtown and usually do not have sophisticated public transportation. Any reduction of access routes into the city center could cause a serious loss of activity in the central business district. Furthermore, because of the grid layout of most cities, banning cars from one street can have repercussions on all downtown traffic. Therefore, pedestrian streets must be created in conjunction with revised traffic patterns. And because cars remain the primary mode of transportation in such cases, adequate parking facilities must be ensured. Failure to take these two elements into account not only affects downtown traffic, but can also jeopardize the success of a traffic-free zone.

Revising Circulation Patterns The point of traffic-free zoning is not to eliminate the automobile, but to separate vehicular and pedestrian movement. In order to accomplish this, most cities have reduced, as much as possible, the number of streets crossing the pedestrian zone, and have rerouted crosstown traffic so that major streets do not cut through pedestrian areas.

In Providence, Rhode Island, a traffic-free zone was created in the central business district by eliminating all crosstown traffic from the area and providing only limited access for deliveries. Ten bus stops, many of which were new, were established around the pedestrian core. In Fresno, California, eliminating cars has transformed the city core into a completely vehicle-free superblock.

Providing Parking Facilities In order to compete wth the convenience of suburban shopping centers, American cities must provide enough space for people to park near traffic-free zones. Parking is usually a problem in downtown areas, and the creation of pedestrian zones adds to the problem by eliminating a number of spaces. Usually, surface lots have provided most of the off-street parking near pedestrian malls, but they have become battlegrounds of the fight for space between shoppers and downtown employees. Furthermore, these lots have usually provided only indirect access to pedestrian areas. Long-term parking for commuters has been constructed separately.

Part of the success of Nicollet Mall

in Minneapolis has been the creation of fringe parking areas which greatly improved downtown accessibility. In Springfield, Illinois, creation of a traffic-free zone, construction of a parking garage, and restoration of an historic building were part of the same operation. Two streets were closed to traffic, creating a plaza around the city's Old Capitol, which was being rebuilt to resume its original appearance. When the building was dismantled, the city decided to build a parking garage beneath it. Today, there is a 45-foot deep, two-level garage with a 450-car capacity, directly beneath the Old Capitol.

People-mover along Miami Beach pedestrian mall.

Moving goods in downtown Stockholm.

Traffic Planner Van Ginkel's proposal for a mini-bus.

Economic Revitalization

For a number of years, improving business conditions in downtown shopping areas has been a top priority in American cities. Because of rapid suburban expansion, traditional Main Street shopping has suffered such severe setbacks that in many places it has begun to seem a relic doomed to extinction.

City planners and administrators have been attracted to traffic-free zones as a strategy for reversing this trend. They are realizing that a pedestrian area, when properly implemented and managed, has the potential for helping central business districts remain viable commercially through a combination of improved retail trade, new investors, and new development.

IMPROVING DOWNTOWN RETAIL TRADE

To compete with regional shopping centers, however, downtown commercial districts must offer a wide range of shopping opportunities to customers and present a vital economic image. They must also provide easy access, security, and comfort. For it is clear that not only are shabby storefronts and vacancy signs unattractive, they also discourage shoppers.

The step of eliminating traffic from major downtown shopping streets puts cities in a position to show their commitment to revitalizing their inner cores, while at the same time stimulating a similar commitment, both moral and financial, from merchants. A healthier downtown economy increases tax revenues to the city and ultimately to the community. Property values and assessed valuations are likely to grow, which brings the city increased income, and while new investments create new jobs, they also support the community's economic health.

Reduced vacancy is the first sign of success. Even the announcement of a pedestrian project can often generate enough interest that empty stores are reoccupied in anticipation of increased business. Vacancy rates in Pomona, California, and Knoxville, Tennessee, for example, dropped from 25 percent to zero during the first year of their pedestrian district's existence.[1]

Once the initial momentum has begun, it is necessary to stimulate shopper patronage in order to increase retail sales. The very existence of a traffic-free zone, with its environmental and social benefits, can do this. Some cities have registered sales increases as high as 111 percent, along with increases of 70 to 100 percent in pedestrian flow.[2] However, that in itself is not enough to ensure a permanently vital traffic-free zone. Initial successes sometimes transmute into failures. In Pomona, California, the first year the mall received nationwide press coverage as a successful model of urban revitalization, there was a 40 percent increase in sales. But the mall was slowly abandoned by its patrons, and now, after 15 years of operation, it is almost totally deserted. However, the mall in Kalamazoo, Michigan, has consistently increased its retail sales 20 percent annually for the last 15 years. Over the same period, more than 84 percent of its stores have been remodeled, and $16 million has been invested in new construction. Kalamazoo's success is the result of strong, continuous support from all groups interested in promoting an active downtown area—merchants, businessmen, residents, and the city.

There are times though, when not even public interest and goodwill can sustain the economic gains of a traffic-free zone. The key element to success seems to be timeliness. Sometimes the trend toward decay is irreversible. In such cases, even a well-designed, easily accessible pedestrian district fails. Riverside, a suburb of Los Angeles, is a prime example of bad timing. The project was begun when major department stores were not strong enough to make up for the loss.

Though merchants are the first to benefit from a mall's success, they do not always support traffic-free zones. They sometimes oppose car limitations, fearing a loss of customers, or else are concerned with vandalism and changes in the types of shoppers. Merchant pressure based on these fears was largely responsible for the defeat of the proposed Madison Avenue Mall in New York, though a survey of the businesses along the street shows that only jewelers and clothing stores voiced strong opposition.

In many cities, it was the business people themselves who helped create traffic-free zones. The crusade of local merchants associations to "save downtown" in both Fresno and Minneapolis began even before the com-

Opposite page: In November 1962 automobiles were banned from the first shopping street of Copenhagen. Shop owners feared that trade would drop, but found that in 3 years business rose 30 percent.

Tourist crowds gather on Munich's Rathaus Square four times each day to watch the performing figures on the city hall clock.

A mall in Riverside, California did not help to revitalize the declining downtown economics. When the mall was created business had already left.

petition from suburban centers had affected its vitality. In these two cities, the creation of pedestrian streets was part of a larger overall plan for revitalizing the downtown area, which brought a 30 percent increase in Minneapolis' already healthy sales volume.

One of the most common results of conversion to pedestrian streets is a change in the type and quality of shops. Luxury and specialty stores seem to stay and thrive, bringing regional and national attention to the central shopping areas.

When shopping and sightseeing are combined in a traffic-free area, tourism profits. In Munich, 3.7 million visitors are attracted annually to the city. During the tourist season, 300,000 people make daily use of the pedestrian area.[3]

Ideally, a traffic-free zone should be used during the day as well as at night if the maximum economic potential is to be realized. But modern cities, in which housing has been eliminated from the downtown area, sometimes breed a situation in which central districts are active only during working hours and deserted at night and on weekends. In several cities, the creation of traffic-free zones has heightened this contradiction. In both Europe and America, cities which are realizing the benefits of a mixed balance of functions in central areas have begun to invest large sums of money towards making such a blending possible. The introduction or reintroduction of housing near traffic-free zones has been given top priority in order to stimulate round-the-clock activity. Recreational facilities, including theaters, restaurants, and movie houses, are being included in the plans.

ATTRACTING NEW INVESTORS

When a stable environment for retail business and other commercial activities exists, local and external investor confidence grows. This in turn generates new construction, more jobs, and increased tax revenues. Very often in the United States, the need to attract new investment has been the sole motivation for introducing pedestrian zones, whereas in Europe these economic goals have been given a lower priority than solutions to the problems of mobility and the desire to restore historic environments.

In Springfield, Illinois, a business organization was the initiator in the creation of the city's traffic-free zone, along with restoration of several historic buildings downtown. The group hoped primarily to strengthen the city's drawing power for new investment and construction, and it shaped a master plan which focused on these objectives. Largely as a result of their efforts over the past 10 years, $200 million was invested in the city, with the greater part of it coming after the mall.

There are other examples of similar achievements. From 1964 to 1967, Fresno, California, issued $818,000 worth of building permits for remodeling pedestrian areas and $19.3 million for new construction. Since the traffic-free zone opened, $40 million has been invested in the central business district. Included in the redevelopment were a new convention center, office buildings, and hotels, all of which served to enrich usage of the city core.

Land values generally increase after the opening up of traffic-free zones: property assessments are raised, and rents go up as the demand for space near pedestrian sites increases. This trend sometimes creates a conflict between the desire to attract business and the reluctance, particularly on the part of small enterprises, to invest in downtown stores because of higher rents and increased property assessments. However, this reluctance is usually more than offset by the increased volume of business which merchants on the mall enjoy.

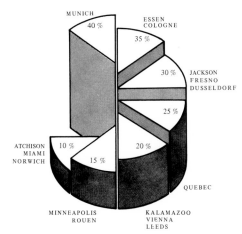

RETAIL SALES INCREASE IN EUROPEAN AND NORTH AMERICAN PEDESTRIAN DISTRICTS

Data obtained from Laurence A. Alexander, *Downtown Malls: An Annual Review*, Vol. 1 (New York: Downtown Research and Development Center, 1975); and *Streets for People* (Paris: OECD, 1974).

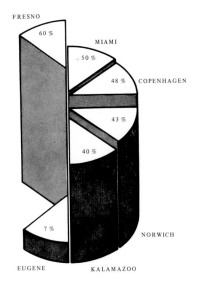

INCREASED PEDESTRIAN FLOW IN TRAFFIC-FREE ZONES

Data obtained from Laurence A. Alexander, *Downtown Malls: An Annual Review*, vol. 1 (New York: Downtown Research and Development Center, 1975); and *Pedestrian Streets* (London: Greater London Council, 1973).

Environmental Improvements

In recent years, more and more people have become aware of the automobile's negative effect on the urban environment. The creation of traffic-free zones has been considered a useful tool for the reduction of pollution levels, as well as the improvement of the downtown areas' appearance and the preservation and enhancement of historic districts.

REDUCING POLLUTION LEVELS

There are two factors which influence urban air quality: street level pollution and upper level pollution. Upper level pollution, which is less concentrated but distributed throughout the city, comes from vehicles as well as stationary sources and is rapidly dispelled in most cities. Street level pollution, however, is highly concentrated, but local, and is not so easily dispelled. Therefore, the most effective way to clean the air is to limit traffic.

In the United States, concern about air pollution led to the passage of the Clean Air Act of 1970. This act required cities to establish air quality controls in their central business districts. Midtown Manhattan, which has one of the worst problems, is being obliged to lower its carbon monoxide level by 72 percent to meet federal clean air standards.

Mobile air pollutant sources account for roughly 95 percent of carbon monoxide emissions, 65 percent of hydrocarbons, 40 percent of nitrogen oxides, 15 percent of suspended particulates, and 50 percent of photochemical smog formed by atmospheric reaction of hydrocarbons and nitrogen oxides.[1]

Combustion engine-generated hydrocarbons, nitrogen oxides, particulates, and smog also attack the surfaces of buildings, damaging them beyond repair. Residential property damage of $43 million and $650 million in damage to buildings were caused by motor vehicles in 1970, according to a U.S. government survey.

In Bologna, Italy, where intensive studies were conducted on the disastrous effects of exhaust fumes on the architectural details of buildings, statues, and frescoes, the photographic documentation of such damage was used as part of the city's promotional campaign to ban traffic from the central core. Evidence was also found that the continuous vibrations of automobile traffic weakened the structure of buildings in several cities. In Venice, vibrations from motor boats have affected foundations along the Grand Canal.

In Copenhagen, in the Stroget where cars were eliminated, street noise levels dropped between 10 and 15 decibels, the equivalent of cutting the original sound level in half. Today, instead of honking horns and roaring engines, mostly the sound of voices and footsteps is heard.[3]

Octave-band analysis has shown that traffic control gets rid of a large percentage of high-frequency sounds, leaving only those low-frequency noises which originate in the surrounding area. The size of a traffic ban makes a difference; the area affected can influence the noise level of an entire urban center.

IMPROVING THE PHYSICAL IMAGE OF DOWNTOWN

The physical image of downtown is seriously affected by the presence or absence of cars. Aside from the effects of the indiscriminate use of traffic and commercial signs, a pedestrian's perceptions are disrupted by the spectacle of cars in perpetual motion. When a stream of traffic separates the two sides of a street, views of historic and architecturally important buildings are obstructed, and it is difficult to have any sense of scale or perspective. When European cities banned cars from streets and squares, whole buildings and streets became visible where before there had been only car tops.

Pedestrians don't need large conspicuous signs to draw their attention when the distraction of traffic isn't hindering their ability to perceive their environment. Coordinated and subdued graphic schemes are enough; they invariably work in traffic-free zones.

Once traffic has been banned from a street, the real character of the street can be brought back into focus. Repaving, lighting, landscaping, and street furniture all add to the safe, attractive, and efficient environments which planners and designers can begin to create.

Repaving Repaving streets to sidewalk level has the effect of eliminating the inhibitions established by a separation of road, curb, and sidewalk, while adding a sense of formal unity to the entire street. Without such repaving, habit tends to influence shoppers to stay on the sidewalk instead of venturing out into the now empty streets.

Lighting Pedestrian-oriented lighting helps to restore a more initimate and natural scale to converted streets. Usually, overhead lighting is controlled so that it won't overpower illuminated shop windows, though many American cities, influenced by security problems, have adopted high-intensity lighting.

Landscaping Linear parks set into an existing right-of-way are elements in the design of traffic-free zones, particularly in the warmer regions of the United States, such as California and Florida. They enhance the appearance of the central business district, setting a mood and tone which go along with the green areas. One of the arguments against them is maintenance cost. After Ottawa's Sparks Street was converted to a pedestrian mall, its yearly maintenance costs increased from $26,000 to $300,000.

Street Furniture In the historic districts of Bologna and Norwich, England, no street furniture was ever required. In Bologna, once the streets were repaved in their original brick surface, the medieval unity of the city was once again restored. Most cities are not so fortunate, however, though they should always try to retain those elements of the original environment which might lend themselves to use as street furniture. Since the needs of pedestrians are varied and complex, they must be fully accommodated if the street is to retain its life. This sometimes results in a complete reorganization.

By and large, the design of traffic-free areas has followed the standards set in the 1940s by such well-known projects as the Lijnbaan in Rotterdam and the Torg in Stockholm, though there have been modifications which are oriented towards greater flexibility. Vienna, for example, introduced responsive street "toys" providing entertainment, instead of conventional furnishings.

In North America, a greater variety of street furniture has been introduced, and cities have relied heavily on design to lend character to the downtown environment. In North America, the desire to introduce human scale and amenities into urban centers has become a conscious aspect of the effort in shaping the design of traffic-free areas.

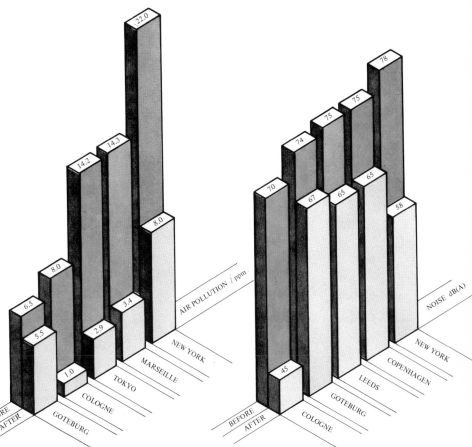

AIR POLLUTION LEVELS BEFORE AND AFTER THE BANNING OF VEHICULAR TRAFFIC FROM CITY STREETS

Data obtained from *Pedestrian Streets* (London: Greater London Council, 1973). *Streets for People* (Paris: OECD, 1974).

NOISE POLLUTION LEVELS BEFORE AND AFTER THE BANNING OF VEHICULAR TRAFFIC FROM CITY STREETS

Data obtained from *Pedestrian Streets* (London: Greater London Council, 1973). *Streets for People* (Paris: OECD, 1974).

PRESERVING AND ENHANCING HISTORIC DISTRICTS

In numerous cities, traffic-free zoning has been used as a conservation measure to restore the unity of the historic urban fabric. The scope of these plans varies depending upon the city's size and the amount of its traffic, but today elimination of cars is considered a necessary step towards the restoration of historic districts.

After closing the commercial district to traffic, Norwich, banned all but local residents' vehicles from its historic district, with the immediate effect of returning it to the original pedestrian scale.[4]

In Bologna, this renewal process was taken a step further to include restoring the social integrity of the historic core. The city has retained its traditional residential mixture of workers, artisans, students, and the elderly. Behind this effort is the concept that a historic center is not a museum, but a living organism. Moreover, it is capable of performing many functions once the constraints and difficulties created by traffic have been eliminated. Although building restoration costs are high, the environmental returns are equally great.

Piazza Navona in Rome before and after the traffic ban.

4

Social Benefits

The pedestrian as an individual and not a moving "vehicle" has only recently been recognized by urban designers, who used to think of pedestrian movement strictly in terms of safety—the need to ensure that people were not run over by cars. The personal and behavioral needs of the person on foot rarely even entered the picture. The neglect of those areas which are responsive to social needs has been a chronic disease of major urban areas. It is most apparent in central business districts where emphasis was placed on exploiting land values and making use of decreasing open space for building construction and the accommodation of more vehicles.

New York's shrinking sidewalks illustrate this erosion of pedestrian space. The minimum standard width has decreased from 15 feet/4.6 meters in 1912 to 13 feet/4.0 meters in 1925 down to 11 feet/3.4 meters in 1963.[1]

As density increases in cities, allocation of open space decreases to the point where pedestrians are squeezed into the leftover spaces between traffic and buildings. In central business districts, property values make it difficult for municipal administrators to find room for pedestrians. However, space has been created by banning all or nonessential vehicles on existing rights-of-way, by permitting increased building height in exchange for reduced site coverage, and by construction of underground concourses and bridges.

There are many methods for locating usable space, though their essential social purposes are to create an environment for pedestrian activity, improve the social image of the city, protect the pedestrian, and reduce vehicular accidents.

PROVIDING SPACE FOR PEDESTRIAN ACTIVITIES

Pedestrian activity has more scope and complexity of movement than any other form of transportation. The unpredictable and imaginative movements of people cannot be handled adequately by the simple linearity of most streets in the central business district. "High-quality spaces," as they have often been called, are the ones which give the greatest range to pedestrian activities; an environment free from the restraints imposed by traffic can begin to offer unhampered

movement, social amenities, and comfort to pedestrians. A comparative study of 32 German cities indicates that people favor flexible environments, while they dislike static design elements that clutter public spaces and interrupt or channel their movements.[2] Banning traffic from centrally located streets provides an opportunity, which has not always been fully exploited in pedestrian design, for creating socially stimulating spaces even in the midst of heavily used downtown areas.

The movable stacking chairs in Munich's traffic-free zone are among the best examples of furniture that offer an almost infinite range of movement and uses. However, the rigid display cases in other German cities with traffic-free zones have aroused criticism.

This criticism of such overdesign is echoed in the United States. In Sacramento, a majority of shoppers objected to the large concrete forms erected along the city's pedestrian street. In Trenton, New Jersey, colorful canopies designed to lend a proper scale were recently removed.

Providing socially responsive places in crowded downtown areas is an important service to an urban population, particularly to those people rarely considered by planners—children, people with infants, the elderly, and the handicapped.

Senior citizens, for example, who constitute a large percentage of the people using downtown areas, are able to take advantage of malls which are immediately accessible. Adults with infants are drawn from nearby residential areas into the downtown areas, where the children can be occupied in playgrounds while their parents shop.

People's attitudes about being a pedestrian have begun to change. Pedestrians who have tasted the pleasure of pursuing leisurely activities become used to the rhythms of the street, the chance to socialize, relax, and watch other people go by. When the sense of the unusual nature of pedestrian zones passes, people's habits created by such spaces develop and grow.

ENHANCING THE SOCIAL IMAGE OF THE CITY

Visitors and residents alike are affected in their image of the city by the existence or nonexistence of pedes-

New York City's Fifth Avenue has been occasionally reserved for pedestrians only.

trian activities. Towns in which the streets are populated both day and night seem welcoming, especially for visitors whose perceptions of a city's character are determined by its street activities. Urban spaces often represent an entire city; they are places with a constant stream of people and activities. For centuries, squares and plazas were places where people gathered for various social purposes, including public meetings and political rallies; today their equivalent is a traffic-free district.

Cologne's two pedestrian streets are more crowded, at any time, than the plaza facing the Gothic cathedral which was once the center of the city. Millions of visitors who come to the city each year are not drawn away from the cathedral square, whose importance is everywhere recognized, but are instead given an added option.

In Bologna, Italy, the emphasis in banning traffic from the central Piazza Maggiore and surrounding streets has been on social considerations. Bologna's planners, involved in the city's restoration effort and the reintroduction of a resident population into the central city, place as much emphasis on pedestrian streets as on schools, hospitals, day-care centers, and other social institutions. The streets as outdoor living rooms provide a gathering place for the larger family that comprises the community. The city takes maximum advantage of its traffic-free zones by promoting theater, concerts, and processions, in the belief that use of the historic city center is a social and cultural right of all its citizens.

Most American cities do not support a large residential population in their centers; they rarely provide the spaces needed for outdoor social gatherings. Therefore, traffic-free zoning has had a tremendous impact, acting as a catalyst for public and private efforts, such as the promotion of public events, fairs, art displays. Successful traffic-free zones often become the symbol of the city and a source of pride to its residents. Previously, cities sought identity through their "tallest building," "biggest astrodome," or some other landmark of historic and promotional value. Now they associate themselves with "their" pedestrian streets.

Kalamazoo, Michigan, advertises itself as "Mall City—USA." Many other cities use the names of their pedestrian streets extensively in advertising and promotional tourist guides.

In European cities, identification with traffic-free zones has also occurred; there, popular names given to pedestrian districts add to the distinct character of the areas. Copenhagen's central commercial spine was named Stroget, which means "to stroll" in Danish. In Stockholm, a major pedestrian area was popularly named the Torg (the Haymarket) after the open-air market once located there. The fame of these streets has spread far beyond their immediate sphere of influence. Both are renowned shopping places throughout Scandinavia.

IMPROVING PEDESTRIAN SAFETY

Pedestrian zoning has often been created for the purpose of reducing traffic accidents. There is always an acute conflict between people and cars in central areas, as well as a greater possibility of accidents. The central portion of London Street in Norwich, England, was closed "to insure the safety of persons using the road," after Norwich's sidewalks had been so trimmed down that pedestrians overflowed into the street. In Stockholm, traffic was restricted and completely eliminated even in some sections of residential suburbs.

In Copenhagen, before and after studies were made of accidents in traffic-free zones and were compared with analogous statistics for areas around the central business district. It was found that accidents rose in number as one moved away from the pedestrian zone toward the outer parts of the central business district. City officials were reluctant to admit, however, that there had been a net reduction on traffic accidents due to the traffic-free area.[3]

Pedestrian deaths caused by automobiles represent 20 percent of all traffic fatalities in the United States and 30 percent in Europe. This makes safety in downtown areas an important issue.

Crowds of people help to create an atmosphere of security which in itself discourages crime. Several cities have introduced special police patrols, emergency phones, and bright lighting in their traffic-free zones. Usually, most of this proves to be unnecessary. Confidence in their downtown areas has been restored by the very existence of pedestrian streets.

Providence, Rhode Island.

The Hague, Holland.

How Pedestrian Zones Work

This section focuses on some key factors in the creation of traffic-free zones. The information, which has been gathered from a number of North American and European cities with operational pedestrian areas, has been organized into the following chapters: Involving the Community, Legislation and Finance, Planning and Design, and Managing Implementation.

   The complexity of creating a traffic-free zone requires that the overlapping nature of these factors must be recognized. Not only are they functionally interdependent, but they must be developed in conjunction with one another.

Oldenburg, Germany.

5

Involving the Community

Traffic-free zoning proposals have usually generated enormous controversy. Opponents fall into several categories: those who are most directly affected by the project, such as merchants on the site who fear a loss of business if the project fails; taxpayers who object to public funds being spend on a pedestrian zone; taxi-drivers, truckers, and private bus companies which see traffic-free zoning as a threat to their interests; and automotive firms which tend to object to any street being closed off. Even city traffic planning agencies often resist the idea of having their present street system disrupted. And conservative political organizations add their objections to the rest, arguing that pedestrian zones represent a bureaucratic intervention in the private sector—one more threat to free enterprise and freedom of choice.

Often people who think that their economic interests are threatened couch their objections in lofty terms, claiming that they are acting in the public interest. Or their opposition may result in covert support of "citizens groups" against the project, as well as financing of litigation against it.

Whatever the scope of a pedestrian project, it affects the lives of everyone working or residing in the area. For this reason and because the forces of opposition are themselves often powerful and well organized, it is necessary to have a well-organized approach to the development of plans: the success of a traffic-free project can depend upon a group's capacity to involve the right people in the implementation and planning processes, as well as in the sharing of actual (not token) leadership.

Those who are affected by pedestrian projects should always have the opportunity to participate in the decisions which influence their various roles in the community.

ROLES OF THE PUBLIC

As a project is developed, the time comes when the public is called on to support it, whether for rezoning, patronage of business, or payment for improvements. In the most successful examples, the public has been involved from the very outset of the process—during its inception, throughout planning and implementation, and on into the operational phase. In cities where projects have been developed without public participation, the results were often disastrous, and in the final analysis, it was the community that made a traffic-free zone viable or allowed it to die.

It is important to determine which people should be involved when and how their participation can be obtained. Residents are voters and taxpayers with the power to approve public expenditures of money and influence boards, the city council, and local officials on new ordinances, zoning, and building codes. Unresponsive officials can be voted out of office, and people can try to stop civic projects which they do not consider to be in their interest. As consumers, residents shop in the area of a planned pedestrian precinct. Adolescents and young adults, although they are not taxpayers, are major consumers and supporters of the theater, arts, and other activities. Property owners and renters may be required to rehabilitate business properties and their homes or else may have to move if demolition, rezoning, or reorganization of the area is required as part of a traffic-free zone.

The people living in a community are valuable sources and collectors of information. Each person has opinions about the community and its activities or lack of them, as well as strong views about their own neighborhoods and the appearance and services of their central city. These people are all essential elements in the organization of support for pedestrian zoning, and it is necessary to make provision for open discussion of the issues and for channeling their potential input. Not every city that has established a traffic-free area has solicited public understanding and support of it. In far too many cities, either because of the central bureaucracy of governments or because of special interests, the public was ignored in the process.

Bologna, Italy, and Norwich, England, are positive examples of cities which have adopted specific methods for obtaining citizens' participation in the city planning process. The municipal administration of Bologna operates on two levels. As in other Italian cities, its council is a deliberating body which operates through a central executive. However, Bologna has also instituted 18 district or neighborhood committees. Each is made up of 20 members nominated by the city

Copenhagen, Denmark.

Chicago, Illinois, street fair.

Painting contest in Tokyo's Ginza.

TWO EXAMPLES OF PEDESTRIAN STREET BATTLES

The following 2 examples of pedestrian street battles (with different outcomes) point out the importance of public participation in traffic-free projects.

Battle Creek, Michigan, was the scene of dramatic schemes to halt plans for a downtown pedestrian street. The merchants had agreed to pay 60 percent of its costs, and the city had approved the plan, using public funds to pay for the remaining 40 percent. Then, an opposing group forced a referendum on the issue. At an August 1972 primary, the antimall forces turned out and won their case. However, the project's advocates returned to their mission with new enthusiasm and perspective. They gained the support of labor and other organized groups, and then resubmitted the issue to the electorate the following November. A large turnout rewarded their efforts, and the pedestrian zone became law.

The story of New York City's proposed Madison Mall did not have as happy an ending. Madison Mall was first proposed in 1970 as part of a traffic control plan for midtown Manhattan, which recommended that because of the unbearable congestion, noise, and stress of the area, automobiles be banned from five streets. Madison seemed the one on which the initial step might most easily be taken, and Mayor Lindsay quickly adopted the idea. But he ran into opposition from merchants, who charged that the mall would disrupt traffic and discourage business. The mayor proposed a 90-day test of the project, which was also opposed, and the courts eventually ruled that the test required the approval of the City's Board of Estimate, which the mayor did not control. When the mall test was heard by the Board of Estimate, it was defeated by a vote of 12 to 10.

The "More Streets for People" tent theater in New York City featured educational audiovisual shows on city planning. The exhibit traveled to cities across the United States and Canada for more than two years.

council. The district committee is an advisory body with a decentralized executive structure. Decisions of the city council are submitted to the district where they are discussed, often in public meetings, before the city acts on the proposals. This system has been in use for 15 years and is highly successful.

British procedures require that municipalities publish proposed alterations in local newspapers. Twenty days are then allowed for objections. In Norwich, this procedure was expanded, and a 6-month temporary street closing was instituted prior to permanent implementation in order to evaluate the effects of traffic-free zoning and to allow public comment based on firsthand experience.

OUTLINING THE PROCESS
The following is a tentative outline based on results from a number of positive experiences, which illustrates the creation of a traffic-free zone through all its stages from inception to operation. It serves as a reference for involving the public and delegating responsibilities. The stages involve identifying key participants; expanding community involvement; organizing meetings; developing an organization; setting goals; preparing surveys and special studies; setting objectives; establishing concepts, plans, and implementation procedures; and monitoring operation.

Stage 1: Identifying Key Participants The first step is taken when a private citizen, public official, or organization makes a decision to begin the action process in support of a traffic-free zone. The potential actors in the local theater of action must then be identified: local government, prominent citizens, the business community, civic groups, the academic community, and the media, all of whom will play a major role in various phases of the overall project.

Stage 2: Expanding Community Involvement Once the potential participants have been identified, they must be contacted. The first meetings and discussions on how to proceed will most likely have a ripple effect; word should spread establishing preliminary interest throughout the community.

Stage 3: Organizing Meetings The first meeting should both explore and generate public interest: potential difficulties should be highlighted, local problems and concerns reviewed, additional participants included or identified for future involvements, and essential information located and collated.

Stage 4: Developing an Organization As soon as a certain level of energized interest has been generated, it is necessary to begin channeling that energy into an efficient organizational structure. This is a difficult stage; the real workers are separated from those whose interest is temporary, and attempts must be made to engage as many people as possible in a satisfying way and convert their capacity for ideas into the capacity for action. Existing and potential resources must be evaluated, including funds, human power, and services; it must also be noted whether these sources involve city government, private organizations, or individual citizens. A staff, responsible for planning, administration, and promotion, must be selected and divided into different categories of personnel. The staff should include program management, responsible for planning and administration; special consultants, responsible for specific aspects of the plan; and survey workers.

Up to this point, media and public communications may have been sporadic. They must be clearly established, and procedures must be set up for consulting with and advising the community, city officials, and business groups on a regular basis.

Stage 5: Setting Goals Setting goals gives a focus to the project: it educates and inspires participants, crystallizes the intent of the project as an aid to communication and publicity, provides a guide to determining which studies and surveys may be necessary, and establishes clearcut reference points for choosing among alternate solutions.

Stage 6: Preparing Surveys and Special Studies Studies and surveys are divided into two general categories:

Comprehensive Surveys, in particular, feasibility studies, are needed to formulate local planning. These surveys cover such areas as land use, building conditions, economics, and preparation of base maps.

Detailed Studies of a more specific nature are required for particular aspects of the project. These focus on such areas as parking, traffic analysis, truck deliveries, and bicycle paths.

Areas of investigation are usually defined at the outset, since data from one study will often be applicable to that of another study. In addition, existing research should be studied, because each community has quite a bit of information already on hand. This can save a significant amount of time and money.

The responsibility for carrying out studies and surveys is often split into two groups: those responsible for supervising the studies and those who will do the actual survey work. There is enormous potential for community involvement in survey work. Not only does using citizen volunteers save money while producing results, but it also helps build local support for the project.

Once the coordinating organization is set up, it is ready to proceed with gathering information, making critical reviews, tabulating and analyzing data, and developing recommendations based on its findings. Analysis of the information can take place in joint planning workshops, with community goals serving as the framework for discussions. It is important that the community be made aware of the findings. The more information available to the public during the initial stage of the process, the greater the possibility of its support.

Stage 7: Setting Objectives In contrast to general goals, objectives represent a synthesis of the recommendations from various surveys and studies, a comprehensive list which forms a plan of action for determining the ultimate aim. These objectives should be quantified and scheduled as far as possible. Together with general goals, they represent a statement of the community's specific desires for the area.

Stage 8: Establishing Concepts, Plans, and Implementation Procedures Any conflicts that have arisen among objectives should be resolved at this stage: idealism and practicality must be reconciled on a fundamental level. Some objectives will be modified and others eliminated altogether for reasons of suitability or because

prospects for their realization are simply too slim, too costly, or too time consuming. Planners and urban designers at this point help to focus on the technical aspects of execution. Careful evaluation of alternatives, different land use patterns, desired "images," services, facilities, and so on should always draw upon as much public participation as possible. Public hearings or a series of smaller meetings with various local groups can help to settle on a single concept for the project.

The plan resulting from these deliberations is then presented for acceptance by the municipality as official policy. Usually, this is when a series of public hearings will be held, prior to taking any formal action. All segments of the community should be involved in these public hearings; they can both review the decisions which have already been made and provide additional ideas, criticisms, information, and evaluation. These hearings represent a critical turning point for the project—a time when community support is either gained or lost. To ensure their greatest effectiveness, the plan should be fully disseminated beforehand, and communications with the media should be firmly established.

Stage 9: Monitoring Operation Successful managing of the implementation process requires careful monitoring of the project's progress, since the long-term success of a traffic-free zone depends on an awareness of changes both within and around the project and upon an understanding of all the elements which have the power to influence it. Timely completion of the various stages must be assured; necessary changes in the planning strategy must be made; individual projects in the area must be made consistent with the ultimate goals of the plan; and construction must be coordinated with the existing needs of the local community.

ORGANIZING FOR ADVOCACY
Advocacy efforts should always be designed keeping in mind the need to gain the support of the community and its leaders. Facilities can be minimal, but they must be reliable and effective. The formalization of a leadership or steering committee helps to focus problems which may develop and prevent cross-decision making.

THE QUESTIONNAIRE

Here is a sample of the kind of questionnaire that will help you take the pulse of your block.

Dear Neighbor:

Some of your neighbors on the block are interested in improving it by making it more attractive. Your answers to the following questions are to let us know if you are interested in the idea as well, what you feel should be done, and how much you'd be willing to do to improve it. We'll get back to you with the results of the questionnaire shortly.   Thank you!

Please return the completed questionnaire to either (give the name and address of the president of the block association or the temporary leader if one hasn't been elected yet) or (give the name and address of the vice president of the association or another temporary officer or leader).

1. How long have you lived on the block?

2. Do you like living on the block?_____

3. Do you rent or own the place where you live?_____

4. Do you work?_____ If so, what do you do?_____

5. Age_____ Male or female_____

6. How many people live with you?_____

7. What are their ages and sexes?_____

8. Do you find the block attractive-looking?_____
unattractive?_____
neither?_____

9. Do you ever use the street as a place to chat, sit in the sun, play games? Please describe briefly the ways in which you use your street. _____

10. If additions were made on the street, which of the following would you like to see:
a. additional lighting_____
b. banners_____
c. benches or seats_____
d. community bulletin board_____
e. more attractive paving_____
f. painted wall murals_____
g. fresh paint on fences, building fronts, etc._____
h. trees and plants_____

11. If a vacant lot on the block or nearby is available, would you like to see it cleaned up, decorated, and turned into:
a. a small park_____
b. a playground_____
c. a garden_____

12. If street changes are made, should they be designed especially to serve any of these groups:

children_____ elderly people_____
young adults_____ adults_____
teenagers_____ everyone_____

13. Where on the block would you like to see changes? At the ends (which one? or both?)_____ in the middle_____ elsewhere_____ (please say where)_____

14. Do you think the kinds of changes suggested in this questionnaire would be popular or unpopular on the block?_____
Please give the reasons for your answer:
_____

15. Would you help to make the street more attractive by contributing:
time?_____ money?_____

16. Do you have a skill that would be useful in making changes on the block, such as carpentry, masonry, painting, sewing, designing, working with electricity?_____

17. Would you be willing to volunteer this skill—using your own talents and perhaps teaching or supervising others—to help improve the block?_____

18. Are you in a profession whose services might be of use to a block association (such as law, insurance, communications)?_____

19. Would you be willing to contribute time and advise to help your block association in a professional capacity?_____

20. Do you have any suggestions for improving the block?_____

Source: Mary Grozier and Richard Roberts. *New York's City Streets* (New York: The Council on the Environment of New York City, 1973).

Once a fundamental network has been established, it is possible to begin informing the general public, generating their support, and beginning feasibility studies which require considerable investments of time and money.

PROMOTION

Promoting a traffic-free zone can be as important as the resulting improvements. Often, after years of decline and congestion in a downtown area, people have forgotten its potential and are not even aware that a pedestrian project could benefit them. Local merchants, fearing change, imagine a loss of retail trade. It is often necessary to stimulate their imaginations in a direction which has lain dormant for years, or has never existed at all. An ambitious and aggressive promotional campaign has the capacity to accomplish all this by sponsoring numerous popular events throughout the year and introducing creative merchandising programs, thereby attracting customers to the traffic-free zone who would otherwise shop elsewhere.

Participation is an essential ingredient in promotional campaigns. Retailers, downtown merchant associations, municipal officials, the media, clubs and civic organizations, and representatives of consumers, all contribute to the success of the project. Promotion is an ongoing activity, which includes the formulation of slogans, the design of logos or symbols, the organization of special events, media campaigns, parking rate reductions or free public transportation rides, as well as better retail services and attention to customers. Beyond that, ingenuity and sensitivity to the environment and needs of the community serve as the best guide.

SPECIAL EVENTS

Special events are among the best ways to promote the pedestrian zone. Through games, happenings, star attractions, contests, and prizes, a traffic-free district can be publicized before and after completion. The events should be clearly identified with the site by name, location, or sponsor, but preferably all three.

Promotional events not only lend identity to the place, but also attract people there—a place where they shop, do business, have lunch, or otherwise participate. Special events

Environment	Energy	Sense of Place	Safety	Property Value
Recreation	Preservation	Business	Comfort	Participation

TEN GOOD REASONS TO CREATE TRAFFIC-FREE ZONES

The arguments in favor of traffic-free zoning speak for themselves if the project has been well thought out and well documented within the context of a city plan. The most persuasive arguments are those demonstrating that the proposal is a response to the specific needs of the local community. The following list of 10 good reasons to create traffic-free zones was prepared as part of a demonstration program sponsored by the United Nations in conjunction with 1976 World Environment Day. It cannot substitute for uniquely local arguments, but the list provides some general, useful points.

1 To attract people. More people means more opportunities for shopping, socializing, business, and fun. More business means more money for both the citizens and the city.

2 To provide a sense of place that strengthens community identity and community pride. This improves community relations and reduces feelings of alienation, while creating a place for all types of people to congregate.

3 To reduce noise and air pollution.

4 To provide a safe and attractive environment in which children can play and senior citizens can meet and rest.

5 To improve the visual environment. Signs, lights, spaces, colors, and textures can be designed to relate to the person on foot, rather than to the person on wheels.

6 To promote urban conservation, environmental preservation, building restoration and renewal.

7 To increase property values and, consequently, the city's revenue from real estate taxes.

8 To special rights-of-way to be reserved for bicycles and public transportation vehicles. This improves mobility through the city center and helps save energy.

9 To decrease the number of motor vehicle-related accidents, saving lives, police work, and judicial time.

10 To promote citizens' participation in the inception, management, monitoring, and improvement of the pedestrian area. Thus, the project becomes a lively instrument for public education in urban life.

Santa Monica, California.

Providence, Rhode Island.

Children's judo contest in Manhattan's Grand Army Plaza.

bring people into the area, but the traffic-free zone itself is responsible for keeping them there.

Different kinds of events attract different kinds of people. Women, children, and the elderly are the most frequent users. However, office workers are frequent visitors, particularly during lunch hours and immediately after work, and daytime promotional events should also cater to their interests.

Special activities are often planned to bring people into the area who might not otherwise come or to encourage use during nonbusiness hours. For example, evening outdoor concerts bring teenagers and older people together. Though such activities do not necessarily mean greater sales, they do make a traffic-free zone an urban amenity. Theaters, restaurants, bars, or shops open at night benefit directly. In any case, off-hour events help maximize the use of a pedestrian precinct in addition to building a strong community image for it.

Special children's events include circus acts or acrobats, contests, races, pet shows, costume parades, kite-flying contests, and puppet shows.

Events that attract people of all ages include appearances by well-known personalities, homemade food sales, dances or dance exhibitions, martial arts demonstrations, concerts, school or civic performances, car, bicycle, or motorcycle shows, flower shows, antique furniture or arts and crafts displays, coin and stamp shows, "grand openings," book fairs, art exhibits, and so forth.

Not only does putting on special events require the energies of a large number of organizations, citizens, and merchants, but it also requires suitable facilities in which they can be held.

Merchandising Practices   No matter how frequent promotional activities may be, or how many people are attracted by them, the volume of retail sales ultimately depends on sound and up-to-date merchandising practices. Traffic-free zones are usually in the heart of the central business district where retail trade has been based on long-established traditional methods. In contrast, competing suburban shopping centers urge their store tenants to use dynamic retailing practices. Merchants in traffic-free zones have had to reexamine their sales techniques and displays. In particular, they have taken advantage of the new opportunities for pedestrian browsing. While promotional activities bring people to the pedestrian zone, only the merchants can get them inside their stores.

Merchandise promotions gain an advantage by coinciding with special events. For example, spring flower shows complement Easter and Mother's Day sales. Similarly, vacation and travel shows in June and July increase sales during the summer.

Advertising   In most successful examples, good advertising reflected the same excitement and creativity that special events conveyed. Advertising is an essential tool in portraying the traffic-free zones as both a shopping area and a place for people. The public should continually be kept informed of sales as much as advertising funds will permit; and the image of the pedestrian mall as an area of constant human activity should be kept before the public. The pedestrian mall is not a place to visit once simply for curiosity. It is a permanent addition to a city's life, and advertising should reflect not so much its momentary specialness, but its importance to the daily existence of the community.

6

Legislation and Finance

Very few laws exist on the subject of pedestrian malls. Except in a few states, where specific pedestrian legislation has been passed, lawyers have had to use ingenuity to make the most of related but unspecific laws and to create or push through new legislation where necessary.

The importance of understanding the law and its potential impact on a mall program cannot be overstressed. Not only do legal mechanisms designate authority for carrying out a mall project, they may also provide for its maintenance, financing, and programming. A mall can only become a reality if the legal and financial mechanisms for implementing and maintaining the project are clearly understood and the planning survey incorporates indications of any specific legal or financial provisions which apply to malls in the city or state.

The complexity of the legal issues will require the participation of a lawyer early in the planning process. Except where a clear precedent is commonly known, law and finance are areas that must be handled by appropriate professionals beyond the initial formation stages.

There are many kinds of legal decisions to be made when instituting a traffic-free zone—from narrow literal decisions which involve the choice of limiting or banning vehicles and installing improvements to broad decisions concerning a city's land use, traffic control, and transportation policies.

This chapter will deal first with the overall urban policy decisions, then with the more specific aspects of creating pedestrian zones, and finally with funding strategies. The assumption in all cases is that fully qualified professional help is available.

LEGAL ASPECTS OF URBAN POLICIES
In America, the creation of pedestrian zoning has been seen largely in economic terms as one more attempt to reverse the decline of downtown areas. In Europe, in contrast, banning automobile traffic has been part of a broader perspective, which involved an overall policy program.

Pedestrian zoning can be linked to a variety of citywide objectives, which can be pursued through a number of legal tools. One objective is to lessen urban sprawl while increasing the density of development. Greater density requires that land be used for buildings instead of vehicles. Zoning is a major land use control device for achieving this aim. Zoning specifies the ways in which particular sites and districts can be permitted to develop by regulating the height and bulk of buildings, the size and location of open space around them, and the intensity of development.[1]

A zoning plan is usually prepared by a zoning commission or city planning department and then approved by the local government body. Traditionally, central business districts are zoned for the most dense development. It is possible to clearly delineate areas of high commercial and residential density by specifying the precise limits of what is permitted and what is not in any particular area. This includes both structural and site requirements, such as height of buildings, lot coverage, ratio of total floor area, and setbacks.

A city's land acquisition policy can also be used to control density indirectly. By prohibiting or restricting development on its edges, a city raises land values, encouraging more dense development of central areas. This policy has been effective in Europe, where cities have an easier time acquiring, and thereby controlling, the development of land on the periphery of the municipal area.

In the United States, where real estate taxation is a much larger source of urban revenues than in Europe, it is possible to use this as a potentially powerful tool for affecting the density of development. A city can encourage dense development by heavily assessing land values rather than improvements so that developers will build more extensive facilities to generate revenues for the high taxes on the land. This is a device rarely used, since the usual practice is to tax improvements more heavily than land.

Another indirect means of discouraging new development in order to promote greater density in the central cities is for the city to deliberately refuse the extension of sewer and water facilities into undeveloped areas on its perimeter. As a growth deterrent, this will help to push development inward rather than outward.

On the surface, open space creation would seem to be inconsistent with policies to create greater density. The reverse, however, can often be

Nassau Street's lunch-break mall in New York City.

Box from City of New York, *New Life for Plazas* (New York City Planning Commission, 1975).

so; it is possible to actually increase density while providing for more open space, wherever the creation of pedestrian-auto restricted zones is used as a complement to open space policies in inner cities.

For example, New York City's zoning law allows office building developers 20 percent additional floor space (greater density) but requires them in return to put in a plaza (open space). It has also been proposed that the development of several building lots be planned conjointly so that open space can be pooled to create a larger, more usable area.[2]

Open space can also be created by a land acquisition policy through which a city buys, through negotiation or condemnation, land which it wishes to preserve for, or convert to, open space use. This policy can be facilitated whenever the city acquires property from the nonpayment of real estate taxes.

Urban renewal programs, which develop a portion of the city according to a plan based on a completely renewed street pattern, are a further source of open space. The city acquires much of the land, clears it, installs new improvements such as streets and sewers, sells the land to redevelopers, and provides in the plan for a pedestrian district.

The availability of adequate public transportation can be an essential element in traffic-free zones. This means that such a project must taken into consideration a city's total transportation policy. In both Europe and the United States, where public trans-

---

NEW LIFE FOR PLAZAS

Since 1961, New York City has allowed builders up to 20 percent increases in allowable floor space as a compensation for providing generous plazas as part of their projects. The formula has proven successful, and most new buildings are now surrounded by open space. These spaces, however, have not been as successful in human terms. Following are the requirements for a new zoning provision concerned with the quality as well as the quantity of urban plazas.

1 Plazas should take advantage of southern exposure where possible. Orientation on avenues should be restricted according to the amount of open space in the immediate vicinity.

2 Plaza dimensions: minimum of 750 square feet/75 square meters; not less than 10 feet/3 meters deep.

3 Plaza proportions should not exceed a ratio of 3:1. A 40-foot/12-meter minimum width is imposed on through-blocks.

4 The plaza, as a public space, must be open at all times. Access must be provided along at least 50 percent of front lot lines.

5 The elevation of a plaza must be within 3 feet/0.9 meters of the curb level. If the plaza covers 10,000 or more square feet/1,000 square meters, 15 percent of the area can be within 15 feet/4.6 meters of curb level.

6 Permitted obstructions:

Area of Urban Plaza		Maximum % of Obstruction
in square feet	in square meters, approximately	
Less than 5,000	Less than 500	33
5,000–5,999	500–600	36
6,000–6,999	600–700	39
7,000–7,999	700–800	42
8,000–8,999	800–900	45
9,000–9,999	900–1000	48
10,000 or more	over 1000	50

7 In general, there must be 1 linear foot/30 centimeters of seating per 30 square feet/3 square meters. For a through-block or a site sloping 2.25 percent, 1 linear foot/30 centimeters of seating is required for every 40 square feet/3.8 square meters.

8 Four trees are required for a plaza of 1,000 square feet/100 square meters; 6 trees for plazas of 5,000 square feet/500 meters; and 1 tree per 2,000 square feet/200 square meters on plazas of 12,000 or more square feet/1,200 square meters.

portation runs at a deficit, it must be underwritten by some government to keep the fare low enough to attract riders. In Stockholm, a special county tax covers the $75 million operating deficit of the transit system, and New York's massive transit deficit is underwritten by the city, state, and federal governments. It is the efficiency of these public transit systems in carrying large numbers of people—who become pedestrians at their destination—that allows for dense development.

Limiting arterial construction is one other device for preserving, if not encouraging, high densities in central cities. Vancouver, British Columbia, has built almost no urban expressways, with the result that sprawl has been discouraged and city property values have been maintained at a high level. This is one reason why the city has a thriving central business district.

Historic preservation and reduction of noise and air pollution are other citywide aims which can be partially achieved by pedestrian zoning. Restricting vehicles by the imposition of taxes and/or reduction of parking go hand in hand with creating auto-free zones in areas where national or local policies require steps to reduce air pollution.

Historic preservation programs may also require that old structures threatened by vibrations and emissions of vehicles be protected by removing traffic.

LEGAL TOOLS

From country to country in Europe, and from state to state within the United States, the ease of taking the first step in creating traffic-free zones varies widely. What may initially appear to be a simple administrative decision often requires approval from the highest levels of government. In seeking the appropriate legal tools for a particular pedestrian project, it is necessary to know whether the project can be built solely through administrative action or if legislative action will be required as well.

In the United States, perhaps because of the heavy dependence on automobiles, violation of the "sanctity" of a street as a place for vehicles is usually a major production. Since American cities are governed by individual states, the power to ban automobiles varies considerably from state to state and often depends upon

---

TWO EXAMPLES OF
PEDESTRIAN MALL LEGISLATION
IN THE U.S.

In the United States, a number of states have enacted laws specifically directed towards creation of auto-restricted or pedestrian zones. These laws allow cities to implement those zones, provided certain procedures are followed to allow objections to be heard. The two laws on which many other states have based theirs are those in California and Minnesota.

California: 1960 The law states that certain areas of the city and particularly retail shoppping areas may be designated to separate pedestrian from vehicular travel to protect public safety and otherwise serve public interest and convenience.

Specifically, the state delegates the cities the authority to:

Establish a mall district.

Restrict and prohibit vehicular traffic.

Pay for the mall improvements from general funds.

Levy assessments on mall properties.

Construct desired improvements.

A peculiarity of the legislation is that it specifically notes that "No money available for expenditure within the city from the proceeds of any tax, license or fee imposed by any public agency upon the ownership or operation of vehicles or the fuel used therein shall be used to pay such (mall) cost or expense."

The law also provides for public hearings and majority approval of affected landowners before a mall can be officially undertaken by the city.

Minnesota: 1962 Laws pertaining to pedestrian districts are incorporated into overall chapters concerned with streets, parks, and parkways. A mall is defined as the solution to problems of congestion, and authority is extended to the cities in such cases to "limit" the use of such streets by private vehicles" in the interests of the city and the state.

There are several stipulations for designating a street as a mall:

It must be located in the central business district.

Traffic must be allowed on intersecting streets.

Mass transit must be allowed to continue operating where it is "in the interest of the city."

The mall must benefit the "movement, safety, convenience or enjoyment of pedestrians."

The law also extends power to the cities to levy assessments and condemn needed properties for public use. And it includes provisions for financing improvements. The city may use money for the mall that it would otherwise have used on the unimproved streets.

It may assess benefited properties in proportion to benefits from the mall. It may recover leftover costs by assessing property values equal to the net amount of the estimated costs remaining after deducting the amounts to be charged to the general funds of the city and received on account of use by vendors. The limit shall be $0.50/$100 of assessed valuation. Public hearings and majority approval by landowners are required according to state law.

CONSTRUCTION FUNDS USED FOR
The DOWNTOWN PLAZA:
FEDERAL TAXES   0
STATE TAXES   0
COUNTY TAXES   0
CITY TAXES   0
PRIVATE DOLLARS 100%
Project of GREATER DOWNTOWN FREEPORT INC.
JAMES PARENT, ARCHITECT

the degree of a city's autonomy in determining its own policies. All cities, however, have the power to regulate traffic and impose certain kinds of land use controls; in most cases, a city's governing body may close streets to traffic entirely or restrict it by allowing only buses and trucks. If a street is entirely closed, this may constitute a "demapping" of it. This term is significant because it implies that some sort of legislative activity by the city's government and approval by the city's planning commission is required.

It is obviously simpler and faster to begin with already existing city laws by finding out, whenever possible, whether the necessary powers can be derived from park, public safety or health, highway and traffic, or related legislation. For example, Galveston, Texas, and Decatur, Illinois, established their downtown pedestrian streets under existing state and county laws for "municipal improvements." Special district zoning may also accommodate residential project proposals.

Additional or broader powers, which probably will be needed, will have to be granted by new local legislation, and this, in turn, may require state legislation.

Several states (California, Colorado, Minnesota, New Jersey, Oregon, and Washington) have passed legislation specifically enabling cities to undertake pedestrian projects in central business districts. Pedestrian legislation is pending in several others states, including New Hampshire.

If a state law does not allow city initiative in the areas appropriate to pedestrian zones, then it may be necessary to commit time and resources to obtain enabling legislation.

FUNDING STRATEGIES
Despite its comparatively uncomplicated nature, a traffic-free zone is not inexpensive. Surface improvements, such as lighting, repaving, and amenities, can be costly. Also subsurface improvements, such as reconstruction or relocation of utilities, are very expensive, often consuming far more resources that the surface work.

City budgetary practices and current tight money situations demand that the advocate make clear the financial priorities for pedestrian projects which must compete with many other projects seeking limited city funds. The legal means selected for the mall's development will, to a great extent, determine the finanical plan.

Funding for a project can come from individuals, businesses, and government, though in Europe and America the latter two are most likely to make the most extensive contributions.

In Europe, the local administratiion is more likely to carry the government's share of financing a traffic-free zone than in America. Because of the complicated nature of the federal-state-local government relationship in America, and the variations between different state and local jurisdictions, it is difficult to generalize about the American experience. Funding the traffic-free zone improvements can be a matter of infinite variety. In general, it is important to investigate all possible sources of funds, since public jurisdictions and moneys can sometimes produce surprising results.

Local Financing   In Europe, financing of physical improvements in relationship to pedestrian zoning is largely a local matter, with funds coming from the city's budget. For example, in Germany, "ordinary" local expenses are met from a municipality's annual budget, while "extraordinary" expenses, such as those for a pedestrian zone, may be paid for by loans or bonds. This generally occurs where the improvement is to be paid for over a period fo more than 3 years. In Europe loans or bonds are always liabilities of the entire municipality, whereas in the United States they are usually repaid from specific sources of revenue. Contributions by merchants who benefit from a pedestrian facility may be required, as was done in Essen.

The complicated relationship of governmental levels in the United States is reflected in the ways by which pedestrian zone improvements are financed. There are numerous variations and combinations, changing from locality to locality and state to state. Some of the more common devices will be discussed here, since they may provide methods which could be adopted wholly or in part in other situations.

At the local level, probably the simplest device for financing improvements is the capital budget. The capital budget pays for physical

---

FUNDING OPTIONS

Some sources of funding are general enough to cover most or all of the project's cost, while other, more specialized sources can be applied only to specific improvements. In many cases a number of financing methods will be used within a single project.

The following is a list of the major tools available in the United States.

General obligation bonds

Revenue bonds

Special assessment

Special service area tax

Voluntary assessments

Special private contributions

Motor fuel tax funds

Federal-aid urban system transportation funds

Urban renewal

Urban mass transportation funds

Federal revenue sharing

Housing and Community Development Act, 1974

SPECIAL ASSESSMENT PROCEDURE OF BURBANK, CALIFORNIA

In April 1967, a municipal ordinance was approved, defining the boundaries of the pedestrian zone. The initial cost estimates were set at $917,855. This amount was to be funded by a bond issue to be retired by revenues from a special assessment district including only those properties having frontage on the proposed pedestrian area. An assessment engineer was hired by the city to establish an equitable means of taxation. Evaluations were made on a front-foot basis which included an adjustment factor for varying property depths. The average figures were computed to be approximately $238 per front foot. Following is a table illustrating the property depth assessment factor, based upon a standard 50-foot / 15-meter wide lot.

| **Depth** | | |
In feet	In meters	%
75	23	87.5
90	28	93.5
100	30	100.0
103	31	101.5
120	36	110.0
125	38	112.5
138	42	119.0
150	45	125.0
160	48	130.0
170	51	135.0

---

improvements to the city "capital" structure, that is, its schools, fire stations, sewers, and so on. Facilities eligible for funding through the capital budget vary. If physical improvements to auto-free zones are not specifically eligible, it may still be possible to take advantage of the capital budget. For example, judicious scheduling of street reconstruction or park improvements makes it possible to channel funds for those purposes into a pedestrian district. Since much of the cost of an auto-free zone lies beneath the surface where utilities must be relocated or rebuilt, it is often possible to get a utility company to replace, repair, or modernize its equipment as part of its ongoing operation in conjunction with pedestrian zone construction. This will save large expenditures by the city.

Most communities also fund certain types of projects from bond issues paid off by special-purpose property taxes, the receipts of which can only be used for specified purposes, such as playgrounds, street lighting, or recreational facilities. All these may be incorporated as part of the improvements in an auto-free zone.

The Special Assessment District is a traditional way to finance public improvements. This is a designated area in which the parties that benefit have their real estate tax assessment increased according to the degree of benefit they derive. Mall levies are usually calculated according to property values, mall benefits, mall frontage, or other easily quantified factors. For example, buildings facing directly on a pedestrian mall have received the highest increase in assessment, while those further away have their assessment increased proportionately less.

Merchants, in particular, have often made malls possible through their willingness to be taxed. Where there are absentee or otherwise reluctant property owners, they may consider leases with tax escalation clauses that pass the mall costs onto the resident tenants.

To the extent that a pedestrian area benefits the entire community, a general assessment can be levied against it as a whole. Some states have allowed municipalities to use a special assessment district to finance construction of such projects. Likewise, the states have allowed municipalities to assess commercial and / or business properties within the district for the cost of operation and maintenance.

Other sources, however, should be explored. For example, in 1968, New York City amended a state law so that property assessments were disallowed for such projects as pedestrian precincts. A proposed pedestrian zone for Brooklyn has prompted the city to seek assessment authority again, but the matter remains unresolved.

A more unusual local financing device has been the special service area. Additional real estate and personal property taxes are levied within the designated area for the purpose of providing services not available to the entire community. Unlike the special assessment district, the increased taxes are based on the assessed valuation of property, not the proportionate benefit derived gy the property from the auto-free zone.[3]

When improvements to a traffic-free zone are minor and can be carried out piecemeal, a sidewalk improvement ordinance may be used. An ordinance is a local law. In this case, it requires improvement of a sidewalk by adjacent owners, according to carefully defined specifications. The owners are required to make improvements within a specified time period; otherwise, the municipality does the work and collects a special tax from the owner.

In addition to these special local financing devices used in the United States, one should not overlook voluntary contributions that can be made by benefited property owners and tenants as well as by local businesses and foundations. Sometimes, merchants voluntarily assessed themselves for specific improvements, paying according to the benefits de-

rived, based on the same kind of formula used for the special assessment district.

Nonlocal Financing In the United States, the great bulk of any nonlocal funds available for improvements to auto-free zones comes from the federal government.

A principal source is the Federal Aid Urban Systems Program, which gives localities more flexibility in determining how their highway funds are spent. Thus, localities may now use federal highway moneys for traffic operation improvements, such as control systems, signs and pavement markings, and major street improvements. They also use these funds to create grade separations between traffic flows and public transportation improvements, such as exclusive bus lanes, bus stop shelters, and fringe parking facilities. Used imaginatively, this program can finance many important aspects of auto-free zones.

Community development and "general revenue sharing" programs are less directly applicable, but very useful, sources of federal funds for pedestrian zones. Community development includes many specific loan and grant programs, formerly administered separately by the Department of Housing and Urban Development. Public facilities, urban beautification, historic preservation, and urban renewal programs, all of which have elements applicable to pedestrian zoning, are now eligible under the community development program. In the past, it has been necessary to "play the label game" carefully in seeking improvement with major federal financial assistance from the urban renewal program. Washington, D.C., for example, used urban renewal funds in its downtown pedes-

trian program, linking physical improvements to a public information project funded from other sources. This approach may still be possible under community development, but changes in laws and regulations must be followed closely.

The U.S. Department of Transportation provides grant assistance to localities for constructing and operating transit systems which may be central to the success of a pedestrian zone. Funds may also be used for actual construction costs of the traffic-free zone and special demonstration programs, such as urban transitways. The Department of Transporation has recently announced selection of five cities for auto-restricted zone demonstration projects.[4] This program, jointly funded by the Urban Mass Transit Administration and the Federal Highway Administration, includes preferential treatment for transit services. Two of the five cities will eventually be chosen to implement their plans with Department of Transporation funds.

Other Financing Sources Corporate in-kind and financial contributions have already been mentioned as a source of nongovernment support for pedestrian improvements. Charitable foundations have often helped the implementation of auto-free zones by contributing outdoor sculpture and seating or recreational equipment.

In the United States, the National Endowment for the Arts, an independently operated federal grant program, has funded architectural and graphic design studies for urban improvement programs, as well as public information campaigns aimed at promoting citizen support and participation.

7

Planning and Design

Planning a traffic-free zone is a complex process based on identification of potential problems and possible solutions as well as extensive analysis of local physical, economic, and social resources. When properly synthesized and evaluated, such an analysis may be used to support basic recommendations concerning the desirability and feasibility of creating a traffic-free zone in a given urban area.

COLLECTING AND ANALYZING DATA

The following is a tentative list of basic factors which significantly affect both the cost and visual appearance of a traffic-free zone. A thorough analysis of these factors provides basic information about a city, or a specific section of it, to determine if a pedestrian project is feasible.

Physical Factors Data is needed on the following topics:

Natural Environment Climate, precipitation, wind, and effect of the sun throughout the year must be taken into consideration, as well as topographical features that may be assets of liabilities.

Built Environment This information includes an inventory of existing land uses, building types and conditions, outdoor services, and amenities.

Movement Patterns These patterns include accessibility to and mobility within the area, public and private transport modes, capacity of the street system, peak and off-peak traffic volume, parking, deliveries, and servicing.

Utility Network Pedestrian zones are often proposed for the oldest parts of downtown areas, where utilities are likely to be the most outdated and in need of frequent repair. It is therefore important to know the location of sewers, gas, steam, electricity and telephone wires, and any other subsurface utilities, how they are reached, their capacity, and current condition.

Conditions and Trends These include data on air, noise, and visual pollution sources; analysis as to whether overall conditions are improving or deteriorating in the area; existing plans for new construction; proposed changes in traffic, parking, and public transportation; physical deterioration of structures, roads, and transportation facilities.

Social Factors Data in this category include the following:

Population This includes information on existing and potential users of the proposed traffic-free zone, including data on its residents, employees, and visitors.

Activities Information must be gathered on type, duration, and intensity of activities, as well as shopping and recreation patterns.

Conditions and Trends This subject covers the area's crime rate, occurrences of vandalism, and degree of social openness.

Economic Factors These fall into the following three areas:

Property Ownership This requires data on private, public, and institutional ownership; number of local and absentee landlords; and assessed values of taxable property.

Activities Inventories must be taken of residences, offices, industries, and institutions. Information is collected on the residents' incomes, housing occupancy rates, and market demand; business volume in the area, types of firms, hours of operation, and number of employees; location and types of factories, working schedules, and number of workers, schools, hospitals, nursing homes, churches, and community centers.

Conditions and Trends This includes real estate, sales taxes, and income trends; vacancy rates in stores; housing occupancy; and investment patterns.

In addition to these data, the surveys described below are also important in the planning process.

Physical, Social, and Economic Surveys Surveys must be taken on the following topics:

Streetscape This survey is needed to determine the general appearance of a street or district, its landscaping and furniture, as well as sidewalk curbs and street surface conditions.

Building Appearance This study determines which buildings are of architectural interest and to what extent restoration or maintenance work is needed. Structural conditions have to be assessed before any renovation project. Many old buildings are so damaged that they sometimes require major repair, or worse, demolition.

A CHECKLIST OF POTENTIAL ASSETS

1. General Appearance

☐ a. Interesting skyline if clutter eliminated.

☐ b. Open spaces could be landscaped.

☐ c. Vistas could be created to certain major buildings.

☐ d. Unifying design concept possible among buildings.

☐ e. Unnecessary poles, signs, and wires could easily be removed.

☐ f._____

2. Buildings

☐ a. Buildings with interesting architectural details.

☐ b. Buildings of historical value.

☐ c. Rear entrances could be improved.

☐ d. Vacancies allow space for expansion.

☐ e. Most buildings in sound structural condition.

☐ f._____

3. Signs

☐ a. Obsolete signs easily removed.

☐ b. Interesting old signs to restore.

☐ c. Sign panels harmonizing with building possible.

☐ d. Flush mounted wall signs could be easily viewed.

☐ e. Uniform "under-canopy" signs could be used.

☐ f._____

4. Streets and Alleys

☐ a. Wide main street right-of-way.

☐ b. Pavement width could be reduced.

☐ c. Traffic markings and signs easily replaced.

☐ d. Regular street clean-up program could be initiated.

☐ e. Street resurfacing could be programmed.

☐ f._____

5. Traffic

☐ a. Traffic could circulate around main shopping street.

☐ b. One-way movements could be eliminated

☐ c. Some turning movements could be eliminated.

☐ d. Through traffic could bypass CBD.

☐ e. Better locations possible for loading zones or bus stops.

☐ f._____

6. Parking

☐ a. Some on-street spaces could be eliminated.

☐ b. Locations available for more off-street parking.

☐ c. Existing parking lot design and layout could be improved.

☐ d. Space available for landscaping and screening.

☐ e. Employees could park in locations other than customer spaces.

☐ f._____

7. Pedestrian Facilities

☐ a. Sidewalks could be widened.

☐ b. Spaces for benches, fountains, and restrooms could be created.

☐ c. Landscaped arcade through midblock to parking area possible.

☐ d. Mall or semimall could be developed.

☐ e. Canopy could be installed along entire street.

☐ f._____

8. Land Use

☐ a. Reasonably compact shopping core.

☐ b. Some non-CBD uses would be willing to relocate.

☐ c. No major outlying commercial uses yet.

☐ d. Good variety of retail uses.

☐ e. Adjacent land available for expansion.

☐ f._____

9. Utilities

☐ a. Water and sewer systems feasible to improve.

☐ b. Overhead wires could be relocated or placed underground.

☐ c. Street lighting ready soon for replacement.

☐ d. Storm drainage can be improved.

☐ e. Utility companies cooperative and interested in community.

☐ f._____

10. Merchandising and Customer Relations

☐ a. Good market available for quality goods and services.

☐ b. Experienced and knowledgeable business officials.

☐ c. Active Chamber of Commerce.

☐ d. Aggressive and creative young business people.

☐ e. Some businesses draw from outside trade area.

☐ f._____

11. Community Attitude

☐ a. Strong community spirit.

☐ b. Have worked for educational, recreational, and medical service improvements in past.

☐ c. Progressive local government.

☐ d. Government and business will cooperate.

☐ e. Take pride in high quality of local improvements.

☐ f._____

12. Planning Activity

☐ a. Active planning agency and planning program.

☐ b. Good zoning ordinance.

☐ c. Plan has been discussed.

☐ d. Public officials recognized value of professional assistance.

☐ e. Funds available for continuing planning program.

☐ f._____

13. Area Trends

☐ a. Trade area population has increased spendable income.

☐ b. Larger farms require more goods and services.

☐ c. Our community is center for governmental, educational, or medical services.

☐ d. Good recreational or tourism potential.

☐ e. Metropolitan population decentralizing into our trade area.

☐ f._____

14. Other

☐ a._____

☐ b._____

☐ c._____

☐ d._____

☐ e._____

☐ f._____

Source: *Central Business District Improvement Manual for Iowa Communities* (Des Moines, Iowa: Division of Municipal Affairs, Office for Planning and Programming, 1971).

PROBLEM CHECKLIST

1. General Appearance

☐ a. Cluttered, unattractive entrances.

☐ b. Lack of landscape plantings and green spaces.

☐ c. Dirty, littered streets, sidewalks, and alleys.

☐ d. Visual chaos of poles, signs, and wires.

☐ e. Lack of design harmony among buildings.

☐ f. Lack of views, vistas, and visual focal points.

2. Buildings

☐ a. Poorly maintained exterior appearance.

☐ b. Drab, uninteresting interiors.

☐ c. Functionally obsolete size and shape.

☐ d. Vacant upper stories.

☐ e. Dirty, cluttered rear entrances.

☐ f. Inharmonious remodeling.

☐ g. Absentee ownerships.

3. Signs

☐ a. Excessively large.

☐ b. Overhang public right-of-way.

☐ c. Poorly maintained.

☐ d. Gaudy, garish, and ugly.

☐ e. Difficult to read.

☐ f. Poorly designed.

☐ g. Inharmonious with building architecture.

4. Streets and Alleys

☐ a. Too narrow for traffic and parking needs.

☐ b. Poor surface condition.

☐ c. Inadequate storm drainage.

☐ d. Lack proper markings and directional signs.

☐ e. Rough railroad crossings.

☐ f. Dirty and littered.

5. Traffic

☐ a. Congested, slow moving.

☐ b. Inconvenient circulation pattern.

☐ c. Turning conflicts of intersections.

☐ d. Loading zone conflicts.

☐ e. Poor access routes.

☐ f. Through traffic conflicts.

☐ g. Excessive truck traffic

6. Parking

☐ a. Insufficient number of spaces.

☐ b. On-street spaces conflict with traffic.

☐ c. Unattractive, poorly designed lots.

☐ d. Inconvenient location.

☐ e. Dirty, muddy, or rough surface.

☐ f. Poorly lighted.

☐ g. Slow turnover.

☐ h. Employees use prime customer spaces.

☐ i. Spaces too small, difficult to use.

☐ j. Obsolete fee structure.

7. Pedestrian Facilities

☐ a. Rough, broken sidewalks.

☐ b. High curbs.

☐ c. Pedestrian-automobile conflicts.

☐ d. Dark side streets.

☐ e. Unattractive routes between stores and parking areas.

☐ f. Lack of benches, fountains, rest rooms, phones, trash containers, and information centers.

☐ g. No protection from inclement weather.

☐ h. Narrow sidewalks.

☐ i. Excessive noise, dust, or objectionable odors.

8. Land Use

☐ a. Lack of major shopping store.

☐ b. Noncommercial dead spots in shopping frontage.

☐ c. Excessive vacant buildings and land.

☐ d. Lack of room for expansion.

☐ e. Objectionable uses that produce noise, dust, odors, smoke, or traffic conflicts.

☐ f. Lack of compact, convenient retail core.

☐ g. Outlying retail uses complete with CBD.

9. Utilities

☐ a. Water system old and undersized.

☐ b. Inadequate fire demand storage, pressure, or hydrants.

☐ c. Sanitary sewer old and undersized.

☐ d. Poor storm drainage.

☐ e. Tangled mess of overhead wires.

☐ f. Inadequate, unattractive street lighting.

☐ g. Streets continually torn up for repairs.

10 Merchandising and Customer Relations

☐ a. Limited selection and variety.

☐ b. Lack competitive pricing.

☐ c. Poor quality.

☐ d. Unattractive window and interior displays.

☐ e. Lack prompt and courteous attention to customers.

☐ f. Lack of product knowledge.

☐ g. Irresponsible service and maintenance practices.

☐ h. Obsolete styles.

☐ i. Failure to recognize potential markets.

11. Community Attitude

☐ a. No community concern or pride in CBD.

☐ b. Businessmen not interested in improving their stores.

☐ c. No public-private cooperation.

☐ d. It's too late to save the CBD.

☐ e. No imagination.

☐ f. Nobody wants to spend money.

☐ g. Don't need any help.

12. Planning Activity

☐ a. No active planning agency.

☐ b. No plans prepared for improvement.

☐ c. Plan prepared, but gathering dust.

☐ d. Inadequate or no zoning ordinance.

☐ e. Inadequate or no construction codes.

☐ f. Inadequate or no sign regulations.

13. Area Trends

☐ a. New regional shopping center within 60 miles.

☐ b. New highway connection to major cities.

☐ c. Declining rural population.

☐ d. Neighboring community has improved CBD.

☐ e. Unstable employment base.

☐ f. Workers commuting farther to larger cities.

14. Other

☐ a._____

☐ b._____

☐ c._____

☐ d._____

☐ e._____

☐ f._____

☐ g._____

Source: *Central Business District Improvement Manual for Iowa Communities* (Des Moines, Iowa: Division of Municipal Affairs, Office for Planning and Programming, 1971).

Exchange Street

Little London Street

Swan Lane

Bank Plain

Opie Street

Along London Street, the central pedestrian spine of Norwich, England, shop owners upgraded their properties and signs along esthetic guidelines established by an advisory committee.

Shoppers' Opinion Polls   Polls are made to determine customer preferences and habits.

Merchants' Surveys   Interviews with local merchants are useful to assess the retail strengths and weaknesses of a specific area.

Traffic Management   This survey includes data on traffic volume, number of accidents, pedestrian and bicycle movement, parking demand and supply. In particular, three detailed studies are necessary for pedestrian planning: (1) safety studies to identify existing or potential conflict points between pedestrians and vehicles; (2) sidewalk inventories to determine location and characteristics of various features that interfere with pedestrian movements; (3) pedestrian counts at stretegic locations in the area to verify existing and potential intensity of activity and possible congestion.

Market Analysis   This investigates the potential for additional retail and office space, as well as housing, hotels, and institutions.

Surveys provide a better understanding of local assets and problems. In addition, they form the basic premises for establishing goals and objectives of traffic-free zones.

DETERMINING FEASIBILITY
A feasibility study is actually the first step in a chain reaction which leads to sound planning policies and a viable design scheme. It provides a means of identifying social, economic, legal, and physical problems, while indicat-

ing potential responses, resources, and solutions. Many cities have prepared feasibility studies at the very beginning of the planning process to evaluate the cost benefit of a traffic-free zone in their downtown districts. They have relied upon the combined services of a team of experts, including market analysts, architects, land use and transportation planners, engineers, realtors, and financial specialists, all of whom contribute to the complexity and comprehensiveness of the study. In Europe, such studies have traditionally been carried out by local city agencies as part of the government process of planning and development, while in America, they have often been prepared by private planning consultants in cooperation with local city agencies. Once the feasibility of a project has been thoroughly determined, it is possible to begin work on formulating a design program.

Design programs involve careful management and organization of the groups and individuals who are participants in the project. It is necessary to maintain a forum in which all viewpoints can be expressed, as well as the possibility for continuous feedback between the community and its technical, design, and construction suppliers.

DESIGN PROGRAM
The design program is the basic reference point for the physical design. The soundness of the program depends upon the establishment of design performance criteria; the consid-

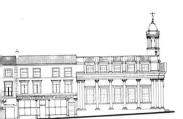

Bedford Street

Bank Plain

Castle Street

Gentlemans Walk

eration given to the social aspects of design; and the quantitative aspects of the design—that is, the relationships among the dimensions of the space itself, the facilities provided and the number of users, and the kinds of activities planned for the traffic-free zone.

Establishing Design Performance Criteria   It is necessary to begin with a set of design objectives which are responsive to the requirements of the community. Once this has been accomplished, the objectives should be formulated into a set of performance criteria to be used by participating professionals in their own determinations, as well as by the community as a basis for evaluating the designer proposals.

In formulating design objectives within a community, it is essential to keep in mind that the experience of another city is not applicable in every situation. The professional team can help to determine which proposals are feasible under which circumstances and to map out alternative design proposals, which should follow a careful analysis of the community's expectations for the mall. The design must be made to support the intended activities in the mall area, not the reverse, since the ultimate goal of design is to translate functional, economic, social, and environmental objectives into concrete terms. Grouping a list of daily activities into a reasonable number of categories can facilitate design proposals. The following divisions may be a workable model:

Functional Objectives   Operation and use of the mall, its accessibility, mobility, maintenance, and services.

Social Objectives   Participation in, as well as the observation of, activities such as resting, talking, playing sports or games, celebrating festivities and events, monitoring children at play, babysitting, promoting educational and cultural performances.

Economic Objectives   Meeting the needs and requirements of income-producing functions related to office and commercial activities.

Environmental Objectives   Improving the quality of the physical environment by preserving and restoring historic landmarks; providing green areas, flowers and trees, fountains and ponds; and enhancing the visual aspect of the overall street scene.

All these elements are described in detail below:

Improved Access by Car and / or Public Transit   This may involve updating street or highway patterns, modifying existing bus and / or subway lines, or adding a few more facilities. Signs, lighting, and traffic information may need improvements. The project should also include adequate parking for residents, employees, and visitors within walking distance of the mall; public transit stations on the pedestrian area; and visually and functionally effective corridors between parking areas and the mall proper.

Improved Mobility for People, Goods, Service and Emergency Vehicles, and

Access for Operation and Maintenance of the Utility System   Easy mobility should minimize conflicts between pedestrians and vehicular traffic, and may require instituting a mini-transit system along the length of the mall when the distance is too great for pedestrian comfort. Mobility of goods calls for easy loading and off-loading provisions for merchandise, supply, and equipment. The circulation of fire trucks and police, ambulance, snow removal, and garbage collection vehicles must be ensured, since they require horizontal and vertical clearance and adequate maneuvering space. Access and maintenance of the utility system are also needed for inspection and repair of storm and sanitary sewers, water mains, telephone lines and cables, power transmission cables, lighting conduits, fire and police alarm conduits, steam pipes, and television cables.

Income-Producing Activities for Employees, Clients, Shoppers, and Residents   Types and locations of these activities should be identified by clear graphic information. Pedestrian flows across the mall and along its length should be encouraged. People should be protected from uncomfortable weather conditions. Building entrances, window displays, views, etc., should be visually and functionally related to the mall. Shopping and business activities should be integrated with adequate supporting services and outdoor facilities restrooms, restaurants and cafeterias, playlots for children, telephone booths, etc.)

*Strong Recreational Appeal by Allo-
cating Spaces and Facilities That Respond to the Various Needs of the
Mall Users*   The mall is essentially a
gathering place. There should be
playlots and playgrounds for children,
sitting arrangements and sheltered
spaces for the elderly, small tables for
those who want to use the mall as an
outdoor cafeteria and during work
breaks, exhibition facilities for students and artists, stages for concerts
and ballets, etc.

*Improved Visual Environment by Re-
storing Existing Buildings, Repaving
the Street Floor to Unify the Entire
Space, Planting Trees and Flowers,
and Promoting Wall Paintings and Informational Graphics Design*   Sculpture can enhance the unique-
ness of the mall. Removal of unsightly
utility cables improves the overall
streetscape as well as the coordination of individual innovations into an
overall beautification scheme. A unified system of signs, street furniture
and building facade decorations can
greatly contribute to the restoration of
human scale and the enhancement of
local architecture.

The final operation is the translation
of general and specific goals into a
set of performance criteria. The following two examples illustrate this operation:

Objective   Mobility for emergency
and service vehicles. *Performance
criteria:* emergency traffic route large
enough for appropriate vehicles; vertical clearance for the tallest equipment; adequate turning radii at convenient locations; ladder clearance
for upper building floors; maneuvering room for equipment without ob-
struction from street furniture, lighting, signs, etc.; low and easily
mountable curbs, if any.

Objective   Easy utility access, operation, and maintenance. *Performance
criteria:* emergency traffic route large
enough for various facilities and pull-
off space for maintenance vehicles.

Qualitative Aspects of Design
Designers often concentrate on
refining the formal architectural
components of public spaces without
understanding how people use the
space and what makes a place successful.

Extensive observations of pedestrian areas indicate that it is not the
weather, the shops, the urban
spaces, or architecture that is the
focus of people's attention, but other
human beings. Space, building materials, and street furniture are only a
frame around the interactions of
people. If the frame is good, it helps; if
bad, it hampers this activity. Although
good design features are important
components of a high-quality public
space, the main consideration should
be the generation of high levels of activity.

Designing for the pedestrian landscape requires knowledge about
what is going to take place there. Pedestrian activities can be grouped
into six primary actions: walking,
standing, sitting, lying, running, and
playing. Walking, standing, and sitting are the most frequent.[1]

A distinction can be made between
the actions that are "necessary" and
those that are "optional." Examples
of necessary actions include walking
to buy groceries, standing while waiting for a bus, and sitting to rest after a
long walk. These actions take place
throughout the year under practically
all conditions and independent of
weather or space arrangements. Optional actions include strolling, standing to enjoy a view, sitting in the sun,
and watching a passing scene. In
most cities, for example, only necessary actions occur during the winter,

but as the weather improves during
spring, a growing number of optional
activities take place.[2]

Physical limitations appear to have
a rather strong effect on the choice
of where to walk. Direct routes and
shortcuts are preferred, while steps,
slopes, and long stretches are usually
avoided.

Providing adequate seating is essential to the creation of a high-quality space. There is sometimes a tendency to cut back on seating in order
not to "distract" shoppers from their
"mission" or to discourage "undesirables" from frequenting the area.
This strategy, however, has proved
self-defeating because it makes pedestrian zones less desirable places
for everyone. Often, increasing seating capacity has prevented those
"undesirables" from monopolizing
the area.

Important design criteria for seating
facilities include orientation toward
the sun, view, weather protection,
and dimension and form.

Scandinavians almost make a cult
of the sun. Places to sit in direct sunlight are in demand three-quarters of
the year.[3] Cities located in hot climates apply the opposite criteria to
the location of seating facilities. Munich, Germany, has resolved different
seasonal needs by providing movable
chairs in its pedestrian zone.

View is perhaps the most important
factor affecting the use of seating. If a
bench is not facing anything, it will either remain empty or be used only in
case of necessity. Sitters want to see
as much as possible of the activity
around them.

Good weather protection guarantees use of seating facilities during
rain, wind, or hot sun. The dimensions
of a seat are also important, as well as
the provision of back and arm rests.

Seating facilities do not necessarily
have to be traditional benches and
chairs. Anything can be used, especially by the young. Examples include
planters, fountains, low walls, or
steps. Many cities prefer to provide
secondary seating because it increases capacity, yet does not make
a place look empty when unused. In
most European historic centers, the
steps of monuments or public buildings and the rim of fountains usually
serve as secondary seating. In North
America, the rim of planters and fountains or fire hydrants are the casual
choices.

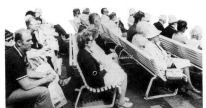

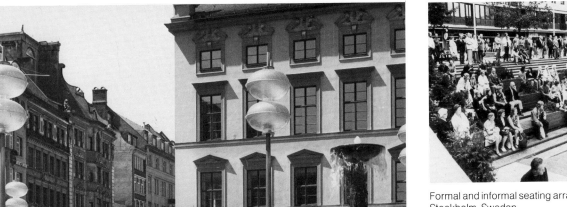

Formal and informal seating arrangements in Stockholm, Sweden.

Stackable chairs that people can arrange as they please, as shown here in Munich, Germany, are a positive innovation in the design of public open spaces.

DIRECT ESTIMATION OF
PEDESTRIAN DENSITY

Pedestrian density can be determined through the following procedure:

1 Measure the building floor space on a block or block face.

2 Measure the walkway space in the same area.

3 Count the pedestrians to be found in that area at an instant during a selected peak period by means of aerial photography.

4 Develop a statistical relationship that shows what number of pedestrians at an instant are associated with a unit of floor space and a unit of walkway space.

5 On the basis of flow analysis, postulate a comfortable rate of flow.

6 Convert the comfortable flow rate into a space allocation per moving pedestrian.

7 Multiply the number of pedestrians expected to be found in front of a building during the peak period by the desirable space allocation per pedestrian to obtain the needed walkway space.

From Boris S. Pushkarev and Jeffrey M. Zupan, *Urban Space for Pedestrians* (Cambridge, Mass.: MIT Press, 1975), p. 26.

Quantitative Aspects of Design   The design of outdoor spaces has seldom been approached in a way to maximize pedestrian activities and comfort. Streets and squares have been shaped to the requirements of motor vehicles, while pedestrians have been herded onto shrinking sidewalks. Design of the public outdoor environment is similar to that of indoor spaces and facilities. Among the questions to be answered are those dealing with identification of local activity, analysis of movement patterns, the relation of walkway space to buildings, the establishment of dimensions and locations for pedestrian services and facilities, and ensuring accessibility for the handicapped.

A widely used technique for the study of pedestrian flow and density and performance of seating facilities is time-lapse aerial photography. It is important to determine the spatial elements which encourage or disrupt pedestrian flow, such as physical obstructions, traffic lights, steps, and broad uninterrupted spaces.

A recent study of space requirements for pedestrians in New York City outlines some basic steps to determine the amount of walkway space a building requires. This procedure, termed "direct estimation of pedestrian density," simplifies the process of conventional traffic demand analysis. The same method can be applied to a larger area to determine space requirements for pedestrians in a traffic-free district.

In general, urban advocates should be aware of the need to investigate local pedestrian traffic demands and people's need for space in different circumstances and activities. For example, the amount of room a person occupies may change drastically depending on the weather. In case of rain, someone with an open umbrella occupies an area 10 times larger than that he or she regularly needs for walking. Practical considerations aside, many psychological factors also affect pedestrian movement.

The amount of available space has an effect on human behavior. If there is too little room to perform physical tasks or if objects and other people in a given space interfere, the natural pedestrian flow will be inhibited. On a more basic level, people need to be able to choose between sitting together with others or remaining separate, communicating or reflecting,

participating or observing. All this depends not only on design, but on individual preferences, cultural factors, social conventions, and taboos, and the design should take into account the kinds of communication the mall hopes to encourage or develop.[4]

DESIGN PROJECT

The overall design project takes the performance criteria one step further by translating them into a comprehensive system of proposals for the detailed arrangement of the pedestrian zone. This process has two stages: (1) presenting a series of design options to the community for evaluation and (2) preparing working drawings as a first step towards implementation. This should include a preliminary cost estimate. The architect's project translates ideas and concepts into physcial images which should be understandable to the community. Drawings should visualize plans, elevations, sections, and perspective views showing the basic spatial design of the traffic-free zone and the location of its activities, clear spaces, and markers. This project is a summary of all the findings in the planning process and is used as a framework for detailed studies of transportation, engineering, landscaping, graphics, street furniture, and lighting.

Transportation   Transportation studies result in recommendations for adapting and improving existing traffic systems so that the area is accessible and parking is close to it.

Engineering   This study supports recommendations for technical repairs, modifications, and innovations in the structural components of the area as well as in the utility system.

Landscaping   Landscaping studies involve the selection and arrangement of various plantings, grassy areas, and water. This is an area of great public interest because the various design options have profound functional and environmental implications. There are many alternate approaches to landscaping, depending on local drainage problems, the growth and seasonal requirements of different plants, and maintenance. Plants create interest and beauty in urban settings; they muffle the noise of traffic, absorb noxious gases, and retain dust and dirt particles. They can also reduce glare, not only from

Low-cost street roof in Wupperthal, Germany.

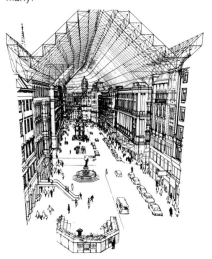

Proposed transparent roofing for Vienna's Graben.

In Trenton, N.J., kiosks and canopies designed to provide human scale to the mall and to shelter a variety of activities have been recently removed and substituted with trees and shrubs.

natural sources but from automobiles, building materials, signs, and other objects. From the standpoint of climate control, trees and shrubs provide shade in the summer, building insulation in summer and winter, and an effective shield against strong winds. Plants of all varieties can also be used to direct and guide pedestrian traffic.

Esthetics, however, is the essential element in the greening of urban areas. Planting creates a sense of intimacy as well as expansiveness and draws the visual elements of a space together, giving it a focus even in diversity. Successful landscaping in urban areas is determined largely by local conditions of soil and climate, though proper planting and maintenance are essential.

Graphics The graphic study encompasses treatment of street pavements, walls, store signs, window displays, and building entrances, as well as directional and informational systems. Signs not only contribute information and vitality to the urban environment, but if well designed, also improve the character and flavor of the area. However, they can often be confusing or fail to deliver their messages. A number of cities have encouraged careful design of private signs in accordance with the character of the local environment and its architectural elements. Others have adopted municipal regulations which control the design and location of signs.

Street Furniture Street furniture includes benches, outdoor seating, telephone booths, children's play equipment, trash receptacles, display and exhibition structures, book and newspaper kiosks, fast food vendors, game and cafe facilities. Information signs, planters and tree grids, bus shelters, fountains, amphitheaters, and lighting may be purchased from existing manufacturing lines, while most furniture needs to be custom designed to fulfill local requirements.

There are two basic approaches to street furnishings: they can be distributed throughout the entire mall to enhance the overall interest of the area, or they can be concentrated into multipurpose groups. For example, telephone booths, bus shelters, drinking fountains, and benches form groupings that attract increased activity. Graphic and lighting systems can add direction and identity, giving a certain "feel" to an area even when it has relatively little actual street furniture.

Top: Sensitive lighting and landscape arrangements in the Riverside, California mall. Above: An imaginative and informative wall painting in Minneapolis, Minnesota advertises a music store located in the building.

Proposed street information system for New York City designed by Massimo Vignelli: a series of poles, color coded for easy identification of the elements they contain, such as telephones, mail boxes, fire and police alarm boxes, and litter bins. The poles also provide for advertising, directional signs, announcements of special events, and bus stop and subway signs. The top of each pole houses a light fixture.

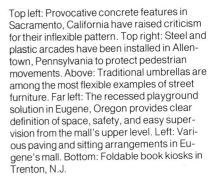

Top left: Provocative concrete features in Sacramento, California have raised criticism for their inflexible pattern. Top right: Steel and plastic arcades have been installed in Allentown, Pennsylvania to protect pedestrian movements. Above: Traditional umbrellas are among the most flexible examples of street furniture. Far left: The recessed playground solution in Eugene, Oregon provides clear definition of space, safety, and easy supervision from the mall's upper level. Left: Various paving and sitting arrangements in Eugene's mall. Bottom: Foldable book kiosks in Trenton, N.J.

Lighting   Lighting allows for night use of a traffic-free zone and increases the safety of the area by acting as a deterrent to crime. Lighting enhances the user's appreciation of the urban scene; advertises stores and displays goods and services in shop windows and through luminous signs; and provides direction and information. It is far easier to set standards for determining the amount of necessary indoor lighting than to determine what is required outdoors. Very often this depends upon the function and purposes of the lighting system, as well as on increased efficiency and pleasurable usage of a traffic-free zone. When this has been determined, it is easier to proceed with the development of a specific lighting study which will best complement the pedestrian district.

Too often street lighting comes from high sources, which results in strong and even, but monotonous illumination. Such failure comes about because designers don't take into account the varieties of pedestrians' needs and perceptions, which are best served by lower light posts and more varied levels of illumination. Changes in light intensity, with some areas highly illuminated and others bathed in shadows, create a more stimulating environment. Some cities have codes establishing the minimum level of light; some have tried to formulate a ratio between maximum and minimum levels. Ultimately, the minimum level of light should always be enough to convey a sense of well-being.

Lighting has been used to accentuate important pedestrian features such as crosswalks, bus stops, turns, steps, and ramps. In most pedestrian zones, a mainstream of light indicates circulation routes, signs, window displays, etc. In Minneapolis, for example, the brightest lights are reserved for store interiors, while the mall itself is left much darker. This focuses public attention on store merchandise, rather than on the mall—a useful sales mechanism.

Two principal components of outdoor lighting fixtures, the luminaire and the post, are among the most important design elements of the traffic-free zone. If light poles are spaced regularly and fairly close together along a pedestrian way, they can help create visual rhythms with other elements of the street environment.

Besides being supported by poles, lights can be attached to buildings, trees, or street furniture or integrated into shop windows and signs. The primary lighting fixtures on a pedestrian walkway are usually kept out of the reach of people, 10 to 15 feet/3 to 5 meters in the air. Where low-level lighting is used, fixtures are placed in such a way that they do not produce glare.

The color of light is different according to the types of lighting sources. It may blend or contrast with the surroundings, depending on what the designer feels is the proper effect to be achieved.

In New London, Connecticut, an ingenious two-level lighting system was implemented. White mercury vapor lights on 35-foot/11-meter poles were set in the same pattern as the original street lights, providing enough illumination to discourage crime. Smaller lights on 10-foot/3-meter poles were spaced throughout the grassy areas to add sparkle and bring the scale of the space closer to eye level.

Pedestrian-scale lighting fixtures in Bremen, Germany.

8

Managing Implementation

In the context of this book, implementation of a traffic-free zone does not simply refer to construction, but rather to the entire process which prepares for, includes, and follows the construction. Therefore, this chapter will cover the following issues: selecting materials; estimating construction cost; identifying participating agencies; promoting vitality during construction; and planning for proper maintenance.

SELECTING MATERIALS

Throughout the design process, the mall must be thought of on a long-term basis; maintenance, material replacement costs, the sustaining of esthetic values, and general appearance must be taken into consideration. Cost estimates should be based on a life-cycle cost analysis so that designs and materials are evaluated for initial cost, life span, maintenance charges, replacement costs, and the cost of money. The result will present a true picture of long-term expenses which first cost estimates cannot provide.

Durability and climatic effects on materials and maintenance represent major factors, since climate can, for example, affect expansion or contraction of materials. Rain or ice conditions can be particularly influential. Also to be considered are the kinds and amounts of activities to be performed in the mall, the posibilities of vandalism, and the importance of proper drainage channels to material integrity.

Some materials may be combined visually, functionally, or economically to perform what a single alternative cannot. For example, a combination of paving materials can create patterns that facilitate movement and a variety of uses in a given area of the mall. Asphalt blocks, for example, can be combined with green or earth areas to create soft paths through gardens and parks. Fresno, California, used material variations to create a mall pavement patterned with undulating stripes across its width. The result encourages pedestrians to cross from one side of the mall to the other.

Textures in a traffic-free zone are an essential visual element of the urban landscape. Because repaving an existing open space is a fundamental aspect of a pedestrian project, the materials selected for walking surfaces are of great importance. An annotated list of the commonly used paving materials follows:

Concrete Relatively inexpensive and durable, it can be finished in a variety of colors and textures.

Precast Concrete Slabs Produced by compression or poured in open molds, they have the same characteristics as concrete.

Natural Stones Commonly used paving stones include slate, granite, quartzite, sandstone, marble, and blue stone. Though relatively expensive, granite is the longest wearing and the most widely used of all. Stone for sidewalks and other pedestrian paths must have a safe and even surface. Accordingly, they are used in large regularly cut slabs, as paving bricks (pavers), or in the form of "setts"—stone cubes that have long been popular for paving European streets and plazas. In addition, there are a number of stone aggregates, "cast stone," which resemble the natural material but are less expensive.

Cobbles Obtained from beaches, river beds, and gravel pits, naturally rounded stones can be laid in random rough courses or in fairly exact patterns. Though the initial cost of cobblestones is high, maintenance is low and they are extremely durable.

Brick As a material for paving pedestrian areas, brick is rapidly regaining popularity. Although significantly more expensive than concrete, it is highly versatile for its range of textures, colors, and sizes. It is also durable.

Cities	Total Cost	Invisible Cost	Ratio
Fresno, Calif.	$1,841,000	$1,181,000	64%
Danville, Ill.	110,989	45,521	40
Michigan City, Ind.	1,794,000	1,300,000	72
Poughkeepsie, N.Y.	3,400,000	2,800,000	82
Knoxville, Tenn.	313,000	125,000	40

ESTIMATING CONSTRUCTION COST

There is no single standard that can be applied to the construction costs of a pedestrian zone. Such factors as when it is built and regional geographic differences cause major price variation. However, changes in construction costs are mainly due to differences in the quality of materials and work used to develop a pedestrian street.

A great amount of the construction cost of a pedestrian zone goes into invisible improvements, such as modernizing or moving utilities, ripping out and replacing pavement, installing new drainage, and other site preparation. Nonconstruction costs, such as legal expenses, planning, and design studies, can also be expensive.

The U.S. examples in the box on the left indicate the ratio of invisible improvement costs to the total cost of implementing the traffic-free district.[1]

In terms of visible improvements, the basic walking surface of the district—its area, materials, and design—is responsible for the remaining direct expense. Undoubtedly, construction of the project stimulates private investment in building renovation, new signs, and so forth. Thus, the value of improvements to a public space is usually greater than the public investment.

Indirect costs should also be taken into account. New parking facilities, changes made to accommodate rerouted traffic, new signs, and the cost of additional services to the area are all examples of indirect costs. If a traffic-free zone is a success, many of the costs will be recouped by the additional real estate and sales tax revenues it generates.

Following are detailed cost breakdowns for two cities. Pomona's pedestrian area was built in the early 1960s; New London's was completed in 1974; therefore, inflation must be taken into consideration.

POMONA, CALIFORNIA

Construction

Removals and earthwork	$ 69,036
Storm drainage	72,431
Reinforced concrete	34,532
Special pavements	107,682
Water distribution	7,585
Electrical	158,688
Stone masonry facing	50,000
Precast concrete stone	10,000
Structures	5,000
Waterproofing sculpture pool	1,000
Metal trash receptacles	1,000
Travertine facing	3,000

Others

Legal	11,049
Title	4,520
Assessment engineer	9,330
Bonds and advertising	1,660
Engineering consultants	51,930
Miscellaneous materials	12,155
Streetwork	17,674
Traffic signals	17,254
Trees	43,500
Blueprinting	740
Engineering and inspection	7,472
Total	**$712.477**

POMONA, CALIFORNIA:
SECOND STREET PEDESTRIAN MALL

Cost Summary

Total
(as of February 1966) $712,477.00

The project extends 2,976 feet/900 meters and covers nine city blocks. Commercial properties run along both sides of the mall for a length of 2,316 feet/700 meters. Of the project's total length, all but 125 feet/38 meters received special paving treatment. The total improvement area was about 225,000 square feet/2,200 square meters.

Cost per front foot
(of commercial properties) $153.00

Cost per linear foot
(of physical improvements) $239.00

Cost per square foot $ 3.17

NEW LONDON, CONNECTICUT

Summary

General costs	$ 54,200	
Pavement	349,260	
Mounds	29,250	
Lighting	45,863	
Canopies, kiosks, and panels	375,000	
Plantings	65,700	
Gas	80,000	
Telephone	50,000	
Parade	77,000	
Underground utilities	299,936	
Total	**$1,426,209**	

Detailed General Costs

Mobilization	$ 10,400	
Traffic officials	15,200	
Flagpoles	6,000	
Clock installations	1,500	
Maintenance and protection	6,000	
Ship's ventilator mailboxes	3,600	
Miscellaneous	11,500	
Total	**$ 54,200**	

Pavement

Temporary sidewalk	$ 23,500	
Sidewalk and curb removal	25,000	
Roadway excavation	1,500	
Common excavation	19,000	
Preparation of subgrade	22,860	
Resetting existing surface units	23,300	
Enclosing sidewalk hatchways	22,000	
4 in./10.16 cm cobblestones	87,000	
8 in./20.32 cm cobblestones	40,000	
Steel bollards	7,800	
Concrete sidewalk and curbing	40,600	
Asphalt preparation and paving	32,300	
Total	**$349,260**	

Mounds

Planting soil	$ 9,150
Concrete sitting wall	12,000
Filter mat	2,100
Drainage pipes	6,000
Total	**$ 29,250**

Lighting

Underground electricity lines	$28,083
Pedestrian and roadway lighting	17,600
Total	**$45,683**

Canopies, kiosks, and panels

Footing sockets	$ 19,800
Central canopies	101,250
Kiosks	42,250
East canopy	52,650
West canopy	51,300
Design changes	6,600
Display panels	15,200
Graphic panels	14,400
Extra	71,550
Total	**$375,000**

Plantings

Wooden tubs	$13,000
Sodding	3,900
Seeding	100
Plants and trees	46,000
Irrigation	2,500
Underdrain	200
Total	**$65,700**

Underground utilities

Pavement removal	$ 39,860
Traffic control and maintenance	15,500
Fill	23,500
Trench excavation	53,300
Storm system	51,496
Water system	75,080
Sewer system	16,200
Irrigation	10,000
Completion incentive	15,000
Extra	7,076
Total	**$299,936**

NEW LONDON, CONNECTICUT:
CAPTAIN'S WALK

Cost Summary

Total $1,426,209.00

The project extends 1,200 feet/360 meters and covers four city blocks, only two of which are totally traffic free. The length of the fully pedestrianized area is 800 feet/240 meters. The two outer blocks are semimalls with improved sidewalks. The following figures refer to the 800-foot/240-meter long pedestrianized stretch, which accounted for 75 percent of the total project cost.

Cost per front foot
(of commercial properties) $ 668.00

Cost per linear foot
(of physical improvements)   1,337.00

Cost per square foot   26.00

The construction of a new mall in Boulder, Colorado.

IDENTIFYING PARTICIPATING AGENCIES

Implementing a traffic-free zone requires political, legal, and technical expertise, as well as establishment of a working partnership between public agencies and private groups. Among public agencies usually involved in the process are the following: the city planning department in charge of overall planning, the highways or public works department that oversees construction, and the traffic department that reroutes traffic in the area. The fire and police deparments and ambulance service can assist in coordinating compliance with regulations and insuring access, as well as resolving special problems. Utility companies can help coordinate plans for access, reconstruction, relocation, and maintenance of gas, electric and telephone lines, as well as water, steam, and sewers. New routes and stops on or near the traffic-free zone will be coordinated with the city transporation agencies.

Private companies that should arrange their schedules and services to accommodate the needs of the pedestrian area include trucking firms, parking lot operators, and taxi companies. Owners of abutting property must give permission for access during construction.

Consultants such as planners, lawyers, traffic and civil engineers, landscape architects, urban and graphic designers will continue to provide services at various stages in the implementation process.

PROMOTING VITALITY DURING CONSTRUCTION

Because construction of a pedestrian area often takes months to complete, plans must be made to maintain customer traffic to stores during that period. In many cities, torn up sidewalks, noise, dust, and other inconveniences to customers were overcome as follows:

Buffers were constructed to shield shoppers from heavy construction. These were decorated with colorful graphics by school children or design consultants. Temporary landscaping and street furniture were introduced.

Alternative Paths were established through the rear entrances of stores and businesses. Existing paths in the traffic-free zone were made as safe and attractive as possible.

Promotional Activities and special sales, contests, and events were organized to maintain public interest during construction.

PLANNING FOR PROPER MAINTENANCE

Since a pedestrian area generates intense activity, maintenance is an important consideration. Necessary services, such as litter and snow removal, landscaping, and public facilities upkeep, must be studied carefully to determine how they will be carried out and what the costs will be.

Ground maintenance can be provided by the municipality or the downtown organization charged with administration of the zone. In most cases, landscaping and plant upkeep is handled by the municipal parks department or by a private landscaping firm.

Assessing stores that front on a pedestrian zone is a common method of meeting part of all maintenance costs. The upkeep of Freeport's downtown plaza totaled approximately $7,000 in 1975. Merchants on the plaza were assessed $3 per front foot to cover this cost. The maintenance cost of the Kalamazoo Mall was $8,500 in 1960. By 1972, this figure had risen to $18,000. About 50 percent of these costs were met by assessing businesses along the mall $4.25 per front foot, with the balance coming from the city.

Police Protection Pedestrian zones which retain some vehicular traffic can be protected, to a degree, by police cars. In some cities, police can patrol the area from cross-through streets. In the other cases, they can utilize the special emergency vehicle right-of-way included in the design of pedestrian districts. In other cities, special mini-vehicles and motorcycles have also been used. However, the most common method of policing traffic-free zones has been by foot patrol.

Access for Emergency, Service, and Delivery Vehicle Service and emergency vehicles require easy access to all properties along a pedestrian street. Accordingly, a special right-of-way, which blends into the pedestrian scheme, is always provided. These special lanes must respond to spe-cific requirements in terms of width, vertical clearance, and turning radii.

The U.S. National Board of Fire Underwriters recommends the following fire protection specifications: trees, benches, lighting poles, and any other fixed objects should be located so that they will not hamper fire fighting. While hydrants and alarms boxes should be designed to harmonize with street furnishings, they must be easily identifiable and properly spaced.

At least 12 feet/4 meters of open space must be provided for emergency vehicles along the entire length of the pedestrian street, not including existing sidewalks.

All manholes, hydrants, alarm boxes, sprinklers, and fire department Siamese connections must be readily accessible. Canopies should permit clearance for large emergency vehicles and should be made of non-combustible materials. They should not restrict access to upper floors.

Whenever possible, deliveries in pedestrian districts should be made from rear and side streets. However, many cities allow delivery vehicles to penetrate the area during restricted hours.

Above: Special police vehicles for patrolling New York's Lincoln Center and, left, snow removal in Copenhagen, Denmark.

The European
Experience:
Selected
Case Studies

This section describes 10 European pedestrianization experiments. These particular case studies have been chosen because they reflect the diversity of planning approaches, legal methodologies, and financial strategies that have been applied to the creation of pedestrian zones throughout Europe. Although the implementation of urban pedestrian malls in America has focused primarily on downtown economic revitalization, a close look at the European situation reveals a greater number of reasons for traffic-free zoning. The goals sought by European planners have ranged from strictly functional ones dealing with traffic control strategies to humanistic ones dealing with conservation of the urban fabric and improvement of residential conditions in central areas. The broad acceptance of traffic-free zoning has been based, primarily, on its capacity to achieve these goals. However, the conditions in Europe—the political climate, the postwar economic situation, the fact that no special legislation was necessary for municipal improvements, and a financial structure where costs for such improvements could be allocated directly from city budgets—further contributed to an atmosphere very favorable for such a radical change in planning policies, regardless of geographical and linguistic differences.

The pedestrian phenomenon also had its roots in the fact that most European cities underwent a similar development pattern and therefore were experiencing similar environmental and traffic problems. Throughout Europe, the transition from the old to the modern city has been characterized by the built-up areas first reaching, and then spilling outside, defensive walls that were built in successive rings from the Middle Ages through the Renaissance.

As a result of the Industrial Revolution, people began moving into urban areas faster than public and private housing enterprises could accommodate them. The defensive walls were demolished. In most cases, boulevards, ring roads, and plazas replaced them, serving as dividers between the aristocratic inner city and the new, low-cost housing sprawling around the perimeter.

Cities became organized around a system of radial routes converging on the center, which was the optimal form for the rational development of the outlying areas. New residential quarters were laid out in a grid pattern. Railroad lines, as well as the radial arteries, ran through the core areas. The necessary space for these transportation lines was created by demolition. Toward the end of the 19th century, zoning and building regulations became necessary to

The city of Rotterdam dramatically exemplifies the process of growth and change that many European cities undertook following the destruction of World War II. The top photograph shows the city center in 1933, and the middle photo shows the city center in 1945 after the rubble had been removed. Buildings that were not too badly damaged were restored, as shown in the bottom picture of the city center in 1970. In the foreground is the "Lijnbaan," one of the best models of pedestrian design.

curb the uncontrolled development of peripheral areas, as well as the construction of inadequate and unsanitary housing for workers.

Only in the beginning of the 20th century did cities begin to develop instruments to control, and in some cases radically modify, the concentric pattern of the late 19th-century development. In the Netherlands, the introduction of the Housing Act in 1901 obliged municipalities to draw up extension plans for future growth. Under the Berlage Plan of 1907, Amsterdam began to develop toward the south and west of the core, while the eastern and northern areas were protected for low-density development.

A similar approach was followed in Copenhagen, with the 1947 Finger Plan. City planners proposed that future development take place along five major transportation axes stemming from the core. The plan was aimed directly at stopping the concentric ring of low-cost housing developed after 1850. It did not, however, eliminate the tremendous pressure brought to the core by the road system, which converged in the center of town.

The growing congestion in city cores reached the point where strong remedial action was unquestionably necessary. Controls, such as one-way streets and restricted parking, were introduced. But these strategies proved only partially effective. European cities were primed for pedestrian zoning.

Politics has played a great role in the implementation of pedestrian streets. Urban policies reflect decisions made at the national level. In the past years, conservation of historic districts, limitation of traffic, and protection of the urban environment have become national goals in many countries, where ministries have been specially created to handle legislation and financing of urban improvement programs.

In Europe, cities have great control over their territorial development. The decision-making process is directly under the auspices of the city council. Generally, once a master plan is approved, it is rigidly enforced.

Expropriation of land has been a powerful tool in successfully implementing European development plans, and it was instrumental in postwar reconstruction. Ownership of land gives cities the power to control

expansion of new urban developments and location of peripheral shopping centers. In core areas, this device enables city administration to control the type, size, and quality of redevelopment.

Since 1851, the Netherlands has had compulsory purchase legislation which gives municipalities power to expropriate land for new developments or land use changes. When Rotterdam was redesigned after World War II, its reconstruction was possible only because of this power. Expropriation capacity was directly responsible for the creation of Lijnbaan, the city's pedestrian zone.

Stockholm, Sweden, began acquiring land as early as 1912, although some of those parcels have only recently been developed.

Economics is an equally important factor in pedestrian zoning. In recent years, the general economic recession in Europe has forced planners and administrators to review their planning attitudes, and the focus has shifted to utilizing resources rather than creating new ones. The restoration of housing stock, the reuse of abandoned buildings as community centers, and the recycling of streets into pedestrian spaces have all been results of this rearrangement of priorities.

In addition, the weakened economy has halted costly urban highway projects. For example, in Norwich, England, only one-third of the proposed highway encircling the city was constructed, due to lack of funding. However, this did not decrease the success of the pedestrianized area in the city's central commercial and historic district as was expected.

In specific situations, the reduction of private vehicles through traffic-free zoning has met with the national economic interest. In Denmark, the national government strongly supported banning traffic because the country does not have an auto industry. Therefore, reducing car imports can improve Denmark's economic balance.

In most cases analyzed, pedestrian streets in Europe have been implemented before there was specific legislation for the process. Most of the streets were closed to vehicles by simply redirecting existing traffic patterns, a procedure which does not require parliamentary action.

One of the simplest legal methods

for traffic-free zoning is available in the Federal Republic of Germany, where amendment of traffic regulations by specific authorities is done through agreement of the city's police department, the city's traffic commission, and its bureau of road circulation. A similarly straightforward method is found in Denmark, where the proposal originates with the city planning commission, it is then approved by the city council, and then a traffic plan is worked out with the cooperation of the police. In both cases, restriction of vehicular access is viewed as a traffic issues, not a major land use question.

At the other end is the United Kingdom, where a street closing requires publication of a notice, a 21-day objection period, approval by the local planning commission initially responsible for the plan, and submission to the Secretary of State, who has the final power to make the order official. Until a permanent closing is approved, no landscaping can be installed.

The cost of pedestrian amenities and physical improvements to existing structures in the traffic-free area is often absorbed by tenants or landlords. In a number of cities, merchants have volunteered to pay for display cases, sculpture, and fountains; storefront improvements have been covered by shopkeepers. In other cities, however, government subsidies have been available for the renovation of facades in historic districts. For example, in Rouen, funding came through the Malraux Law, a national landmark preservation statue.

DESIGN FEATURES
The physical dimensions of pedestrian streets vary with each project's scope. In general, streets closed for commercial reasons tend to be shorter and more complexly designed than those for conservation and environmental purposes. Streets with prominent commercial functions display a greater variety of improvements and amenities to attract people.

Location of the street in the central area is a key factor. The success of Hohe Strasse and Schildergasse in Cologne is due to their strategic position between the railroad station and the bus terminal—very functional for both tourists and residents.

The length of pedestrian streets does not affect people's willingness to use them. Moreover, the intensity of human activity and scale of architectural setting make long streets like the Stroget in Copenhagen very pleasant places to walk. Special vehicles to move shoppers were not necessary for the success of European pedestrian projects. However, mini-buses were adopted in some cases to increase mobility from railroad stations, bus terminals, and parking areas to the central business district.

With few exceptions, the design of European malls has been less than innovative. Elimination of sidewalks, pedestrian bridges, covered walkways, and broken vistas are all part of a standard vocabulary for pedestrian streets. Lijnbaan in Rotterdam and the Torg in Stockholm set those standards in the 1940s. The impact of these projects resulted from their use of pedestrian design as an organic part of the overall project rather than as added beautification. No furniture was needed in Copenhagen and Bologna, where the major goal was to recreate public spaces to allow the interaction of people without the pressure of automobile traffic. Both cities proved that creating pedestrian zones can be accomplished very inexpensively.

Pedestrian zoning has proved essential to the revitalization of Europe's historic urban cores. However, traffic-free streets cannot solve all of a city's problems. Restoration of historic buildings must be combined with programs to attract people back to the historic centers, for these centers cannot survive on their own beauty as museum pieces. Amsterdam has one of the most beautiful central districts in Europe, with more than 7,000 historic buildings. However, today it faces severe decay because the city has not been able to create the right balance of functions in its core.

A number of European cities have made great progress in the area of housing rehabilitation. This is a major priority in Copenhagen, where speculative building practices in the early 1900s accelerated the deterioration of the city's housing stock. Between 1960 and 1975, over 5,000 dwelling units were restored as part of the city's revitalization effort.

In Bologna, the major goal over the past 10 years has been to restore decayed neighborhoods and keep people of different incomes and pro-fessions in the central area. To avoid the center's transformation into an enclave for the rich, the high costs of restoration are being underwritten by the city.

The newest trend in Europe is to bring pedestrian zoning into residential areas. This has been done experimentally in Stockholm, both in the central area and in the suburbs. In Bologna, too, pedestrian zoning has been extended into the residential neighborhoods of the core. This is done through citizens' committees which decide whether or not creating pedestrian walkways is functional for a particular neighborhood street.

Thus Europe is opening up a new direction in the pedestrian concept. This coincides with a new awareness on the part of planners, who now realize that the problems of large cities must be approached on the neighborhood scale with community participation.

Greater Amsterdam's development plan.

9

Stockholm
Sweden

During the past 30 years, the city of Stockholm has applied pedestrian zoning to a variety of situations relating both to traffic control and environmental improvement. While most pedestrian streets in Europe are glamorous but short, Stockholm's pedestrian system now extends throughout the entire city.

The major traffic-free area in downtown Stockholm is the Torg, a multi-block mix of office towers and commercial and cultural buildings. Planned in 1946 and largely completed by 1962, the Torg has been a model renewal project for the past 15 years. In 1961, Stockholm began to implement car-free zones in the central commercial district. And in 1972, a major experiment was initiated in two residential areas—Ostermalm, close to the downtown, and Aspudden a suburb built in 1910. These particular experiments were aimed at eliminating all through-traffic from residential districts by segregating it to peripheral walkways. The dramatic improvement in the environment and safety of the residential streets resulted in the permanent adoption of the concept and its extension to other residential neighborhoods in the city.

CITY PROFILE

Stockholm, the capital and largest city in Sweden, is regarded as one of the most beautiful cities in the world. The city was founded in the middle of the 13th century and was officially recognized as the capital in 1436. The medieval nucleus of the city remained intact, and today the street network and many of the buildings from that period still exist, forming an area of great architectural interest which has been protected from change. The modern central business district developed within the so-called stone town, a district which dates back to the 17th century and still reflects the original layout.

The shortage of land reserves has resulted in a slowly decreasing city population. Stockholm presently has 750,000 residents, but this figure is expected to decrease by 50,000 within the next 5 years. Large-scale renewal efforts in the stone town contributed to the loss of residents. The greater Stockholm area includes some twenty-eight communities and a total population of 1,350,000.

JOINT TRANSPORTATION AND HOUSING POLICY

Both housing and transportation policies in Sweden are initiated at the national level. However, the joint development of transportation and housing has been the particular guiding philosophy of Stockholm's Department of Planning and Building Control, which supervises all planning in the greater Stockholm region.

TRANSPORTATION

As a national policy, "transportation is expected to be a neutral factor in development. No single mode is favored for its own quality, desirability or profit."[1] Public rapid transit, as well as the highway system, is expected to be economically self-sufficient. However, the city has to contribute a large part of the rapid transit system's running expenses.

In the early 1940s, the Greater Stockholm City Council approved the construction of an underground railway system which constituted the basis of a proposal to cope with the city's accelerated growth. The overall proposal envisioned new housing districts as beads along the rapid transit strings, which would intersect beneath the city center.

Today, planners recognize that social and environmental factors are not quantifiable, but important elements in evaluating the cost and benefits of transportation systems. Therefore, Stockholm has tried to improve the appearance of its very efficient rail and subway systems. At present, two subway lines cross Stockholm's central area, and a third is under construction. When it is completed, the central business district will have rapid transit entering it from six different directions, and no station within it will be more than 2½ minutes from any other.

Consistent with the national policy of neutrality in transportation, the public as well as Stockholm's Department of Planning and Building opted for extension of the subway system. In addition, the city has consciously discouraged the use of private cars in the downtown area by not increasing the capacity of the streets and by initiating stringent parking controls.

As in many other European cities, Stockholm's traffic pattern is based on a radial road system. The system of arterial highways built around the city after World War II is heavily used.

Since 1950, private car ownership in Sweden has increased by 750 percent, to the point where Swedes own 2 million cars, with per capita ownership rising from 50 to 300 vehicles per 100 inhabitants.[2] To increase the capacity of the radial road system, a belt freeway system some four miles in diameter is now under construction to deflect and control the increased incoming traffic on roads leading to the city.[3]

HOUSING

Improving housing quality is also a national goal in Sweden. All housing is either publicly built and maintained or privately built under strict leaseholds; there is very little segregation of low-, middle-, and upper-income residential areas.[4]

In spite of a national policy favoring the growth of smaller towns and cities, the housing shortage in Stockholm has been severe.[5] In greater Stockholm, new clusters of housing are built along the transportation spines. High-rise buildings comprise 85 to 90 percent of this construction, with the remainder in row or terrace houses. To lessen transporation cost as a deciding factor in the choice of urban or suburban housing, people can purchase monthly unlimited rapid transit passes at a cost of about $10.

Because almost all areas within the city boundaries are completely built up, planners have directed their efforts toward revitalizing existing housing. An integral part of this program is improving the environmental conditions of Stockholm's central area, which has been adversely affected by increased automobile traffic. Public response to revitalization programs has been excellent. In sections of the city undergoing restoration, integrated traffic control and housing rehabilitation programs are initiated at the same time. This greatly facilitates creation of traffic-free zones in the city. Joint housing and transportation development is possible because the city owns most of the land within its boundaries.[6]

THE TORG

Planning for the Torg began in 1946. This office, commercial, and entertainment complex was conceived as the anchor of a large urban renewal project—part of an ambitious modernization program for Stockholm's stone town and central business dis-

The Torg's organizers experimented with a "free wall" that citizens used to express their views or leave messages. The wall was continually repainted at the city's expense; later it was torn down during the completion of the House of Culture.

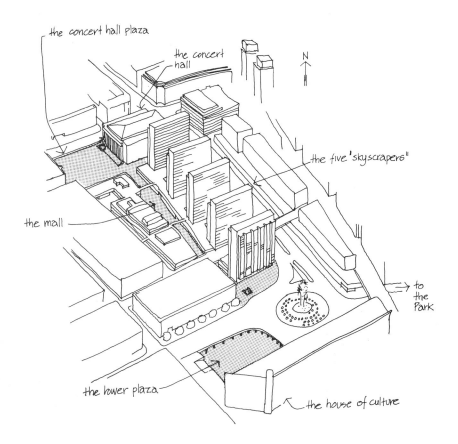

the concert hall plaza

the concert hall

N

the five "skyscrapers"

the mall

to the Park

the tower plaza

the house of culture

Fifteen years after its completion, the Torg is still regarded as one of the most significant examples of downtown renewal in the world. The five towers and two-level commercial center complex provides vertical separation of different movement systems. Architect David Hellden was the designer of both the urban layout and the first office tower completed in 1959.

trict. This plan called for new housing, establishment of the subway system, reconstruction and widening of streets, and construction of parking garages. In 1946, the city center still had essentially the same gridiron structure as that recorded on maps from 1640. Three- and five-story buildings from the 19th century lined streets seldom more than 30 feet / 70 meters wide.

The area now occupied by the Torg was traditionally Stockholm's open air market. In the center of a dense commercial district, the complex has become the heart of the downtown area and of the greater metropolitan district as well. Spread over several city blocks, the Torg consists of a two-level commercial center designed around a pedestrian walkway. The upper level forms a pedestal for five 20-story office towers. The area is served by subway stations and contains a number of parking garages, underground service railways, and storage areas.

At either end of the main concourse level is a large plaza. One is modern in conception, reflecting the design of the new House of Culture that faces it. The opposite plaza faces the old Concert Hall and is maintained as a small, traditionally open-air flower and crafts market.

DESIGN FEATURES

With a hard-edged design and little greenery, the Torg is nevertheless lively. There have been very few changes since it was conceived in the 1950s, and the hard, glossy materials reflect the esthetic of that decade. A series of recurring elements convey a sense of cohesion and modernity; pedestrian bridges connect terraces and wide stairways connect the two levels. Uniformly spaced suspended light fixtures in the center of the pedestrian street give a sense of scale. In general, the dark paving of the pedestrian walkway and the building materials of the Torg have been used skillfully.

The pedestrian system was designed as an integral part of the overall renewal of the central business district, not as a superimposed cosmetic decoration.

Walking through the Torg is a pleasant adventure. Both the bridges and the stairways provide vantage points for the daily pedestrian show. During Sweden's relatively short

A VIEW FROM THE MERCHANTS

Stockholm's traffic-free experiments have largely been initiated by merchants. Their attitude toward pedestrianization, therefore, has usually been positive. In 1969, a comprehensive survey of the country's pedestrian streets was carried out by the Chalmers Institute of Technology in Gothenberg. Businessmen on 24 of the 30 streets surveyed were 75–100 percent in favor of traffic bans; on five streets, 50–75 percent of the merchants approved; and on one street only 25–50 percent were satisfied.

Because of the complicated interrelation of factors affecting sales volume, it is hard to determine exactly how influential pedestrian zoning has been. Numerous studies, however, do reflect a satisfactory level of sales on Sweden's pedestrian streets, which coincides with the attitude of shopkeepers. A 1965 survey made by the Swedish Retail Federation, which took into account 110 companies located on traffic-free streets throughout the country, recorded either stable or improved conditions for 90 percent of the business establishments, with the remainder showing a decrease.

Opposite page: Arranged like seats on a bus, the benches on Stockholm's pedestrian streets allow citizens to take maximum advantage of the sunny months in Sweden.

warm season, benches are added on the street, arranged like seats on a bus, so that Stockholmers can take advantage of the scarce sunlight.

Connected directly to the lobbies of the office towers, the second level of the Torg consists of roof gardens which lead to more small commercial stores. The upper-level stores run parallel to those at ground level and are linked by pedestrian bridges at several points. Unlike most two-story shopping malls, the second-level shops maintain high-quality merchandise, taking advantage of their proximity to the office lobbies.

The Torg is the "in place" in downtown Stockholm. When special events take place on the concourse level, the complex is at its best. This success is not due only to the people working in the office towers. People from all over downtown Stockholm are drawn to the place. Elderly people, housewives, teenagers, and children make the Torg lively throughout the day. Regrettably, this is not true at night. Only when there are events at the Concert Hall or the House of Culture does some of the daytime vitality continue into the evening.

The Torg still works after 15 years, but there has been a shift away from the mentality that created it. The present emphasis on environmental conservation has caused a change in planning, and it is within this context that Stockholm's planners are expanding the city's traffic-free system.

A TRAFFIC-FREE DOWNTOWN

In spite of new parking lots and the rapid transit system provided by the 1946 renewal project, the central business district could not absorb the increasing number of cars that were pouring into it. Nor, for that matter, could the residential and commercial districts in the city or even the older suburbs surrounding Stockholm. For the past 15 years, planners have been experimenting with different approaches to pedestrian zoning in order to deal with the problems of congestion and deteriorating environmental quality.

The first steps toward pedestrian zoning in Stockholm were taken in the late 1950s, with negotiations between shopkeepers along Vasterlanggatan in the medieval nucleus of the city and the Stockholm Retail Trade Association. The consequences of a traffic

ban on retail trade were discussed, and in 1960 the Retail Trade Association recommended that Vasterlanggatan be converted to a pedestrian route during peak hours. The city authorities agreed, and in 1961 Vasterlanggatan became Sweden's first pedestrian street. All motor vehicles are banned from 11 A.M. to 5 A.M., with general traffic permitted at other times to allow for necessary deliveries. Vasterlanggatan's pedestrian stretch is 1,950 feet / 600 meters long, making it the longest single pedestrian street in Stockholm.

Between 1963 and 1967, vehicular patterns were reorganized in the city's central business district, and traffic was completely eliminated from two major streets, the Drottingatan and the Biblioteksgatan, with strong support from local merchants. Drottingatan connects to the Torg, and all the major department stores and better shops are on this street. Traffic was banned for six blocks; outside of eliminating cars, the only other improvement was the repaving of a few blocks. When delivery and services to the stores on Drottingatan cannot be made from parallel or side streets, trucks are permitted on it between midnight and 11 A.M.

Three blocks east of the Torg is the Biblioteksgatan, the main vehicular spine of a characteristic small-scale commercial district. This street was closed to traffic in 1963. After the street was pedestrianized, it remained alive day and night. Its restaurants, discotheques, and movie theaters have not suffered any loss of patronage.

Converting these streets into pedestrian walkways was not part of beautification efforts for the central Stockholm shopping district, but simply a strategy to eliminate conflict between pedestrians and cars. The two streets are no longer hazardous for walking, and the relative accident rate involving pedestrians and cars has sharply dropped.

However, improvement has only been local. Environmental conditions of central Stockholm in general have not benefited from these two traffic bans, nor has there been any appreciable change in the traffic pattern of the city. Completion of the ring and crosstown roads is expected to reduce the number of cars in the central area, but construction has stalled. The adverse environmental effect of present automobile traffic in the older parts of Stockholm is so severe that political priority has been given to reducing it.

OSTERMALM
A central Stockholm Traffic Policy Committee was appointed to carry out experimental traffic reorganization in Ostermalm, a residential and commercial area of the inner town, as well as in the residential suburb of Aspudden.

Ostermalm was chosen as a test case because it had a typical city street grid. In 1970, the first preliminary plans were presented at a public exhibition. The public was kept informed as plans developed, and on April 10, 1972, the final proposal was formally submitted to the city council. The council approved the plan, which was implemented in August of that year.

Ostermalm is now divided into four segregated traffic zones, and through traffic has been diverted to four peripheral roads. Goal traffic, that is, traffic destined for one of the four zones, now enters through a few gateways to primary local distribution streets or "spines." From these, traffic moves to local streets. Pedestrians have been completely separated from vehicular traffic by a network of routes among dwellings, workplaces, shopping areas, and schools within the district.

ASPUDDEN
The suburb of Aspudden was designed in 1910, before the age of the automobile. The district is densely built up and is served by streetcars. In Aspudden, traffic was congested, and increased car ownership by local residents further thickened the snarl. Compounding this crush was a stream of cars from outlying districts which used the streets of Aspudden instead of a parallel arterial highway. In this district, through traffic was rerouted by blocking one secondary arterial road and two local streets. This greatly reduced noise, pollution, and accidents and has put through traffic where it should have been—on the arterial highway. Local residents strongly supported these changes; and there has been excellent communication among politicians, planners, and the public.

These urban and suburban experiments in traffic control have proven successful. Now Stockholm is ready to implement the concept on a wider basis. Both lay people and professionals agree in the evaluation that the pedestrian streets have been a positive step toward improving the life condition and preserving the character of older parts of the city.

The lower plaza in front of the House of Culture.

10

Cologne
Germany

During World War II, 90 percent of Cologne was destroyed by Allied bombing. After the war, reconstruction efforts were implemented in two separate, but interrelated phases. Redesign of the city's circulation network was planned to accommodate the expected increase in the number of private motor vehicles, and the city's older central section was rebuilt with land use modifications that provided a framework for the introduction of a major pedestrian spine.

Cologne's pedestrian zone extends from the city's world-famous cathedral to the Neumarket, the most popular meeting place in the city. The train station and the bus terminal constitute the other poles of the district, and people move between them at all times of day. The system is like a conveyor belt, funneling shoppers and tourists back and forth through the heart of the city; only around the cathedral does the stream of people slow down. Neither Hohe Strasse nor Schildergasse provides many pedestrian amenities. Nevertheless, they are among the most successful commercial traffic-free streets in Europe.

CITY PROFILE
Cologne was founded by the Romans in the 3rd century. It grew rapidly in the Middle Ages because of its strategic position at the place where the Rhine flows into the North Sea. Goods from England, France, and the Low Countries passed through the city on their way to Eastern Europe. Famous for the variety and beauty of its Romanesque churches and its Gothic cathedral, today Cologne has a population of 830,000 and serves a region of 1.2 million people, which makes it the fourth largest city in Germany. Like many cities in Europe, Cologne has experienced a decline in population. Over the last 4 years it has lost 40,000 people.[1]

The city has regained its prewar prominence as Germany's major Rhine port. Annually through it move 10 million tons of freight, much of which comes from the heavily industrialized Ruhr region.

POSTWAR RECONSTRUCTION
The devastation of World War II permitted Cologne's planners to consider a wide range of reconstruction alternatives. However, they chose to rebuild the city's medieval central section according to the original plan.

The majority of narrow streets in the area were retained, and most buildings were restored to their original prewar scale. Land use in this core area shifted to a high concentration of office and commercial facilities.

A new vehicular circulation system, consisting of three ring roads, was created around the inner city, simultaneously with core reconstruction.[2] To facilitate mobility through the city's center, two widened streets were laid out, cutting through the central area and connecting to bridges over the Rhine. These two streets divide the city into quadrants. Incoming drivers have the option of parking away from the core and transferring to the subway system.

Cologne leads Germany in the construction of multistoried parking garages. In all, it has 21 garages, with the total capacity of 7,300 cars. Most of these were built in the central business district; since the garages brought automobile traffic too close to the inner city, planners have begun siting garages along the rings. These are accessible to the recently improved subway, which operates in the central business district, with stations opening onto the pedestrian zone.

HOHE STRASSE AND SCHILDERGASSE
Hohe Strasse and Schildergasse, the commercial heart of the city, were closed to vehicular traffic in 1949 for a few hours each day. Shopkeepers and building owners had financed reconstruction of Schildergasse after the war, but they were strongly opposed to a 1955 proposal to ban traffic permanently from that street. City planners realized that before the street could be converted, a new east-west traffic alternative would have to be created to serve one of the three bridges crossing the Rhine. In 1960, when the new Caecilienstrasse was completed, the way for the pedestrianization of Schildergasse was open. Merchants who had opposed the concept soon changed their minds. They became so enthusiastic that they formed an association which contributed 60 percent of the cost for repaving and lighting improvements. They also paid for special display cases and street sculpture along the street. Then merchants on Hohe Strasse decided to ban traffic, and they organized themselves to do so. The street was converted in 1962.

The Cologne Cathedral survived although 90
percent of the city was destroyed during
World War II.

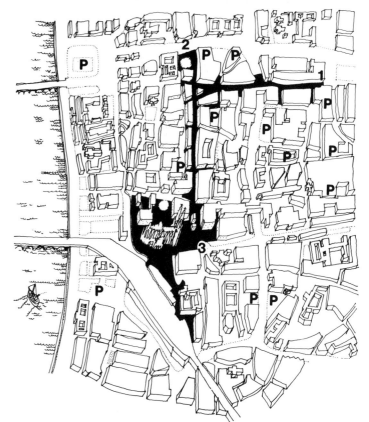

Right: Cologne's pedestrian system is based
on two perpendicular commercial streets,
Schildergasse and Hohestrasse, connected
with Domplatze, the Cathedral Square, and
the railway station. Key to the plan: (1) Schildergasse, (2) Hohestrasse, (3) Domplatze,
(P) parking.

Opposite page: Domplatze.

Hohe Strasse.

Schildergasse.

DESIGN FEATURES

Hohe Strasse and Schildergasse are extremely different in their physical and commercial makeup. Hohe Strasse is narrow, reflecting its ancient Roman character. It is lined with medium- to high-priced boutiques and jewelers that give the street an air of elegance. Its small cafes and fast food restaurants cater to the 1.4 million tourists and visitors who come to Cologne each year. Schildergasse, in contrast, is wide, with large department stores along most of its length.[3] Street vendors selling fruit, flowers, and toys are permitted on both streets, adding color to the area.

The design of both streets is based on their commercial nature. As a consequence, pedestrian amenities, such as places for people to relax, are not provided. The linear configuration of the streets and their function as connectors of the city's major attractions contribute to the "conveyor belt" effect of this pedestrian system. Numerous large, aggressive signs define the appearance of both streets. Although these signs create visual confusion and are not scaled for pedestrians, they make up for the lack of amenities to a certain extent. Together with the moving crowds of shoppers and tourists, the bold advertising adds color and excitement to an environment that would otherwise be bleak and monotonous.

ENVIRONMENTAL IMPACT

The traffic bans on Hohe Strasse and Schildergasse caused a number of side streets to become de facto walkways, greatly improving the overall environmental conditions of the old city.

Cologne's planners were among the few that took before and after readings of noise and air pollution in the pedestrianized area. Air pollution levels dropped from 8 ppm (parts per million) of carbon monoxide to 1 ppm. Noise levels were reduced by 15 decibels, which is equivalent to cutting the original sound in half. These results were much publicized at the time and have constituted a strong argument for introducing pedestrian zones in Germany and Europe.

THE DOMPLATZE

Cologne's pedestrian system has been enriched by the recent renovations to the square around the city's famous cathedral, directly connected to the Hohe Strasse. The square is also linked to the pedestrian concourse of the railroad station via bridges and escalators and to the traffic-free promenades along the riverfront by a pedestrian bridge over the Rhine. Seats, trees, and open-air cafes have been installed, and the square now provides a place to rest and view the celebrated dome. The design elements also shield the flank of the cathedral from the modern station, which is on a slightly lower level. This important area of Cologne has a quiet dignity which contrasts sharply with the intense activity in the core area, particularly that on the pedestrian streets.

11

Copenhagen Denmark

By the early 1950s it became evident to Copenhagen's planners that the increasing number of private automobiles could not be absorbed by the narrow streets in the city's historic core. In addition to creating unbearable congestion, motor vehicle traffic was causing environmental deterioration and affecting the social and economic potential of the downtown area. After experimenting with a number of traffic control strategies, city planners proposed pedestrian zoning as a solution. However, the idea of traffic-free areas was strongly opposed by many shopkeepers and even by some traffic experts.

In Danish, stroget means "to stroll," a favorite Danish custom and Stroget is also the name for Copenhagen's pedestrian zone, the first in Denmark. Famous for its variety of luxury stores, restaurants, and popular (and legal) pornography shops, Stroget is a model for pedestrian planning throughout Europe and especially Denmark, where smaller towns seek to emulate some of its economic and social success.

Stroget clearly identifies Copenhagen's downtown as a pleasant place to spend time, and it attracts people from all over, as well as outside the country. Here is the finest, most luxurious shopping in the region. Some of the large department stores have found life on the street difficult, but small boutiques, craft and clothing shops have thrived; today there are over 2,000 stores and entertainment areas in the pedestrian zone.

Both the plan and ambience of Stroget encourage participation. The area has been designed to draw people into the mall at one end and involve them along its entire length. Stroget's success can be measured by the fact that Copenhagen's pedestrian system is slowly expanding, with the goal of eliminating traffic from the entire central business district.

CITY PROFILE

The population and scale of Copenhagen was limited by the boundaries of the 15th-century walls until 1850, when the military cordon protecting the city opened up. The medieval street patterns remained, but fires had destroyed most of the old buildings and new ones had been built. The population was about 130,000 in the inner city.

By the end of the century, however, the population jumped to 451,488 persons, and the shape and growth of the city changed significantly. Workers moved into the city, and the Industrial Revolution was making an impact. Speculative housing projects were built along the city's perimeter, with intense development occurring between 1870 and 1890. It is possible to read the phases of this development in the three concentric rings of high-density housing that start in the medieval center and move outward.

Housing production diminished during World War I, which also led to an unstable economy. The continuous demand for housing was satisfied at this time by building in courtyards or by adding floors to old buildings; bigger apartments were subdivided; young families began to move out of the central city.

The population grew to 770,000 from 1900 to 1950, after which it began to decrease at the rate of 6,000 people each year. Today, Copenhagen has 600,000 inhabitants.

THE FINGER PLAN: 1947

Modern urban planning for Copenhagen started in 1947, when the Finger Plan was issued. This scheme called for the end of concentric urban development and proposed concentrating new growth along a radial public transportation system, serving the city with five "fingers." Efforts to coordinate planning for the Copenhagen region had started in the 1920s, but the Finger Plan was the first to be implemented.

The rationale for the Finger Plan was clear: housing and employment should be located as close as possible to the main lines of communication so that daily journeys to and from work could be confined to public transportation connections, thereby reducing traveling time to a minimum. This emphasis on public mass transit prepared the way for pedestrian zoning in the central city years later.

A new plan was issued in 1954 that superimposed new controls on the Finger Plan. This plan calls for a system of inner, intermediate, and outer zones to control the extension of built-up areas, with the outer zone reserved for recreational and park development. Four ring roads would cut across the Finger Plan to define the new zones: an inner road with a radius of 1.6 miles/2.5 kilometers

1650

1750

1840

1920

1947: Finger Plan

1954: Outline Development Plan

Historic development and planning policies.

would encircle the central business district; a middle ring with a 3.1-mile/ 5-kilometer radius would connect the outer areas; a third and fourth ring would run outside the urban area.

Also included in the 1954 master plan was a new ordinance declaring the city center an historic district, which meant that any change in the urban fabric would require approval by the municipal authority. Every new intrusion, elevation, construction, or other change would have to be evaluated according to its impact on existing street relationships or its potential disruption to urban scale.

THE OUTLINE DEVELOPMENT PLAN: 1960

The Finger Plan was finally amended in 1960 with an Outline Development Plan. Designed to control the boundaries of urban growth, this provision was passed to maintain the northern region as a recreational zone, while restricting major urban growth to the west and southwest along the coast.

Copenhagen residents relied heavily on tramway and bicycle transportation during the 1950s. But by the beginning of the next decade, the private automobile had begun to replace the bicycle in such numbers that the city found it necessary to institute controls to ease congestion and prevent environmental degradation.

But the controls, which included one-way street designations and restricted downtown parking, were only partially effective. The number of cars continued to grow rapidly, and so did congestion and parking problems until the quality of downtown life seemed seriously threatened. Pedestrian traffic became more dangerous and less comfortable, and many trades and industries in the area suffered from poor accessibility for customers, visitors, and employees. Furthermore, emissions and vibrations from automobile traffic were damaging the historic architecture of central Copenhagen. The city was obviously primed for pedestrian zoning when the government initiated the Stroget in 1962.

STROGET

The original Stroget consisted of three contiguous streets, running from the Town Hall Square to Kings New Square. An experimental traffic ban was initiated in 1962, and in 1964 the area was declared a permanent

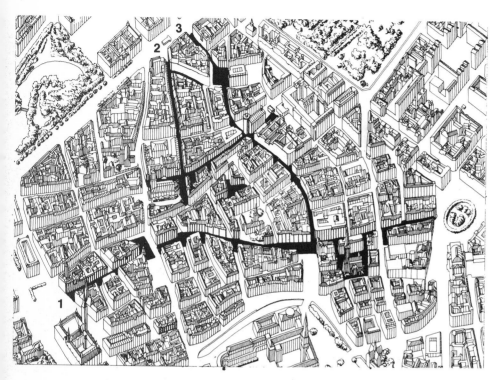

Above and opposite page: Copenhagen's pedestrian system, the most extensive after Venice's, is an intricate web of streets, plazas, courtyards, and alleys which both retains a medieval character and includes a variety of historic landmarks and lively communal places. Key to the plan: (1) Stroget, (2) Fiolstraede, (3) Kobmagergade.

pedestrian zone. The streets were finally repaved in 1967.

The 1962 move to pedestrianize Stroget followed years of debate. Although walking in downtown areas had become difficult, with pedestrians and cars competing for space, there was opposition to the idea of eliminating cars. Merchants feared that banning cars would hurt their business, and traffic experts feared intolerable congestion on adjacent streets. In spite of these objections, the city administration went ahead with pedestrianization. The procedure was an administrative act, enforced by the police and paid for by the city. No special legislation was required.

The positive results of the traffic ban soon convinced merchants that their fears had been groundless. Traffic surveys of adjacent streets revealed no substantial increase in congestion.[1]

In 1968, the Grabrodretorv was declared a traffic-free zone, which added its historic square and church, plus a flowermarket, to pedestrian attractions. Fiolstraede was also pedestrianized in 1968. It includes the city's most important commuter station and connects the Stroget to Norrenport, an old, narrow part of the city with antique shops and a unique Latin flavor.

DESIGN FEATURES
The atmosphere throughout the pedestrian system is pleasant, even though its design is quite simple. The paving is gray, with dark mid-stripes indicating service routes (open to delivery vehicles from 4 A.M. to 11 A.M.). Street signs are modest and tasteful. It is left to the pedestrians to provide color and liveliness. Shops give careful attention to their window displays, which are designed to capture the interest of strollers. Unexpected alleyways and arcades provide variety in the scale of the area.

The pedestrian routes themselves offer little chance to sit and relax; they are quite narrow and there are few benches or seating areas. But the singular thrust of the streets is relieved by open plaza areas, often highlighted by cultural and historic landmarks. Here, there are benches and opportunities to meet and talk or watch informal entertainment. Low-cost amusements such as impromptu pantomime or music are favored. Street vendors are permitted but not encouraged. On warm, clear days, pedestrians frequent the Stroget areas long after the shops have closed, some attracted to the movies and restaurants, but more attracted by the space and views the Stroget offers.

The whole system of pedestrian zones benefits from the urban fabric of the city, which retains a medieval character, although the buildings date mostly from the 18th and 19th centuries. (The city was rebuilt several times, after fires destroyed it in 1728, 1795, and 1807.) The original, narrow street patterns survive, as does the main route comprising the Stroget. Pedestrians throughout the city will frequently turn a corner and suddenly find fountains, historic buildings, or well-delineated towers (Copenhagen is the "City of Beautiful Towers"). The narrow streets form a spider web across the city, with plazas and open spaces at many of the intersections.

FUTURE DEVELOPMENTS
The continuing extension of Copenhagen's pedestrian system, the stress being placed on restoration of the city's historic buildings, the revision of circulation patterns, and the improvements being made to existing

According to city planner Kai Lemberg, "The initial experiment turned out to be a great success. The general public and the press were enthusiastic, the shopkeepers watched the increase in their turnover and were converted into warm supporters of the pedestrian street. Traffice experts and planners observed that the expected difficulties failed to materialize."

housing stock, all reflect a new planning attitude that has arisen from Denmark's current economic state. Up until the past few years, the country's economy grew steadily, based on policies of controlled inflation and large public expenditures. There has been a dramatic change in this situation. Inflation is now a serious threat to currency controls and economic stability, and Denmark is facing its highest unemployment levels in 50 years. The rapidly changing administrations in recent years have further contributed to the overall decline by making it difficult to carry out consistent policies.

As a result, Copenhagen has developed new planning strategies that emphasize the management and improvement of existing resources, rather than the creation of new ones. Using this approach, especially in conjunction with extending the pedestrian system, the city hopes to improve the urban environment for both visitors and residents.

TRANSPORTATION

Transportation improvements have started with extension of the underground railway network by construction of a new city line under the eastern portion of the central business district. This area is also served by buses, partly with reserved lanes.

The city plans to further restrict cars in the downtown area by making parking prohibitively expensive. The government reasons that prime downtown real estate is the most valuable in the city and plans to charge motorists rental rates for parking that are commensurate with the land's full market value. The national government hopes that foreign car imports will drop, which should spur the national economy.

A draft plan for complete pedestrianization of the downtown areas of Copenhagen was published in 1972. Steps have already been taken toward the realization of this plan, including restrictions on traffic crossing the Stroget. The city erected barriers at three intersections, prohibiting all but bus and bicycle transit. In 1972 the city added Kobmagergade to the pedestrian network. While not totally traffic free, this street now routes traffic in opposite directions for one-block stretches, while discouraging all but the most vital service vehicles from entering the area.

All of these measures were considered necessary for the survival of the city and especially for its historic core. The prosperity of central Copenhagen is essential to the functioning of the metropolitan and national trade industries, to tourism, and to the international competitive power and prestige of the city.

HOUSING

Housing rehabilitation has been a special problem for Copenhagen, where speculative building practices have hastened deterioration of the city's stock, despite the fact that most residences were built in the last 100 years.

BUILDING CLASSIFICATION

To establish priorities for reconstruction, the city prepared a building classification that relies on a structure's physical and sanitary condition; its exposure to sunlight and proper ventilation, and its relationship to existing streets, buildings, and open spaces. The city has put special emphasis on clearing up overcrowded courtyard areas.

The rehabilitation program led to the restoration of 2,700 buildings between 1960 and 1972, and over 5,000 more will be restored by the end of this decade.

The program is aided by legislation passed on June 11, 1971, stating that boroughs or private Sanering (rehabilitation) Societies can initiate urban renewal projects on their own. Losses incurred by the process may be defrayed in equal proportion by the city and the state.

Amsterdam Holland

Amsterdam's pedestrian streets were introduced in an attempt to cure traffic problems which developed in the city after World War II. Congestion was especially severe in the old part of the city, where vehicular streets were wedged between canals and bridges and where the particular nature of the subsoil made construction of underpasses, parking garages, and underground public transit systems impossible. Since 1960, nine major streets in the city's core have been totally or partially closed to traffic.

These streets have been repaved, but they offer few pedestrian-oriented amenities. Deprived of its social potential and overcrowded with tourists, Amsterdam's pedestrian network does not hold the attractions of other major traffic-free zones. Merchants and residents alike are not happy with the pedestrian system, criticizing it for its poor accessibility, for creating more traffic congestion, and for being ineffectual against the social and commercial decline of the central district. However, the answer to these problems lies outside the pedestrian streets.

For years, Amsterdam has been a model of rational planning—an ideal, organically developed modern city. But, the central historic core, one of the most beautiful in Europe, was neglected, and today it faces severe physical and social decay.

Ironically, Amsterdam's administration never developed a plan for the center of the city, even though controls were placed on demolition of historic buildings and on the height of new buildings constructed in the core. Social and economic factors changed rapidly after World War II, and these had a devastating effect on the vitality of the historic center.

People began to abandon decayed housing, and businesses either followed their clientele or adjusted the quality of their merchandise to the increasing flood of tourists. Entire sections of the old city were taken over by boarding houses, and the red light district expanded. Liberal prostitution, pornography, and drug laws contributed to increase the crime rate.

Today Amsterdam is divided largely into single-function districts that lack the vitality resulting from a balanced spectrum of day and night activities.

CITY PROFILE
Amsterdam is one of the best pre-served larger European cities, but it is relatively young. Founded about 700 years ago, the city had 210,000 inhabitants by the 17th century, making it the fourth largest city in Europe.

Amsterdam's organized growth began as early as 1612, when the first official plan for the city was adopted. This was the famous Three Canal Plan, which quadrupled the area of the city and allowed for future population growth without need to rebuild fortifications that had to be created on landfill in Holland. This plan provided sufficient land for expansion until 1874. During those three and a half centuries, the city took on its characteristic appearance, which is visible today: a series of concentric canals which have the triple function of defense, transportation, and drainage.

The city's policy of rationalized growth was carried over into the first half of this century beginning with the 1901 Housing Act. This was followed by a series of master plans in 1906, 1907, and 1917.

THE EXTENSION PLAN: 1935
In 1935, the Extension Plan was adopted. This plan, which is still operative, predicted and set down controls for land use and population growth within the municipality until the year 2000. However, the maximum population of 960,000 compatible with controlled development has already been reached.

The Extension Plan was modified in the 1940s to compensate for the increased population and housing demands that followed World War II.[1] Today, the plan has been completely implemented due to the fact that the city owns, or is able to acquire, all the land it needs. In fact, the Netherlands has a long tradition of compulsory acquisition of land for development and expropriation for renewal.[2]

PRESERVING THE HISTORIC CORE
The fragile and beautiful historic center of Amsterdam has never been part of the city's overall development plan. Within its 17th-century walls are 2,000 acres/808 hectares crowded with over 7,000 historic buildings. Today, the heart of the city, with its tree-lined canals, many museums, art galleries, and hundreds of shops, cafes, and restaurants, faces serious decline due to a shift in the residential population, poor maintenance of buildings, the expanding red light district, and severe traffic problems.

13th century

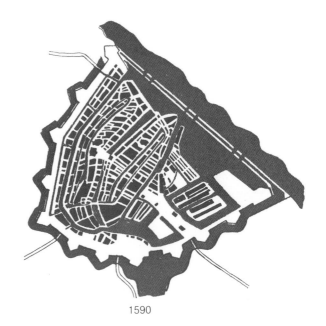

1590

1612

1700

The expansion of Amsterdam's city core
within the protective walls.

POPULATION SHIFT

The old city began to lose its residents after World War II, when new residential districts on the periphery of the city attracted middle- and higher-income families away from houses that were often unhealthy and crowded. Abandoned residential districts were entirely given over to tourist accommodations. Only the elderly and students on one side and the rich on the other stayed on in the city's core.

Most of the buildings in old Amsterdam are in poor physical condition, with the exception of the elegant houses located along the three central concentric rings. As far back as 1940, the national government passed legislation to protect historic buildings, even to the extent of providing funds for improvement. Restoration costs, however, run very high. Even so, there are a number of property owners willing to invest in restoration.[3]

SOCIAL IMBALANCE

Over the past several years, the pornography industry has thrived, and Holland's relaxed drug laws have attracted users to Amsterdam in particular. The city's red light district, which includes pornography shops and prostitution houses, was once confined to a small area. It has slowly spread out, and today it represents one of the most significant land uses in the old city. The highly profitable nature of these enterprises, and their connection with organized crime, make them difficult to eradicate.

TRAFFIC PROBLEMS

Traffic is the last, and possibly the most damaging, factor in the increasing decay of Amsterdam. The city has had restrictions on vehicular traffic since the 17th century because of its narrow streets. Heavy taxes were imposed on private carriages brought into Amsterdam, and there were parking squares for them outside the city's gates. In the early 20th century several canals were filled in to create additional streets, but this did not eliminate the funneling of traffic caused by the city's concentric plan of canals and streets.

When the 1935 plan was drawn up, it was assumed that bicycles would be the major form of transportation, accounting for 70 percent of all journeys. Development was projected on the premise that people should be

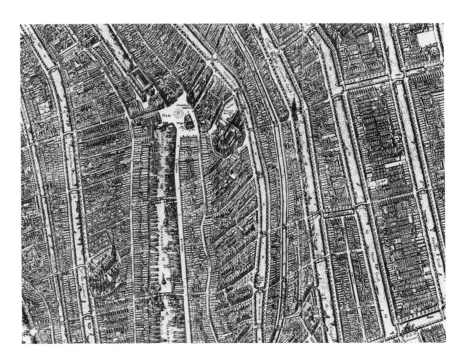

Historically the heart of Amsterdam's urban life, Dam Square is today the center of the pedestrian system and an internationally known meeting place for young people.

Opposite page: Aerial view of central Amsterdam.

Key to the plan: (1) Haarlemmerstratt, (2) Nieuwendijk, (3) Kalverstraat, (4) Heiligeweg.

able to arrive in the city's center in no more than 30 minutes by bicycle. However, only 24 percent of the city's commuters use bicycles today. The dramatic increase of automobile commuting is the result of the distance between the new residential areas and the city's core.[4]

The city took measures to increase the speed, frequency, and capacity of streetcar and bus lines by designating exclusive public transport lanes. However, these lanes have only reduced the available space in the streets, further snarling traffic.

In July 1968, the city council approved construction of metropolitan railway network. Construction on the first line, connecting the central railway station to the new, densely populated Amsterdam-South, was proceding at a good pace; however, increased costs and opposition from residents in the neighborhood through which the line had to pass brought work to a halt.

THE CENTRAL PEDESTRIAN DISTRICT

Traffic congestion in the central commercial streets seriously jeopardized the retail economy of the area. Pedestrian zoning was introduced on a major scale in an effort to reverse this trend. Total or partial traffic bans were introduced on nine major downtown streets, but even this massive effort was not sufficient to halt the exodus of major commercial establishments. Specialty shops have practically disappeared from central Amsterdam. Airline ticket offices, travel agencies, and banks sprang up in their places. Remaining shops have altered the quality of their merchandise from high-quality goods to items that cater to the casual tastes of tourists, rather than to the needs of residents.

A further influence on commercial trends is the high concentration of young people who began to frequent the area beginning in the 1960s. The presence of this consumer group has given vitality to the cafes, cinemas, boutiques, and low-cost eating establishments. However, the more traditional establishments have been forced to close from lack of patronage.

Early in 1960, Kalverstraat and Nieuwendijk were officially closed to traffic during shopping hours, but it was not until 11 years later that they assumed their present appearance. In

1971, they were repaved, and further restrictions were placed on the delivery of goods. The streets are the core of Amsterdam's pedestrian system.

Neither Kalverstraat nor Nieuwendijk has any street furniture, display cases, or special lighting fixtures. However, this lack of amenities is not noticed in the crush of people, mostly tourists, on the streets during the day. After nightfall the pedestrian streets are not as busy, but they are far from deserted. Small shopkeepers leave their windows lighted until late at night, making the evening hours an ideal time for browsing.

A special attraction in the northern half of the Kalverstraat area is the Historical Museum and Beguinage. The museum complex contains one of the two remaining 14th-century wooden houses in Amsterdam. Because admission is free, it provides a welcome place to relax near the busy shopping street.

In July 1971, Leidsestraat was transformed into a pedestrian street, but its streetcar line was retained. This street, once one of the most elegant in central Amsterdam, had lost most of its glamor over the years. At the same time the square in front of the Municipal Theater was converted from a parking lot into a raised cafe terrace; and the pedestrian zone was extended along the southern side of the Singel, a street famous for its permanent flower market. In March 1973, motor traffic was banned from Haarlemmerstraat, which completed a ribbon of pedestrian streets encircling the center of Amsterdam. As a consequence, all the streets which cross the ribbon became de facto walkways. Despite these efforts to control traffic in central Amsterdam, the situation has reached a dead end. The Policy Outline Plan of 1968 for the old city was expected to raise employment, but the restricted accessibility to the center caused many enterprises to move to peripheral districts and suburbs. The reduced number of people employed in the old city has had a negative effect on sales volume. Local activist groups view new hotel construction as a negative development in the center of Amsterdam, especially since Holland's inflationary economy has put a further lid on expansion of the city's tourist industry.

There is a rising demand for housing, but even increased residential population does not seem sufficient to support local commercial facilities. Due to the high costs of restoration, the majority of people moving into the old city have high incomes, which has resulted in social conflict with the original resident population—the elderly, the poor, and students. Students in particular are well organized politically and strongly oppose the trend toward restored housing exclusively for the upper classes.

This dead end situation is not peculiar to Amsterdam. Many European cities with extensive historic districts are experiencing the same troubles. The difference in Amsterdam is that its historic district is one of the most significant in Europe. Furthermore, its decay is all the more dramatic because of the well-planned modern city surrounding it.

Nieuwendijk.

Kalverstraat.

Bologna Italy

Bologna's traffic-free zones were part of an overall effort to revitalize the historic core and control the city's territorial growth. However, the pedestrian district itself was implemented exclusively on the basis of its humanistic and cultural benefits.

"Comprehensive conservation" of the physical and social fabric of central Bologna has been the guiding concept of the administration of this northern Italian city. This implies not only restoration and conservation of a wealth of buildings and monuments in its historic center, but also retaining its traditional residents—workers, artisans, students, and the elderly.

The municipal administration believes that its policy of comprehensive conservation cannot function unless development and growth is controlled in the rest of the city. Therefore, an optimum limit has been established beyond which increasing the size of the city would only endanger the meaning and function of the center.

Controlling growth is expected to curb real estate speculation. This, in turn, will stem the exodus of low-income families to new residential areas on the edge of the city. Retention of this resident group ensures working class participation in the social and cultural life of the city center, and it also protects the area from becoming a strictly commercial and upper-income residential district.

Bologna's pedestrian streets were planned within this city core. Free theater and concerts sponsored by the city in central streets and squares have been enthusiastically received by residents. At the same time, banning traffic has safeguarded the city's historic architecture.

Contrary to other pedestrianization efforts, Bologna's planners were not particularly concerned with improving retail economics. Nevertheless, shops have witnessed increases in sales due to the traffic-free streets.

CITY PROFILE

A glance at maps of Bologna indicates there has been very little change in the city's layout since its foundations. The original Roman grid of 200 B.C. is still visible. One of the major provincial centers of the empire, Bologna maintained its importance in the early Middle Ages when it became a trading center between the indigenous population and invading Visigoths, Huns, and Longobards.

The University of Bologna, which became one of the most famous centers of learning in Europe, was founded in the 11th century.[1]

Until 1884, the city remained within the fortified walls built in 1380, and new buildings were constructed in orchards and other free spaces. After Italy's political unification, Bologna burst through its walls, as it became the most important railway connection between the industrial North and the underdeveloped South.

Bologna's new national role demanded large-scale modifications in the city, the first of which was an inner ring boulevard built on the former site of its walls. In conjunction with this, central axial streets were widened to accommodate increased traffic.

Beginning in 1900, changes occurred more and more rapidly, reaching a high point in the 1930s during the Fascist regime. At this time, large residential areas were demolished and replaced by low-cost public housing, which radically altered the physical and social character of the city.

In the mid-1960s, people began leaving the city, attracted by new peripheral housing. Within the city, traffic congestion was becoming more dense, and environmental conditions were deteriorating. Bologna's social and cultural domination of the region was slipping away as a direct result of population loss. It was evident that remedial action was necessary.

COMPREHENSIVE CONSERVATION

The city's program of comprehensive conservation has become the model for other cities in Italy. Power for implementing this program was made possible by both national and local means. In 1968, the national government gave regional administrations the power to undertake independent planning and financial decisions. For many years, Bologna had been governed by a communist administration, which initiated a strong public service program in the metropolitan area. This program included developing schools, medical centers, and public transportation. When the national government gave regional administrations broader power, Bologna's planners were able to implement the large-scale perservation of the central city and control development of peripheral districts at the same time.

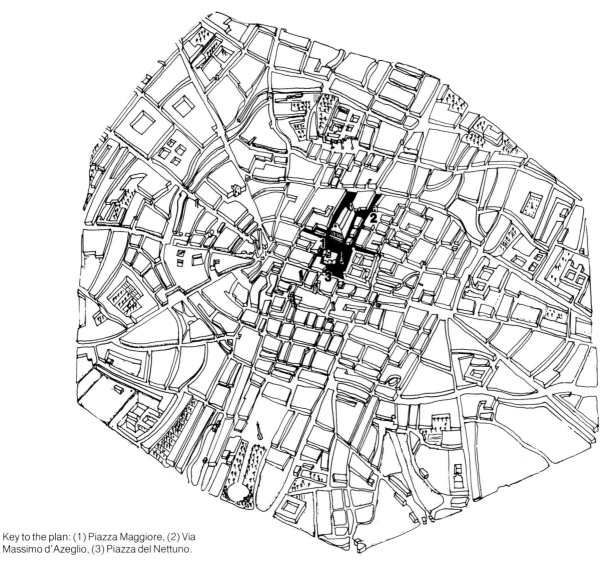

Key to the plan: (1) Piazza Maggiore, (2) Via
Massimo d'Azeglio, (3) Piazza del Nettuno.

Bologna's City Hall.

Piazza Maggiore and surrounding street have been pedestrianized. Empty lots and unused historic buildings have been adapted and restored for community use.

The city's young, aggressive planning department believes that use of Bologna's historic core is a "right of all citizens." As a consequence, the city must not grow beyond the point where the core cannot give all citizens the same opportunity to participate in politics, cultural activities, and entertainment facilities.[2]

Planning goals also include curbing the tendency of the central area towards becoming a commercial district. To infuse greater social and cultural opportunity in the center of the city, the administration is transforming major unused or underused historical buildings into schools, social centers, community meeting rooms, and theaters. By eliminating private speculation from the building restoration process, city officials have removed the one factor which most contributes to changing restored inner-city areas into high-income enclaves.

From the beginning, citizens have participated in the decision making, particularly in determining housing policies. By using empty neighborhood buildings to house people temporarily while their own homes are being restored, the city has avoided the relocation of local residents and the disruption of their social habits. Rent levels in restored buildings are established before restoration. Landlords have pledged not to speculate on the increased value of the restored buildings, and tenants have pledged not to abandon the old neighborhoods.

A PEDESTRIAN ISLAND

On September 16, 1968, the city council approved creation of a pedestrian zone in the center of Bologna. Traffic was rearranged to permit special lanes for taxis and buses, and at the same time two large restricted parking areas called "Blue Zones" were created.

Piazza Maggiore and Piazza del Nettuno, at the geometric center of Bologna, were permanently closed to vehicular traffic. Via D'Azeglio, Archiginnasio, and Pignatari leading into these piazzas were also closed.

Piazza Maggiore and Piazza del Nettuno form the social and cultural focus of Bologna. Religious ceremonies and carnivals have taken place in both piazzas for centuries. Residents continue to take advantage of the piazzas for political rallies and traditional Sunday morning strolls.

GOVERNMENT DECENTRALIZATION

Citizens' involvement has been institutionalized in Bologna. The city has been divided into 18 neighborhoods, each of which has its own citizens' committee. When any decision is made by the city, the residents then participate in an open assembly which decides the issue.

The historic center of Bologna has been divided into "intervention areas," for which individual development plans have been prepared. Restoration is being done on one intervention area at a time. Funding for it is drawn from the national Low Cost/Low Income Housing Program, through which building owners can get loans that are repayable with small interest.

As part of Bologna's restoration efforts, old buildings such as the convent pictured here have been converted into community facilities such as schools, day care centers, and emergency medical units.

One year after the center of Bologna was converted into a pedestrian zone a poll was taken among the city's residents. Forty-three percent of the people interviewed from all over the metropolitan area strongly identified the center of the city with the Piazza Maggiore. When asked what image they associated with the piazza, 28 percent identified it as a monumental space that is part of a unified urban complex. However, 52 percent identified it as an important place for social interaction. Some 15 percent of those interviewed saw it as a place for adult activities such as political demonstrations and festivals. Twenty percent of the people viewed the Piazza Maggiore as being populated by pigeons for children to play with and people to feed. However, the Piazza Maggiore as a theater or setting for collective events was very real to the people interviewed.

In addition to restoring human scale to the center of Bologna, another major consideration in the decision to ban traffic was the protection of historic buildings and their details. A number of buildings had already been damaged by the emissions and vibrations of automobiles. This deterioration has been halted.

Closing off the streets surrounding the two major piazzas was simply achieved by installing flower planters at each intersection. In accord with a 16th-century engraving, Piazza Maggiore was repaved in brick to conform with surrounding buildings. This simple procedure restored the unity which had been lost in the 1930s when curbs and asphalt paving were installed in the plaza.

In keeping with Bologna's social policies, the city promoted annual exhibits and information campaigns, before and after the traffic ban, to define the city center from historic, cultural, and political perspectives. The city continues to sponsor a wide variety of participatory events to intensify citizens' awareness of their heritage.

Encouraged by a positive citizen response, the administration decided to close several more streets. In 1972,

Via Calderini and Via dell'Inferno were closed and traffic on streets perpendicular to them eliminated. After agreement had been reached with shopkeepers, the streets around Bologna's characteristic commercial blocks were permanently closed to traffic in 1973. The banning benefited the entire city center, since the number of cars entering it was reduced greatly.

Creation of the pedestrian "island," as it is called by residents, was a fundamental step in Bologna's transformation. It is a basic element in the new way of life the city can offer its residents. The unexpected overwhelming success of the pedestrian zone has encouraged the city to continue clearing streets and plazas of both parked and moving vehicles, and limiting access to all but resident traffic in selected areas. As the organizations and citizen committees in various neighborhoods become more efficient, pedestrian streets will begin to emerge in residential districts.

The power to evaluate whether or not a pedestrian street extends the functions and services of each neighborhood, and fully develops its social life is, today, in the citizens' hands.

14

Rouen
France

Rouen leads France in the creation of pedestrian streets. It was the first French town to initiate a comprehensive pedestrian system as part of a plan aimed at reversing a trend making the city a mere economic suburb of Paris, some 84 miles away.

The city's initial traffic-free experiment was located along a major commercial street. The pedestrian system was later expanded to ease the flow of tourists around the cathedral. Pedestrianization was implemented in both zones to revitalize the city's central area, improve the quality of street life, and restore the prestigious historic buildings.

The heart of Rouen's pedestrian system is the bustling Rue du Gros Horloge, a vigorous commercial spine which connects the old Market Square with the cathedral—the center of the medieval city.

Since its conversion in 1970 8,000 to 10,000 people use this street daily, enjoying its specialty shops, department stores, outdoor cafes, and street vendors.

CITY PROFILE

Founded during the Gallo-Roman period, the city grew along two axes at right angles to each other that intersect near the site on which the cathedral was built. As the capital of Normandy, Rouen has a rich history. Joan of Arc was burned at the stake in the Market Square. In the 19th century, Ruskin and Victor Hugo made it an important stop on the Romantic itinerary of medieval architecture in France.

Rouen sustained heavy bombing during World War II, and much of its core had to be rebuilt. As a result, this area now contains both narrow medieval streets and wide modern thoroughfares.

The city's population decreased dramatically due to the war itself and the prosperity immediately following it. By 1968, Rouen's population was 30,000, as compared with 60,000 in 1928. Increasing numbers of dwelling units in the city's central area were converted into warehouses and offices, securing the city's role as the major commercial and administrative center for this region of 400,000 people.

In spite of the severe bomb damage in the war, Rouen still offered many architectural attractions, and tourism became an important part of its econ-omy. Most of the historic and architectural landmarks are protected by the Malraux Law of 1962.

PLANNING FOR GROWTH AND PRESERVATION

In the 1960s, Rouen's administrators were forced to recognize a reversal of the trends that prevailed since before the war. Population was on the rise again,[1] and the city's growth had to be controlled while new housing and better transportation had to be provided. In addition, Rouen's role as a regional center had to be strengthened. Rouen could not contain the predicted population expansion on its present site, nor could the right bank core be further developed through high-density urban renewal. The only solution was the development of four new towns, interconnected and tied to Rouen by an effective rail and highway network.

Preservation of the historic center was another of the city's major tasks. Here, the problems were to blend together extremely diversifed activities and control traffic. To accomplish this, the core had to be relieved of those functions which conflicted with preservation and restoration: wholesale trade and industry.[2]

A municipal planning agency, L'Atelier d' Urbanisme, was established to coordinate urban renewal in the eastern slum section of the central core. Gradually, the agency became involved in improving public open spaces throughout the entire central area, and it was finally given responsibility for working out a new master plan. This included improving traffic and parking and formulating a pedestrian scheme.

Gaining Public Support The city's policy of creating pedestrian zones to enhance street life and promote tourism awakened the hostility of merchants in the central area. In 1966 and 1967, preserving the historic center, and therefore its commercial prominence, did not seem urgent to them. However, when several shopping centers were proposed for the outskirts, merchants quickly changed their minds, and chances of implementing the new plan improved.[3]

The local newspaper took up the cause of converting the Rue du Gros Horloge into a pedestrian street. To overcome objections, city agencies held several sessions with the merchants to explain the project.[4]

Rouen's central core of about 465 acres/186 hectares is economically divided into two unequal areas. The western half near the Seine and its port is exclusively offices. The eastern part was the center of clothing manufacture and until recently a slum. On the eve of World War II, this thriving central core was the only truly vital area of the city. The left bank of the Seine was an industrial suburb built around docks, gasworks, and railway yards, which was particularly hard hit during the war, as were the bridges and the right bank up to the Cathedral Square. Present Rouen's pedestrian system is part of an overall traffic plan to restructure the city's right bank and protect its historic areas. Future plans call for an additional 10,000 feet/3 kilometers of pedestrian streets on the left bank. If the pedestrian system is extended to the left bank, a similar hierarchy of traffic patterns and types of transportation will be used. In addition, there will have to be connectors from the highways leading into the central area and adequate parking facilities created near pedestrian streets.

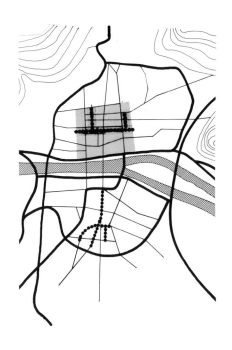

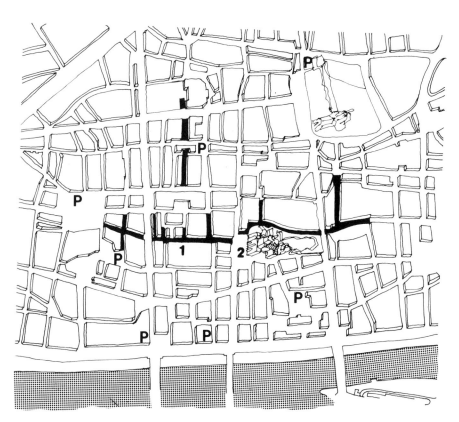

Key to the plan: (1) Rue du Gros Horloge, (2) Cathedral Square, (P) Parking.

RUE DU GROS HORLOGE

On May 1, 1970, general traffic was banned on the Rue du Gros Horloge, between Rue Jeanne d'Arc and the Cathedral Square.[5] This pedestrian stretch, only 24 feet/8 meters wide and 875 feet/260 meters long, is a showcase of medieval half-timbered shops and townhouses. The street forms a vista leading to a Renaissance gate with a clock, the Gros Horloge, set above its archway.

A few months later, sidewalks were removed and repaving of the street began; gray cobblestones were laid in a peacock-tail pattern. Only a few sites were available for providing amenities, but one or two flower planters were installed at entrances into the street and at crossings. Granite slabs laid on edge were used for the planters, and attractively proportioned granite curbstones from the street were recycled as benches.

As the 1970 Christmas shopping season began, the first section of the pedestrian street was ready. After the sidewalks were removed and the street repaved, the majority of buildings along the street were restored.

Though 150 parking places were eliminated when the street was converted to a pedestrian walkway, some 900 additional spaces were created within walking distance.

A few months after conversion, merchants along the mall recorded a 10 to 15 percent increase in sales; and merchants on adjoining streets requested that the pedestrian concept be extended to include them. So far, the city has 4,000 feet/1.2 kilometers of pedestrian streets, and another 9,000 feet/2.7 kilometers are proposed for the district.

However, further development of the pedestrian system requires greater accessibility to the center of the city and improved mobility within it. Planners want to redesign the ring boulevards as feeders and construct parking adjacent to them.

This would allow for the expansion of the traffic-free area, adding several streets in the historic district to the pedestrian network. The remaining streets would be transformed into service or access routes.[6]

The Rue du Gros Horloge was a pioneer effort to accustom the public to pedestrian zoning. Even if the size of the first phase of the project seems too small to grant it the status of a model case, it has had remarkable im-

Rue du Gros Horloge is both the heart of Rouen historic district and an active commercial street. Prestigious medieval architecture leads pedestrians through a Renaissance archway which enhances the scale of the street and the visual perception of its spaces.

THE MALRAUX LAW

Named after Andre Malraux, a former Cultural Affairs Minister, the law was passed by the national government to protect not only isolated monuments but entire neighborhoods—*secteurs sauvegardés* or landmark districts. This legislation not only prevents demolition for slum clearance and urban renewal, but also calls for careful preservation and restoration of worthwhile elements on the site. Ugly annexes, remodeled facades, garish signs and storefronts are removed to reveal the original building beneath the 19th- and 20th-century excrescences.

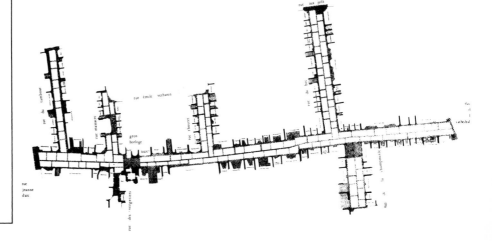

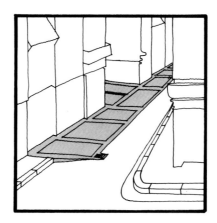

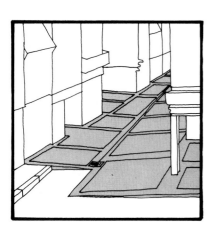

pact at both local and national levels in France.

As a low-cost strategy to develop and protect the center, the pedestrian experiment has been an immense success. No major new construction or urban renewal was required. The principal changes were readjusting flow on the four central bridges to equalize traffic capacity and creating surface parking for the city-owned land. The Rue du Gros Horloge itself was recycled. That is, most of the materials were salvaged from the street and used for paving, planters, and benches. Moreover, the project was conceived and designed with existing city agencies, thus keeping the cost extremely low.

FIGURES AND FUNDING

Redoing the first 3,500 square feet/ 350 square meters of the Rue du Gros Horloge cost $75,555 for repaving, $8,888 for drainage, and $19,666 for lighting. The total initial phase cost only $30 per square yard.

Design and implementation of the first phase was entirely financed by the city. However, the cost of compulsory restoration of historic buildings was borne by individual owners who were partially subsidized.

Extension of Rouen's pedestrian streets will benefit from a 50-50 split in funding with the national government, which has undertaken a program to help local municipalities improve the visual impact of their central zones.

Top: Rouen's gradual repaving process did not disrupt local activities and encouraged merchants to open up their stores so that the new paving could penetrate their premises.

Repaving began in Rouen in 1970 after extensive utility studies. Salvaged materials were used for the street: single-color paving stones laid in straight lines, framing a stone mosaic of a peacock's tail; planters of granite slabs; and benches made from old granite curbstones.

Norwich England

Norwich was the first city in Great Britain to eliminate traffic permanently from a central commercial street. Cars were banned on London Street because they constituted a hazard to the crowds of shoppers that overflowed the narrow sidewalks.

Initially, the ban was temporary, while numerous discussions were held with the merchants along the street to assess the impact of the experiment. The permanent conversion of the street took place only after the traffic ban proved advantageous to citizens and businesses alike.

Moreover, the temporary street closing and discussion among merchants served to strengthen the sense of community along London Street. When the street was permanently pedestrianized, building owners voluntarily undertook the improvement of their own properties.

Norwich is presently experimenting with the possibility of unifying the entire commercial district with a network of pedestrian streets in order to transform the core area into a totally car-free environment. In conjunction with the pedestrian program, the city, with help from private contributors, has launched a massive effort to restore and rehabilitate historic buildings in the core area.

CITY PROFILE
Established nearly 1,200 years ago, Norwich is the largest city in East Anglia, a flat agricultural region with one of the highest population growth rates in Great Britain. By the 11th century, it was one of the largest towns in England, with an economy based on its markets; the city served as an important inland port for the textile industry. In addition, it was an important religious center.

In the early 19th century, Norwich was the third largest city in England, but with the coming of the Industrial Revolution its prominence rapidly diminished. The River Wensum, which flows through the town, could not be used to drive machinery for textile and other heavy industries, which, therefore, moved to sites with adequate water power. Thus the community did not experience the vital but disruptive force of industrial expansion, although by the end of the 19th century, its population had nearly doubled. Even so, it had far fewer inhabitants than other faster growing industrial centers in Britain.[1]

Because Norwich escaped the ravages of the Industrial Revolution, it has retained remarkable examples of English architecture of the 14th through the 19th centuries that are spread along its intimate, winding medieval streets.

PLANNING GOALS
Preservation of its architectural heritage has been one goal of Norwich's planning policy since World War II. The other major aim has been encouraging the growth of the city into an efficient commercial center for East Anglia.

In 1967, the city council adopted a comprehensive urban plan directed toward achieving these two goals. Major elements of the plan included introducing pedestrian zones into the commercial and historic districts of the city's central area. Eliminating vehicular traffic from these areas required the creation of a ring and loop road system in conjunction with controlled parking. However, due to the economic crisis in Great Britain, only the northern and western sections of the ring have been completed so far, and the parking system is only partially finished.

A TRAFFIC-FREE CENTRAL CORE
Beginning in the 1960s, Norwich experienced the clash between pedestrians and automobiles that was occurring throughout Western Europe. The number of motor vehicles had doubled since the late 1950s, and congestion was most severe along London Street, the main link connecting the City Hall, the Market Place area—a lively and colorful outdoor market—and the Cathedral district, the city's tourist center. Many commercial vehicles used the street as a shortcut through the center, making its narrow sidewalks dangerous for pedestrians.

The Commercial District When a sewer burst on London Street in 1965, it was closed for repairs. This proved to be a most fortunate accident. Merchants had expected a sharp drop in sales, but it never happened. Residents were very enthusiastic about the change. The city decided to proceed with an experimental closing for 3 months and eventually extended the experiment to 6 months. The cost of the experiment was small—about $6,000 for the removal of signs and addition of planters and seating.

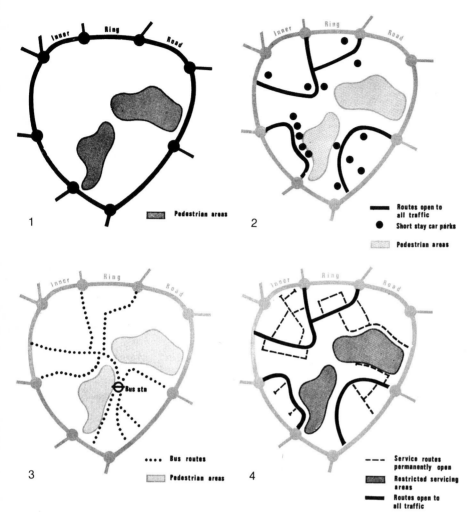

1 | Pedestrian areas

2 | Routes open to all traffic ● Short stay car parks | Pedestrian areas

3 | •••• Bus routes | Pedestrian areas | Bus stn

4 | --- Service routes permanently open | Restricted servicing areas | Routes open to all traffic

The principle of the ring and loop system is that the inner ring road provides for circulation around the central area but that penetration by private transport into the central area is confined to the loop roads. For both environmental and traffic reasons no cross links exist between the loops. The diagrams exemplify the basic principles of the traffic plan for Norwich's central area: (1) pedestrian areas, (2) private car circulation and parking, (3) public transportation, (4) servicing vehicles.

Servicing presented some problems, for only three of the stores could receive deliveries from the rear. The city could not establish fixed service hours because five banks on the street required flexible schedules for delivery, pickup of currency, etc.

After lengthy discussions, two long sections of London Street were permanently closed in May 1968. Goods are now delivered by handcarts a maximum distance of 120 feet / 40 meters from cross streets to the shops.[2]

Closing London Street made more than a single pedestrian walkway—it created a pedestrian district in the commercial heart of Norwich. Perpendicular to it are several Victorian passageways that had been closed to traffic for more than a century. When the London Street experiment proved successful, two small streets nearby, Lower Goat Lane and Dove Street, were made into pedestrian walkways.[3]

Aspects of the district have changed dramatically since it has become a pedestrian area. Restaurant owners note that people request tables near street windows to watch the passing crowd, and in some instances tables have been put outside in the continental fashion. Merchants have seen their sales increase from 5 to 20 percent, and their window displays are no longer soiled by auto exhaust. Building owners on London Street have enthusiastically redecorated their stores according to a color and design scheme established by an advisory committee; graphic controls unify shop signs in the area. About one-third of the buildings are redecorated every year, giving the street a continuously fresh appearance.

Norwich is continuing its pedestrianization program for the business district. Presently Gentlemen's Walk, a major link between the Market Place and London Street, is closed on weekends and is crowded with people. If traffic is permanently prohibited on this street, the entire commercial area would become a unified pedestrian zone as envisioned in the 1967 plan.

The Historic District To protect the residential zone around Norwich's 12th-century cathedral, and the cathedral itself, from structural damage and air pollution, a second pedestrian system was created in that quarter of town. Heavy traffic had already caused some structural deterioration,

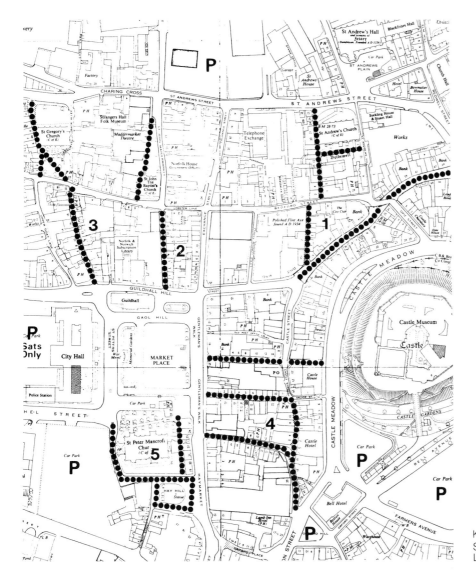

Key to the plan: (1) London Street, (2) Dove Street, (3) Lower Goat Lane, (4) White Lion Street, (5) Hay Hill, (P) Parking.

Lower Goat Lane.

and the city council feared this unique architectural grouping would soon be damaged beyond repair. All vehicular traffic, except the few cars owned by local residents, was banned from this historic area. This second pedestrian zone has been just as successful as the one in the commercial district, though in entirely different terms. With the cars gone, tourists visiting the cathedral experience the Elizabethan charm of the residential district.

In 1967, there was no specific legislation which empowered city officials to close streets to vehicles and improve their environmental conditions. However, city authorities established a precedent by invoking a traffic regulation aimed at eliminating danger to people using city streets and roads.[4] Later that same year, Norwich passed the Civic Amenities Act, which designated seven conservation areas within the medieval walls.

PRESERVING THE OLD CITY

To finance the local conservation program, the city council has allocated an annual sum of $150,000 for acquisition and restoration of historic build-
ings. Between 1972 and 1977, an additional $20,000 was allocated for repair of specific groups of buildings. Although this sum was matched by the Department of the Environment, it covered only a fraction of the cost of restoration. Private funding played the most important role, and the Norwich Trust, a nonprofit foundation established in 1967 and devoted to historic conservation, has recently completed the restoration and conversion of a group of buildings into university dormitories on Muspole Street.

As a complement to the large pedestrian zone and restoration program, Norwich is encouraging more housing in the center of the city to increase the kinds and amount of activity in that area.

In the Colegate area near the cathedral and the River Wensum, the city has just completed a large renewal project. Located on a site of abandoned industrial buildings, the Colegate project combines restoration of historic buildings, some forty new houses constructed by the city council, and improvement of the riverfront.

The redevelopment of a former timber yard is the first step towards the urban renewal of the Colegate area.

Right: London Street before and, opposite page, after its transformation into a place for pedestrians.

Essen Germany

Essen is largely a product of the 19th and 20th centuries. Located in the Ruhr region and home of the vast Krupp empire, the city was radically transformed during the Bismarck era so that today there is very little mix of commercial and residential structures usually found in most European cities.

In the 1930s, city planners took the unorthodox step of creating Europe's first pedestrian street to correct the imbalance caused by increasing automobile traffic. Pedestrian arcades had existed in a number of European markets for centuries, but Essen's pedestrianization effort was the first direct attempt to win back a vehicular street for people on foot. Eight years after the conversion of Limbecker Strasse, cars were partially banned from Kettwiger Stasse and a few small squares and cross-streets nearby.

Because of its strategic role in Germany's industry, the city was almost obliterated during World War II. When reconstruction began, the original pedestrian zone was dramatically extended, so that today the city has one of the most extensive systems in Europe. However, the sharp distinction between commercial and residential zones has heightened the contrast between the intense daytime activity and the nightly desolation of the pedestrian streets. Only 4,000 of the 300,000 people who work in the city live in its center. Thus Essen is atypical among European cities, both in its pioneering response to traffic congestion and in the character of its street life.

CITY PROFILE

Though thoroughly modern, the city was founded in the 9th century. The cathedral dates from 852 when Bishop Altfrid of Hildesheim laid the foundations for it and the Convent of Asnidi. Some 1,100 years later, this is still the heart of the city. The medieval town grew into a kidney-shaped configuration defined by a ring of fortified walls. Today, a road has replaced the walls, and the city has expanded far beyond its medieval quarter.

Eighty percent of the city was destroyed in the war, but in the reconstruction, planners retained the original layout of its medieval center. However, they had to accommodate this area to the contemporary needs of a city of 725,000 inhabitants.

IMPROVING ACCESSIBILITY

Postwar planning strategies for the Ruhr aimed at dramatically improving a polluted environment dotted with coal mines, slag heaps, and factories. In rebuilding a functional and rational central area, Essen's planners have reflected this strategy. As one of the major commercial retail centers for 45 percent of the 5 million people who live and work in the Ruhr, improving accessibility to the city was the major goal.

This goal was achieved by building ample parking and by promoting and improving public transportation. From radial roads, private cars enter the ring around the central business district, where numerous parking lots and multistory garages are provided. From this point, drivers can either take public transportation or use the pedestrian system which extends to most parking areas. Car travel in the central business district is discouraged by traffic diversions and oneway streets.

Another key element in improving accessibility was upgrading rail service into the city and extending the pedestrian system to include the railroad stations on the northern and southern edges of the central business district. At the south station alone, some 80,000 people enter the city each day. The Porchenplatz central bus station on the east also became part of the system. Thus, after the war, the totally pedestrianized core of Essen became the focus of every transportation mode, both public and private, entering the city.

THE PEDESTRIAN SYSTEM

The pedestrian system of central Essen is based on two major streets that cross in the heart of the city, Limbecker Strasse and Kettwiger Strasse. They are respectively 1,800 feet/600 meters and 3,000 feet/900 meters in length. Pedestrian walkways fan out in all directions from these two streets, so that every point within the central business district can be conveniently reached on foot.

On both streets, sidewalks have been eliminated and the road surface repaved with gray slabs in different shades and patterns. The paving is dull, but there are no steps, curbstones, or other impediments to inhibit the pedestrian.

The two main streets differ sharply

in appearance and character. Limbecker averages 27 feet/9 meters in width and is lined with retail shops. It has only one restaurant and no places of entertainment. Consequently, it is busy in the day, but practically dead at night. Kettwiger, however, is 60 feet/18 meters wide and lined with fashionable shops, restaurants, and cinemas that attract patrons far into the evening hours.

Kettwiger's width allows for street furniture, including showcases, benches, flower boxes, fountains, and pavilions. Although the architectural details have been meticulously worked out, the furniture looks obsolete. Kettwiger Strasse is the main thoroughfare between the new town hall and the central railroad station. The presence of street vendors, lottery kiosks, and children's amusements along the street adds to its vitality.[1]

PARKING STRATEGY

In many German cities, postwar reconstruction offered an opportunity to create parking facilities close to the city center. Essen has 6,000 spaces in garages, inside and outside the ring, and 2,000 on-street spaces. The inner-city garages serve pedestrian areas, and walking distance between the car and city garages is generally less than 1,200 feet/400 meters. Garages outside the ring are intended for all-day parking and form part of a park-and-ride system.

The city reserves the right to control fees and policy. Long-term on-street parking is discouraged in favor of short-term off-street parking in garages, where fees are rebated according to customers' purchases.

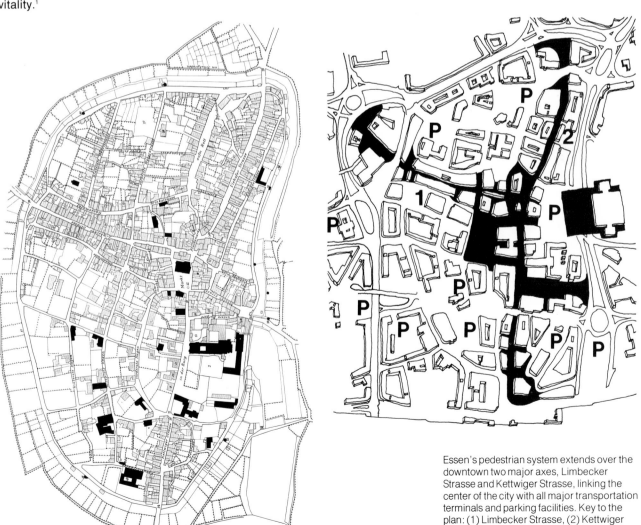

Preindustrial Essen.

Essen's pedestrian system extends over the downtown two major axes, Limbecker Strasse and Kettwiger Strasse, linking the center of the city with all major transportation terminals and parking facilities. Key to the plan: (1) Limbecker Strasse, (2) Kettwiger Strasse, (P) Parking.

IMPLEMENTATION

Essen's pedestrian system was developed gradually, in a series of separate steps, rather than all at once as part of a master plan. Limbecker Strasse was fully pedestrianized in 1930, rebuilt after the war, and opened again in 1960. Though part of Kettwiger Strasse was made into a transitway in 1938, it was not until 1952 that the whole street was completely given over the pedestrians. Viehofer Strasse became a pedestrian street only in 1971. Thus, the city evaluated each step as it converted most of the central business district into a pedestrian zone.

The financing of Essen's pedestrian system was unique within the European context. Construction costs were covered through the creation of an assessment district. Local property owners and long-term leaseholders became subject to special taxes when their streets were converted into walkways.

Though these shopping streets were successful before conversion to pedestrian walkways, customer volume and sales increased 15 to 35 percent after the change. Moreover, property values on these streets have increased considerably. Those merchants who were anxious about losing customers and restrictions on deliveries have changed their minds. There can be little doubt that the pedestrian system in the center of Essen has been a success.

The city plans to extend the pedestrian system to reach a new housing complex to be built near the new city hall. New parking spaces for 3,000 to 4,000 cars are being added along the ring. In addition, a fast suburban rail line and subway are expected to maintain, if not extend, the economic vitality of central Essen. Moreover, attempts have been made to create pedestrian streets in residential districts outside the inner city.[2]

Kettwiger Strasse.

Opposite page: Limbecker Strasse.

FINANCING CONSTRUCTION

Property was taxed on the basis of street frontage. Lease holders were pro-rated according to the length of their leases.

The law stipulates that detailed plans and cost estimates for conversion must be submitted to local authorities and kept available for public inspection and suggestions for one month. Any objections must be resolved before the project can go forward. New pedestrian streets to be built as part of a development program can be financed under the Federal Building Act.

So far, the city administration has spent $1,026,616 on its pedestrian system, and local residents have contributed $418,250 of that amount.

Munich
Germany

Munich's pedestrian system symbolically and physically binds together the medieval heart of the city. The Frauenkirche, New City Hall shops and stores along the Marien Platz, Kaufingerstrasse, and Neue-strasse are a single unified pedestrian scheme which succinctly expresses the governmental, religious, and commercial functions of the city for its citizens and visitors.

The traffic-free zone is part of a comprehensive transportation system which includes a regional subway. Begun in 1970 and mostly completed for the 1972 Olympic Games, the system was initiated to preserve old Munich's glamor and liveliness which were fast disappearing under a glut of car traffic.

CITY PROFILE
Munich is the capital of Bavaria, but is often referred to as the "secret capital of Germany" because of its rich cultural and artistic heritage, which draws more than 3.7 million visitors to the city each year. With 1.3 million inhabitants, Munich is surpassed only by Berlin and Hamburg in population. Over the postwar decades, the city's vital economy has drawn so many immigrants that its population is 11 percent non-German.

The city was founded in the early 12th century, but it was predated by a monastery from which it derives its name. The city is famous for its university and museums, and it is also well known for its industrial output of optical and precision instruments, heavy machinery, and beer.

During World War II, Munich was severely damaged. The scars have remained visible, although medieval and Renaissance buildings still stand in the city's central core. Reconstruction began immediately after the war, and as Germany's economic recovery picked up, the population increased at the rate of 40,000 per year.[1] The inner-city population, however, has decreased by 30,000 people in the last 2 years, and today there are only 18,000 people living there. This sharp decline is due partially to the lack of housing in Munich's center. A new regional transportation system, recently introduced, has induced people to move to the outskirts. Planners view this trend with alarm, for it could transform the inner city into a specialized commercial and office district. As a

countermeasure, they have imposed restraints on commercial expansion in the old city by refusing building permits and by severely restricting the physical expansion of offices, banks, and department stores. The heavily populated area immediately surrounding the inner city has also been protected against nonresidential construction. However, financial and commercial establishments are allowed to expand in selected areas in the peripheral zones.

DESIGNING THE OLD CITY
FOR PEDESTRIANS
When initial reconstruction of Munich began after the war, planners decided that crosstown traffic should be eliminated from the core. A ring was constructed to handle heavy radial traffic coming into the city. However, the German economy grew so rapidly that an extraordinary number of cars poured into the primary commercial district of the old city. In 1964, the condition was so critical that planners were forced to take action.

In the spring of that year, the city council commissioned a local school of urban planning to study the potential effect of creating an extensive pedestrian system in the city center.[2]

The Design Competition As a result of that study, the city council decided to establish a pedestrian street on Kaufingerstrasse and Neuhauserstrasse. A competition for its design was announced; officials stressed the need to conserve and accent the city's charming historic character.

The design competition for the pedestrian area received wide coverage in the local press, and the public followed it with great interest. In general, people were pleased with the winning design, completed in 1970.

As the project was getting under way, the city was building a rapid transit system and improving its highway and street system in preparation for the expected crowds of tourists coming to the 1972 Olympic Games.

The Pedestrian Scheme Munich's first pedestrian street was created between two major medieval gates: the Karlstor on the west side and the reconstructed Rathaus gate on the east side. The city's entire traffic-free system consists of one central spine connecting the two gates. There are several plazas within the boundaries of the pedestrianized area. At only one

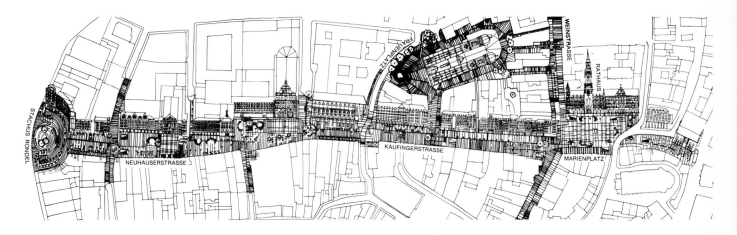

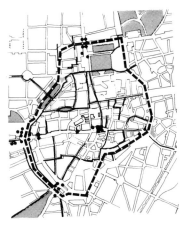

Key to the plan:
—— Pedestrian streets
••••• Subway stations
▨ Parks
▬ ▬ ▬ Inner ring

Aerial view of the central pedestrian spine connecting Munich's two major medieval gates.

point is the major pedestrian street intersected by automobile traffic. The other cross-streets have become traffic-free dead ends.

Planners were concerned about the width of the central spine, which is, at one point, 60 feet / 18 meters. This concern became purely academic once the street was open because of the sheer number of people who used it.[3]

Actually, the width of the main pedestrian thoroughfare is a pleasing contrast to the surrounding narrow side streets. To some degree, this openness is complemented by existing medieval porticos, joined to modern arcades to create a pleasant shopping ambience on rainy days.

The historic buildings in the pedestrian area have been restored and cleaned. They are floodlit at night. The street has been further enhanced with seven fountains, some of which are new and large enough to provide seating. Others, which were formerly in different parts of the city, were moved into the traffic-free district.

Design Features Stackable chairs are probably the single most innovative touch in this pedestrian scheme. People can move the chairs about as they please and group them for special events. Octagonal concrete flower planters are distributed along the street. People often sit on them, though they are not comfortable. Plastic liners in the planters are filled with seasonal flowering plants throughout the years. Trees have been planted in several places.

Relatively low street lights were placed down the center of each pedestrian street to give a sense of scale. Freestanding glass display cases were also installed. However, merchants found that shoppers preferred looking into actual shop windows, as has been true in other pedestrian zones.

The variety of attractions, for tourists and residents alike, makes Munich's pedestrian district vital. Restaurants, cafes, beerhalls, and movie theaters enliven the night life in the heart of the city.

Two new subway stations were coordinated with the pedestrian conversion, so that shoppers have easy access to stores. Lockers are also provided at the stations so that larger packages can be stored and picked up on the way home.

Neuhauserstrasse.

Opposite page: Marienplatz.

Neuhauserstrasse.

PARKING POLICIES

About 40 percent of Munich's citizens own cars; and of the 403,330 registered motor vehicles in the city, 91 percent of them are privately owned passenger cars, which is a very high percentage. To get cars off the streets, the city administration has constructed a number of parking lots and garages. The city has created 13,000 parking spaces. Five thousand cars can be fitted into private parking lots, and another 3,250 in city-owned lots and on the street. Aboveground garages can hold 2,400 cars and underground garages another 2,340. Presently, the city is trying to get people to park in peripheral parking lots and garages.

The amphitheater-shaped fountain in the Frauenkircheplatz.

Legal Aspects   When the city council decided to eliminate automobiles from selected downtown streets, there were no applicable laws in the Bavarian statutes for conversion of streets into pedestrian walkways; and under the German Federal Constitution "creation of pedestrian streets is the sole prerogative and responsibility of local governments."[4]

By declaring a local street a "Limited Public Way," municipal authorities were able to proceed with pedestrianization; and vehicular traffic is considered a special use within the pedestrian district.[5]

TRAFFIC CONTROL STRATEGIES

Parallel to the creation of its pedestrian zone were several strategies that Munich adopted to discourage the use of private automobiles and encourage travel by public transportation. Restricted parking has proved one of the most effective methods of achieving these goals. On inner-city streets, parking spaces have been cut from 16,000 to 4,000.

Highway construction has been implemented to eliminate crosstown traffic by creating a ring and loop road system. The inner ring, a 0.4-mile/0.6-kilometer road, was originally planned as a two-way highway with three lanes in each direction, but local and environmental groups opposed the extensive demolition necessary to construct the road. A reduced version has been put into operation. The ring functions in conjunction with four loops which divide the center of Munich into quadrants and which ease the movement of service vehicles and local traffic. Entrance and exit from each of the quadrants is provided only at the ring.

Munich has also undertaken a massive public transportation program.[6] The city's new underground system links up with the federal railway system, creating an efficient regional transit network connected directly with the city's center.

The city has profited enormously from its pedestrian district. The old core contains not only civic monuments, but also, more importantly, stores, hotels, restaurants, and cafes. The pedestrian zone, together with these attractions, generates a varied street life, day and night.

Top: Outdoor beer halls, fruit kiosks, and planters are among the elements that create a festive atmosphere along the pedestrian district. Above: Munich's movable chairs allow users to choose sun or shade for resting.

Vienna Austria

Vienna presents a remarkable dilemma: either it must convert the whole inner city into a pedestrian zone or abandon the concept. This situation is due to two major factors. Residences, shops, and offices are mixed together to the degree that it is impossible to define a clear-cut commercial district. In addition, the core layout is such that fragmented pedestrian zoning would create an impossible traffic jam on surrounding streets.

As a compromise between totally closing streets in the inner city or leaving cars and pedestrians to fight it out, the city decided to experiment with a temporary closing of its most famous shopping street, Kaerntner Strasse, for the Christmas season of 1971. Using "street happenings," temporary furniture, and other low-cost devices, the city actively involved tourists and residents in the pedestrian environment. Subsequently, this street was permanently repaved and furnished.

Stephansplatz, Graben, and several other streets will be converted pending completion of a new subway. Until then, total conversion of central Vienna into a pedestrian zone will have to wait.

In terms of pedestrian design, Vienna's program of street happenings constituted a unique method of obtaining public participation in urban change. However, the program was eventually dropped because of merchants' opposition. The street happenings concept was never adopted in any of Vienna's later pedestrian streets, nor did other cities consider similar approaches in their traffic-free districts.

CITY PROFILE

Today, Vienna is the capital of Austria, but for most of its history it was the capital of vast empires. The city dominated the trade and politics of central Europe through its position on the Danube. From 806 to 1558, it was the capital of the Holy Roman Empire then the capital of the Austro-Hungarian Empire until 1918. Then it became "an elephant in a backyard," as Winston Churchill put it.

Now Vienna stands outside the political mainstream of Europe, an unused gateway between East and West. This is reflected in the heart of the city. Before the collapse of the Austro-Hungarian Empire, the city had a population of 2.5 million people. Today, its resident population is only 1.8 million.[1]

The Austrian government is Vienna's major employer. In fact, it runs more than 50 percent of the businesses. These enterprises range from low-cost restaurants and motion picture theaters to an insurance company and the third largest savings bank in Austria.

In 1860, the medieval fortified walls surrounding Vienna were torn down and replaced by a boulevard, the famous Ring, which was landscaped with trees and surrounded by public parks and gardens. It became the most fashionable part of the city. About a mile beyond the Ringstrasse, a second outer line of fortifications, the Linienwall, was torn down in 1890 and the Guertel (German for "belt") became the second ring boulevard. As part of this belt, a rapid transit system was constructed which connects the railroad stations. The surrounding area was rapidly built up as a dense residential zone.

Like other European cities of its size, Vienna was severely affected by a dramatic increase in automobile traffic during the 1960s. The city was virtually saturated with vehicles, and the government realized that something would have to be done to keep the city's economy from being strangled by traffic.

PLANNING STRATEGIES

In December 1971, the firm of Victor Gruen International presented the city with recommendations for saving Vienna from the attack of automobile traffic. Conducted in cooperation with the city's planning department, the report suggested banning vehicular traffic from the entire central core as defined by the Ring. The Gruen report argued that a partial traffic ban would be futile for two reasons: (1) streets in the central network were too narrow to support an increase in traffic and parallel side streets to major shopping areas that would allow for an easy delivery system were lacking; and (2) the peculiar nature of the distribution of functions in Vienna's central area, based on a high level of mixed use, including commercial, cultural, and residential, that is, the lack of a distinctly identifiable central commercial district.

Gruen's report also strongly emphasized improving the ring road sys-

PARKING

Finding a parking space in central Vienna is so difficult that commuters arrive as early as 7 A.M. if they start work at 8:30. The city has recently adopted a policy of keeping the number of parking spaces as small as possible to discourage driving into Vienna. At the same time, garage space has been increased; 25,000 spaces in downtown Vienna is considered optimum. People employed within the inner city require 15,000 parking spaces, to which must be added another 7,000 spaces for residents and an additional 3,000 for visitors and tourists. At present, there are eight parking garages with 5,600 spaces, and a additional garage with a 2,500-car capacity is scheduled to open in 1977.

Above: St. Stephan's Cathedral at the center of Vienna's inner city.

Right: Key to the plan: (1) Kaerntner Strasse, (2) Graben, (3) Kohlmarkt, (4) Stephansplatz, (P) Parking.

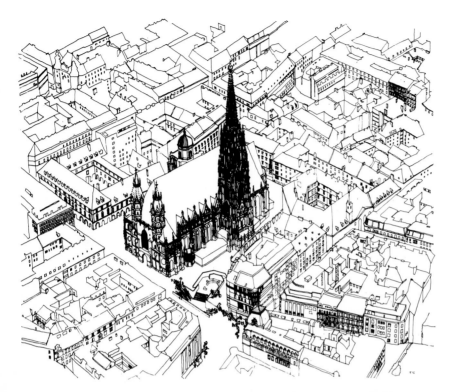

Above: The Graben.

Top: Rendering of the main subway station in front of St. Stephan's Cathedral within the traffic-free district.

tem created in the 19th century. If Vienna's inner city was to become a pedestrian zone, the Guertel must be used as the primary filter for traffic entering the city. The Ring was to serve as a defense against the assault of traffic, as Gruen puts it, recalling the role of Vienna's fortifications.

To implement a complete pedestrian zone in central Vienna, the city decided to build a new subway system rather than rely on buses for rapid transit. To be completed in 1978, the subway will be linked with an expanded regional transportation system. This combination is expected to greatly reduce commuter automobile traffic in the downtown area.

THE STREET HAPPENINGS

When the idea of converting major streets in the inner city to walkways was first aired, merchants were divided in their opinions about it. In a poll taken 2 months before the Kaerntner Strasse experiment, only 52 percent of the merchants thought it was a good idea. That 2 percent edge decided the future of pedestrian streets in central Vienna.

The trial closing began on November 1, 1971, and extended through the Christmas shopping period to February 2, 1972. Rather than a complete traffic ban, the streets were closed between 10:30 A.M. and 7:30 P.M. on weekdays only. This compromise was made to overcome criticism that a total ban on vehicles would turn the long narrow side streets into dead end traffic jams.

A series of street happenings for the Christmas Promenade, as the experiment was called, transformed the previously congested vehicular streets into exciting, if unusual, pedestrian walkways.

The program, which was very inexpensive, included the following:

Illuminating all the facades on the street with flood lights mounted on wooden towers.

Installing loudspeakers for music, information, and announcements of events. No advertising was allowed.

Putting up a tent in the street for small dramatic and musical events.

Placing colorful balls, 12 feet / 4 meters in diameter, for pedestrians to move around and play with.

Setting up a "school for walking" created to stimulate a series of unusual situations—undulating floors, soft surfaces, hanging plastic strips, and rotating rollers—to which the pedestrians were to react.

Special events were also scheduled in the pedestrian area, and traditional Christmas decorations were used to create a festive atmosphere.

Merchants were far from pleased with these street happenings, and during the course of the experiment a number of the attractions were removed. In particular, the large balls and the school for walking generated the most disapproval. However, the program was successful in that it focused attention on the possibilities inherent in the pedestrian street, and only a month after the experiment began, it was given an unlimited extension of time. Moreover, the traffic ban was carried over to weekends and holidays. Nearby merchants wanted their streets included in the pedestrian system—a clear confirmation of its success.

During construction of the subway system, the Kaerntner Strasse was made into a permanent pedestrian street. Completed in August 1974, this conversion enhanced the street's reputation as one of the most elegant shopping streets in Europe. The sophisticated windows of its shops contrast with the understated design of the paving and graceful benches arranged in circles. New lighting, trees, and planters have been added to create a harmonious background for its high-quality shops. Activity on Kaerntner Strasse continues during the evening because of its proximity to the Opera House, famous hotels, cafes, and tea rooms.

There are plans to convert the Stephansplatz and Graben into permanent pedestrian zones as soon as the subway is completed in 1978. However, both streets are actually closed to vehicular traffic now because of subway construction. Also the Kohlmarkt, perpendicular to the Graben, is being turned into a permanently furnished pedestrian street.

Because creation of pedestrian zones in Vienna has been an all-or-nothing proposition, the city has undertaken a far more ambitious program than most European cities. When the new subway system is completed and adequate parking is created on the Rings, the city's historic core will become a unified pedestrian zone.

Left and middle: Kaerntner Strasse.

Bottom: The School for Walking.

The North American Approach: Selected Case Studies

Converting vehicular roads into streets for people is a rather recent phenomenon in North America. The first urban pedestrian mall was implemented only 16 years ago. Nevertheless, the impact of pedestrian zoning has already had far-reaching effects. Banning cars from downtowns has not only affected their physical appearance, but also changed the attitude of people living there. And if Americans are rediscovering—or discovering for the first time—the social potential of urban life, this is due, in part, to the creation of traffic-free zones.

Today, cities are providing more public open space by recycling empty lots and alleys as mini-parks and playgrounds, enlarging sidewalks, and granting rental bonuses for such pedestrian amenities as plazas, fountains, and street furniture. The surrounding storefronts, office buildings, and residences are responding with beautification programs, new lighting, sculpture, and graphics, fostering a new sense of identity and pride in the process. And pedestrians, long relegated to crowded sidewalks, are starting to venture out into streets wrested from automobiles and transformed into malls. A new sense of spatial freedom and participation is emerging, while accepted notions of planning and economic priorities are being challenged.

An overview of North American pedestrianization experiments reveals a uniformity of goals: economic revitalization of downtown retailing and strengthening of shoppers' and investors' confidence in the city center. The extent to which the mall experiments presented here have achieved these objectives varies significantly. Economic trends, retail viability, downtown accessibility, and the condition of public transportation are all elements that have affected the success of pedestrian experiments. The timing of the mall project, the degree of cooperation among merchants, property owners, and city officials, and the relation of the project to overall needs and policies have proved crucial in every case. A mall's design, amenities, and the way in which it is managed have also greatly influenced public response to, and therefore the success of, a pedestrian zone.

Most malls are located in central business districts, although there have recently been efforts to pedestrianize residential or mixed-use neighborhoods. Municipalities have rezoned and redecorated streets and made a strong case for traffic-free environments. The concept does not necessarily require massive amounts of money or major relocation of businesses. Property improvements have often been left to the discretion of landlords, who respond willingly as

New London, Connecticut.

the mall begins to restore confidence in their area. Many malls have been built because merchants were willing to tax themselves. The federal urban renewal program also gave impetus to some malls during the 1960s. Administrative agencies would condemn and redevelop designated areas, according to master plan objectives funded wholly or in part by the federal government.

The degree of pedestrianization varies widely from city to city. The most radical form completely eliminates traffic from the mall area. Emergency vehicles are usually allowed, but even bicycles may be restricted. These totally pedestrian streets were most common when urban renewal funds provided cities with the autonomy and money to implement them. Today, many cities find that transitways are a more feasible alternative now that federal transportation moneys are the most available.

Transitways are pedestrian precincts that restrict but do not ban vehicles. Private cars are usually prohibited, but buses, trams, and taxis are often allowed, subject to pedestrian priorities. The motor routes are narrowed to only one or two lanes of the roadway, while the rest of the street and sidewalk area is repaved and furnished for people. Minneapolis has the classic transitway; its Nicollet Mall has an undulating, two-lane bus route; cross-streets remain open to all traffic; and taxi stations are provided nearby. Yet Nicollet Mall is unmistakably a pedestrian precinct—perhaps the most famous in the United States.

Although enclosing existing city streets is too complex and expensive for most cities to even consider, at least two have accomplished it: Quebec, Canada, and Paterson, New Jersey. Minneapolis circumvented the issue with a system of skyways that introduce three-dimensional pedestrian spaces. The skyways are enclosed bridges that crisscross the mall vicinity to connect second-floor levels of buildings; strollers have the choice of walking on or over the mall, as whim and weather dictate.

A pedestrian mall is a complex legal and financial entity that demands serious, long-term planning. The financial framework of a mall is complicated, both economically and politically. Cities have tried every kind of strategy their imagination and laws would allow. The American experience is difficult to generalize about because of the complicated nature of the federal-state-local government relationship and the variations between different state and local jurisdictions. Funding of traffic-free zone improvements is likely to differ in every situation.

At the local level, the assessment district has been the most common source of funds. In this case, property owners along and near the mall are taxed according to the benefits they are expected to derive from its construction. The levy rate is determined by the amount of front footage and depth of property or according to a property's proximity to the mall. Assessment formulas vary from city to city, but the result is that businesses pay for all or part of the project.

Some cities, however, feel that the assessment route is not practical because of the opposition it can provoke. Trenton, New Jersey, had the legal authority to finance its mall by assessing property owners, but sought alternate funding because it feared legal objections and delays. In the end, it took advantage of a $400,000 HUD Open Space Land grant and state matching funds to pay for one-half of the project. It paid for the second half by diverting $800,000 from a planned city parking garage project.

Diverting capital resources is another funding strategy. Often cities can stretch the definition of road or park construction and maintenance to include pedestrian malls, or they can bury some costs in previously planned construction projects or utility improvements. For example, the Federal Aid Urban System program gives cities flexibility in determining how highway funds are spent.

The costs of urban malls vary considerably, although on the whole they are relatively inexpensive undertakings. Many of the more substantial costs are so-called invisible improvements to underground facilities, drainage systems, and site preparation. Other invisible costs include legal work, inspection, and red-tape related items. Almost two-thirds of the expense in Providence went to invisible requirements, as did 31 percent in Kalamazoo and 82 percent in Pomona.

In 1959, Kalamazoo was the first American city to approach the legal issues surrounding conversion of a city street into a pedestrian space. To do this, it had to identify legal authority to restrict access to a public right-of-way. The question of whether state or local legislation was available or necessary had to be resolved.

Kalamazoo's planning commission, through the offices of the city attorney, made the precedent determination that a pedestrian mall was a valid interpretation of a street right-of-way. This established the city's authority to act without state-enabling action or approval.

The time and legal complexities of introducing and passing legislation at either the state or the local level have prompted many cities to make creative adaptations of existing laws. Relatively little specific law exists on pedestrian malls; related jurisdictions include legal provisions for parks, public safety or health, highway, traffic, and municipal improvements.

Municipalities can pass mall ordinances. Springfield, Illinois, needed only an ordinance to embark on its Capitol Plaza project. But local lawmaking is rarely so simple. Most cities require state-enabling legislation, and this can lead to political and legal delays. There are precedents, however: California, Colorado, Kentucky, Minnesota, New Jersey, and Rhode Island, among others, have already passed mall-enabling legislation.

California was the first to act, when in 1960, Pomona sought the legal authority to create a mall. The resulting California Mall Law not only established legal means, but drew the attention of other cities in that state eager to renew their downtown areas. The law restricts access to public rights-of-way but does not forsake public interest in the street. It includes the provision that a majority of affected property owners can force the city to abandon an unwanted mall proposal. The law, in fact, is very explicit in formally outlining the rights, restrictions, and responsibilities of a city, from resolution to final implementation.

Urban malls are sometimes controversial and competitive in their design. Unlike European cities, where architectural and historic richness can support traditional or even mundane concepts, American cities must rely on the design of the mall itself to lend character to the environment. The unadorned linear street, which often runs through an uncomfortable blend of parking lots, deteriorating businesses, and varying densities, is rarely an inviting pedestrian experience. The design process, therefore, becomes a conscious effort to introduce human scale and amenities, as well as opportunities for social interaction.

The physical characteristics and goals have evolved in three stages. The first was defined by the early 1960s when malls were narrowly envisioned as ways to return shoppers to downtown areas, and design criteria served that single aim. Few distractions to the basic shopping mission were allowed, and amenities were limited to beautification efforts.

By the middle 1960s, designers were gaining a more comprehensive view of pedestrian streets and began to study the relationships between behavior and environment; malls began to serve shoppers as people who might also like to relax and talk between errands. Design themes were introduced, and it became important to articulate human scale.

By the 1970s, however, malls had matured to the point where designers sought to integrate their full potential as social and communal, as well as commercial, places. Shopping still attracted some people to the mall, but many others were attracted by the score of happenings that began to occur there.

The design of the very early malls, in particular, reflected the commercial nature of their origins. Most were initiated by merchants and looked it. Amenities included items to improve the appearance and function of the area and consisted of plants, patterned pavements, decorative sculpture, or new parking facilities. Pomona's Mall epitomizes this emphasis. Similarly, Kalamazoo's first mall version offered trees, fountains, grass, water, and new lighting, but not a single bench. The clear implication was that pedestrians should shop or leave. The next generation, however, illustrated a more complex interpretation of the street. A rich diversity of pedestrian amenities, including playgrounds, sitting areas, flowers, and trees arranged to please and attract casual, as well as shopping, pedestrians were incorporated into these later traffic-free streets. Fresno's pedestrian system exemplifies this trend.

New York's Rockefeller Center skating rink.

The linear park became another popular version of the mid-sixties mall. Designed as urban parks, they are most common in California because the high cost of maintaining extensive green areas is almost prohibitive elsewhere. Ottawa's Sparks Street is not a linear park, but since it became a mall, maintenance costs have increased 10 times, of which a major amount is consumed by keeping landscaped areas healthy and attractive.

The most recent urban malls have been designed not only to provide dramatic or pleasant physical environments, but also to encourage community participation. They have become, in fact, vehicles for integrating a wide variety of urban and social needs. Kiosks or building canopies are often used to articulate pedestrian scale and intimacy. Many of the newest malls provide large open spaces for concerts, festivals, and political forums. New London deliberately left open a large central area for that purpose, at the same time highlighting an architecturally notable church in the background.

The famous skyways of Minneapolis create similar, though enclosed, perspectives. By fulfilling the potential of three-dimensional pedestrian zoning, the skyways have so influenced the city's shopping patterns that the second-floor levels they connect are now considered prime commercial locations, with rents and merchandise quality equivalent to ground-level operations.

On the two-dimensional plane, many cities have provided alternative circulation systems by introducing special vehicles that carry shoppers from store to store and to and from their cars. In Europe, where people are used to walking, this option has not seemed appropriate, but many Americans seem to expect it. The Pomona Mall had two passenger vehicles and still has one. Fresno and Sacramento have introduced similar services. Although the shuttles may add a certain color and excitement to street life, they have not assured the future of any mall and have more often proved cumbersome and uneconomical.

Perhaps the most important conclusion that one can draw from a design analysis is that design alone cannot make pedestrian spaces succeed or fail. The timing of the mall, its operation, and its integration into the surrounding urban fabric are equally important.

A number of malls have been introduced too late or for the wrong reasons. Some pedestrian zones have been conceived without adequate sensitivity or regard for the overall planning needs of the city. Better parking facilities and improved access to the retail area cannot compensate for superficial urban forethought. Not only access to the mall, but access to the city must be considered. Not only the pedestrian street, but its role in the city must be examined.

Pedestrian areas have been an accepted tool for urban renewal since the 1960s, but have only recently matured as an integrated urban strategy incorporating transportation, housing, and open space. In fact, the idea of pedestrian malls serving residential neighborhoods is only now emerging.

Some major cities, after a hiatus of many years, are again attracting residents downtown. The suburban wave has subsided, and people are again responding to the attractions of urban life. In some cases, this positive trend has been influenced by pedestrian malls, which have helped raise the city's regard for itself and its citizens. Providence, Rhode Island, has al-

ready used its urban mall as an incentive to locate several high-rise apartments only two blocks away. Minneapolis plans to extend Nicollet Mall into a residential development planned along the Mississippi River only four blocks from the mall.

Such attempts, however, have been very few. It will be some time before a large number of commercial pedestrian streets are extended into residential zones. Not only funding, but logistical problems promise delays. The federal moratorium on subsidized housing has damaged many cities' efforts to introduce low- and middle-income housing into urban areas under any circumstances.

Hundreds of small- and medium-sized cities have implemented pedestrian zoning with varying degrees of success, but almost none of the largest cities has progressed past preliminary planning stages. Ironically, it is the largest cities that can benefit most from a pedestrian environment. It is they that are choking with traffic and are losing retail trade; it is they that need the diversity and scale that pedestrian environments can provide.

New York City tried to implement the country's largest mall, and it produced the largest debacle. But it yielded some important lessons. Big cities survive on a delicate balance of complex political and economic factors. A mall can threaten this balance of interest, and only the most sensitive planning and leadership can resolve the multitude of factors and constituencies affected. Rarely has such sensitivity been displayed on a large urban scale, and New York's Madison

Mall attempt was no exception. A neighborhood-scale approach, where urban improvements are integrated into the character, scale, and interests of small communities within the city environs, may prove a workable alternative.

Planners, however, cannot decree, but only negotiate; they can make zoning changes and create bonus systems to increase their leverage, but bargaining remains the key issue. New York's Madison Avenue Mall, for example, failed in part because the city tried to impose it on business officials who didn't want it; the prestigious avenue was prosperous, and the merchants along it didn't want the city to interfere with their success by limiting access or creating diversions. The city is now negotiating with smaller neighborhoods that want help and need improving. Some success is already evident in the proliferation of plazas and public spaces along many of the city's streets.

The case for pedestrian malls in big cities is not closed. If the standards for air quality set by the Environmental Protection Agency are enforced, it is hard to see how cities can avoid severely curtailing vehicular access, as cars alone are the single major producer of contaminants.

A new era of pedestrian malls is coming. Major cities and residential neighborhoods, both urban and suburban, will be included. And the pedestrian malls will have fulfilled their promise as instruments for a more humane and responsive environment.

19

Kalamazoo Michigan

Kalamazoo, Michigan, was the first North American city to experiment with pedestrian zoning. In 1959, the first two blocks of its traffic-free system were implemented as part of a major plan to improve downtown economy. Because the project was without precedent in the United States, the legal, financial, and design aspects presented a great challenge to the city's planners. However, the commitment on the part of Kalamazoo merchants and municipal authorities was sufficient to overcome any obstacles, and the initial two-block experiment was integrated into the city's central commercial area.

The mall's success was apparent from the beginning, and over the years Kalamazoo's pedestrian zone has been improved and extended. Today, the city's zone is not only the center of commerce, but also the focal point of community identity.

As planners began to concentrate more and more on human scale and interaction, the objectives of Kalamazoo's expanding traffic-free area changed from purely commercial concepts to those involving community and social concerns. In 1971, the mall was entirely redesigned to reflect this broadened perspective. Pedestrian zoning is still spreading throughout Kalamazoo, and several traffic-free areas are considered for the city's residential neighborhoods.

CITY PROFILE

"Kalamazoo" is the Indian word for boiling pot and takes its name from the bubbling springs in the nearby river. The first trading post was established in the late 1700s by fur traders who found the river easy to ford at that point. The first permanent settler arrived in 1829, and by 1838, Kalamazoo had been incorporated as a village. Its location, about 120 miles/ 320 kilometers midway between Chicago and Detroit, prompted fast growth, and in 1884, Kalamazoo received its city charter.

Modern Kalamazoo likes to call itself the All-American City and Mall City, U.S.A., and it is indeed a typical and progressive midwestern example. Its 75-acre/30-hectare core serves as a trade area for 250,000 people and parts of seven counties. Once known solely as a paper manufacturing center, the city now has a diversified economy and is the home of four universities and colleges.

PLANNING GOALS

The city's merchants first became concerned about the downtown area's economy in 1956. During the preceding year, assessed property values in the central business district had declined by $1 million. Retail sales were also declining, and some businesses were starting to leave the area in favor of suburban alternatives.

In 1957, the downtown began to feel the full impact of competition from outlying areas. The merchants reacted by raising $47,000 and joined with the city in hiring Victor Gruen Associates to prepare a master plan.

Later called the "Father of U.S. Pedestrian malls," Gruen had proposed an ambitious pedestrian plan for Fort Worth, Texas, in 1965 that was adamantly turned down, but it nonetheless identified him with mall concepts. Kalamazoo was Gruen's first mall achievement, growing out of a master plan in which he proposed that traffic routes, pedestrian movement, and parking should be the foci of city development. Specific strategies included the following:

Phase 1 Construction of a one-way loop street around the downtown area. Inside the loop were planned a series of pedestrian malls constructed in former vehicular rights-of-way. Parking lots, within a 5-minute walk from the center, were also indicated.

Phase 2 Expansion of the one-way perimeter road outward and enlargement of the pedestrian areas.

Phase 3 New buildings in the peripheral areas, upgrading of existing buildings, extensive landscaping, and completion of the circulation system.

The City Commission formally received the plan on April 14, 1958, and referred it to the Kalamazoo City Planning Commission for review. The scheme was implemented, and the first step was to design and construct the mall, the first in North America. Its goals soon became familiar to cities around the country: to attract people downtown; to increase downtown retail trade; to promote a safe, pleasant park atmosphere for pedestrians; and to encourage private rehabilitation and development in the core district.

A series of informal meetings confirmed public support of the plan, and in August 1959, the mall was officially inaugurated.

The Kalamazoo Mall eliminated three blocks of one-way traffic that was rerouted on parallel two-way widened streets. Although parking on the mall was eliminated, more than 3,000 spaces are available in its vicinity. Trucking access is provided at the rear of most buildings. Where this is not possible, cross-street unloading is provided. Bus service has been rerouted around the pedestrian zone and in 1964 a tram was provided by the downtown merchants to carry passengers through the mall at a nominal fare. Pedestrian traffic has increased 40 percent on the mall. Downtown parking lot patronage has increased 25 percent.

KALAMAZOO MALL

The two-block Kalamazoo Mall was a clean and comfortable place to stroll and shop. The original design provided a good balance of grass, flowers, concrete, brick, and wood. There were, however, few design elements not directly related to the area's commercial nature. Notably, there was a lack of places for people to sit and relax.

The city soon became aware of its design oversights. When a third block was added to the mall in 1960, benches and a playground were introduced into the pedestrian system. National magazines covered the event, creating curiosity around the country about such experiments. Over 1,500 representatives from other cities came to see Mall City, U.S.A., as Kalamazoo soon started calling itself.

The mall became the success its planners hoped it would. Ironically, the place was so heavily patronized that by 1970, the pedestrian zone was badly in need of renovation. The city and the Downtown Business Association began to assess the amount of rehabilitation required, and the number of recommended improvements was so great that the city finally decided to redo the whole project.

Only the original fountains and grown trees survived the renewal process. The newer version, which still exists, combined rectilinearly patterned concrete pavement with softer midsections of grass. New lighting standards with double globes balanced on a crossbar were installed. Each block was given a central attraction, such as a playlot, a pavilion, or a fountain. The mall's redesign increased its appeal, and during the summer of 1975, yet another block was added.

RESIDENTIAL PEDESTRIAN MINI-PARKS

Today, Kalamazoo is considering further applications of pedestrian zoning, with plans to eliminate traffic from a number of streets in residential neighborhoods.

The city intends to select several secondary streets and close them where they intersect with the neighborhood's major thoroughfare. The area between the intersection and preceding driveways will be closed and landscaped as mini-parks. Not only will the new parks strengthen the pedestrian concept among residents, but the deadends they create will also stop through-traffic.

The city has already initiated studies to establish new bus routes and to evaluate the impact of traffic bans on such services as mail delivery, snow removal, and garbage collection.

Kalamazoo is confident about its neighborhood program, in part because of its success with pedestrianization in the downtown commercial district. For the 17 years of its existence, the Downtown Mall has had a consistently positive impact on the city, as its renewal and extensions confirm.

IMPACT

In the first 5 years of the mall's operation, some stores reported increases of 150 percent in gross sales. The first 10 years registered average annual gains of 10 percent. Some of these were encouraged by the mall's coordination with a parking ticket validation program, financed by the merchants, that provides an hour of free parking for each purchase.

There are no vacancies on Kalamazoo's mall. In fact, the traffic-free zone is the most prestigious address a store can have. As a result, property owners feel responsibility for the upkeep of their buildings, and stores along the mall maintain a fresh, modern look.

Above: The mall's new design alternates grassy areas with the homogeneous concrete surface of the walking paths. The overhead structures were added in the second version.

Left: The clock is one of the few elements that remain from the original version of the mall, first designed in 1959.

Playground along the mall.

The Kalamazoo Center is one of the largest multi-use facilities in the United States. Designed by Michael Severin of ELS Associates, it is a $16 million project, in the northern part of the mall, built by a combination of public funds, private enterprises, and individual philanthropy. The city contributed $600,000 in federal revenue sharing funds; local industry contributed $2.4 million; and the Inland Steel Corporation paid the balance. The city owns the convention center and its outdoor sunken plaza and benefits from an agreement requiring conventions to rent the hotel. The city also gets a percentage of restaurant revenues. Inland Steel owns the hotel, restaurant, and three floors of shopping facilities.

LEGISLATION AND FINANCE

Mall legislation was an entirely new concept in 1959, and Michigan did not have appropriate laws. The city planning commission helped establish a legal precedent when it asked for and received a statement from the City Attorney that "a pedestrian street was a correct use of the public right of way." Kalamazoo was then able to pass ordinances to allow the creation of a pedestrian zone.

The new ordinance established a Pedestrian Mall Advisory Board to control, develop, and promote systematic plans for ensuring a successful mall; the advisory council's recommendations were subject to the approval of the city commission. Other ordinances related to mall signs, building permits, and pedestrian zones in general.

As mall plans evolved, several business officals formed the Downtown Kalamazoo Redevelopment Committee to purchase parking lot sites, which the city eventually bought back from them at cost. By June 1959, the final decision was made to construct a two-block mall along Burdick Street, between Water and South Street.

The original mall cost $58,315. Abutting property owners were assessed $30,000 on the basis of land values, and the city paid the remaining $28,315.

A one-block addition, completed in 1960, cost a total of $24,033. Abutting property owners contributed $12,328, and the city paid the remaining $11,705.

Additional indirect costs for the original mall included street widening ($67,922), utilities ($30,500), and parking ($629,543).

In 1970, the mall was completely renovated at a cost of $300,000. The city and property owners each paid $150,000. Assessments were based 50 percent on land value, 10 percent on square footage, and 40 percent on linear frontage. The utility company also made renovations amounting to $40,000.

The construction division of the City Parks and Recreation Department built the first mall and renovated the second. This made the project less expensive than it would have been through competitive bidding.

The City Parks and Recreation Department assumed maintenance responsibilities. The 1960 budget of $8,472 grew to $18,330 by 1972.

Income from the $4 per front foot / per year / per property owner amounted to $9,588 in 1971, making the mall a 50-50 venture between the city and mall property owners.

More importantly, the mall has returned people to the downtown area. According to police department estimates, pedestrian traffic has increased by 30 percent since the mall opened. The downtown area is now filled with the activity and human interaction that enrich urban life and livelihood.

The mall has, in fact, focused people's attention on their downtown area and the opportunities it provides. Kalamazoo is experiencing renewed interest and participation by its citizens in cultural and social activities, and the city has encouraged this by sponsoring mall events that include concerts, theatrical performances, art exhibitions, and fashion shows.

The mall's economic success is also indisputable and can be measured by the dollars and cents invested in the downtown district by local and out-of-state interests. The prosperity of the pedestrian area and the city's obvious confidence in it have attracted corporations and individuals to the downtown, and Kalamazoo is booming with new construction.

The most visible manifestation is Kalamazoo Center, a convention complex inaugurated during the spring of 1975. Covering an entire block, the project includes a hotel, shops, restaurants, and a theater. The convention facilities have proved so attractive that they are booked up the whole year, promising day and night-time activity in the mall area.

Even before the center's design was completed, rentals on mall properties increased. The retail quality has also improved, and the convention complex has created a new mixture of local and out-of-town people.

Kalamazoo's pedestrian system is the site of, and the incentive for, all the major changes that have taken place in the downtown area. The city's willingness to experiment, and its rational approach to innovation, make Kalamazoo a model from which other urban centers can learn a great deal.

20

Springfield Illinois

Springfield's pedestrian streets were created as part of a major revitalization program, which included a large-scale urban renewal project for the Illinois city's decayed areas and extensive restoration of historic buildings. The city's heritage, especially its identity as Abraham Lincoln's birthplace, has always been an important factor in Springfield's tourist economy.

During the 1950s, deteriorating physical conditions caused a decline in downtown investments and, consequently, in its retail economy. Business executives strongly urged that action be taken by the city and the state.

The resulting program, begun in 1959, included the creation of two pedestrian streets, which are connected to and extend the restored area around the Old State Capitol building. This particular structure is the focus of Springfield's rehabilitation efforts, and the pedestrian streets border the Capitol lawn on the north and south.

The two traffic-free streets are quite different in character, reflecting the split personality of the city's renewal efforts. One is a comfortably scaled commercial stretch lined with old buildings, while the other is dominated by large, new office buildings which are part of the urban renewal project.

CITY PROFILE

Settled in 1818 by pioneer trappers and traders from Virginia, the Carolinas, and Kentucky, Springfield became the County Seat in 1823. It was incorporated as a town in 1832, selected as the state capital in 1837, and chartered as a city in 1840.

Construction on Springfield's first Capitol, the present-day Sangamon County Court House (now the center of the mall/plaza) began on July 4, 1837, and ended in 1853. Larger quarters soon became necessary, and construction of the present Capitol began on March 11, 1868. It was completed in 1888 and cost more than $4.5 million. Still unfinished, the building was occupied in 1876.

Modern Springfield is still in the heartland of American farm country, but it is also a major corporate and government center that evolved from a diversified economy, including retail and wholesale manufacturing businesses; coal mining; and railroad and motor transportation.

PLANNING

In 1959, the Springfield Central Area Development Association (SCADA) was formed to improve the business, cultural, and social potential of the downtown area. Under SCADA auspices, the city planning commission prepared a master plan, Springfield-1980, aimed at increasing investment and construction in the city center. The plan stressed two separate improvement strategies: restoration of the historic buildings in the downtown area and large-scale clearance of decayed areas to open the way for urban renewal.

Since then, many blocks have been renovated, with deteriorating structures slowly giving way to modern office buildings and public facilities. SCADA's special concern, however, remained the preservation and restoration of the Abraham Lincoln shrines and memorabilia in the presidential hometown. These attractions bring about 1 million tourists to the city each year and, with them, about $8 to $10 million of the city's revenues.

THE OLD CAPITOL

The Old Capitol restoration project was SCADA's greatest commitment. The building had so deteriorated over the years that it was condemned. In 1968, the state of Illinois purchased the Capitol building, and serious planning for its restoration began. Two years later, the city and state agreed to dismantle the building completely, numbering each stone for reference, and then rebuild it according to the original plans.

The decision to take the Capitol apart provided the city with an opportunity to solve some of its parking problems. Restoration of the Capitol could only increase the influx of tourists to the area, and already the city had inadequate space for its cars. With the site temporarily cleared, a two-level underground parking garage was constructed; and the Capitol was reassembled over it.

The city's master plan included a recommendation for the creation of two traffic-free streets adjacent to the restored Old Capitol building. The economy of the central area was showing signs of decay, and remedial action was necessary to reverse this trend. Because of their location on the edge of the central business district, the proposed pedestrian streets would affect downtown retail conditions only marginally. However, planners felt that the traffic-free zones would attract people and provide a place for shoppers and tourists to relax.

THE CAPITOL PLAZA

The idea of pedestrian zoning met with strong opposition from merchants and property owners in the area. To increase the credibility of the project, a mall committee was formed which studied traffic-free experiments around the country for 18 months. The committee then carried out a series of extensive traffic studies, and SCADA hired an architectural firm, at its own expense, to draw up plans. Six months later, after more study and modification of the pedestrian scheme, the committee presented its proposals to the public. However, all during this process, communication between the committee and city residents had been poor, and there had been very little exchange of ideas. Because of this, obtaining support for actual implementation of the project was a slow and arduous task.

The mall project, however, was finally completed in 1971 and has met with reasonable success. Neither of the streets is a typical mall, in that both are actually extensions of the Capitol plaza areas into a public

street. The beautifully landscaped and maintained plaza lawns are not open to the public; a metal fence surrounds them. The adjacent pedestrian streets allow people to rest, talk, or enjoy a picnic lunch on the edge of the lawns.

Design Features   Both traffic-free streets are open to the Capitol plaza, with buildings only on the far side of each street. The pedestrian zone to the south of the Capitol is lined with small retail and service establishments and is the more popular of the two traffic-free areas. It is located on the edge of a retail neighborhood, making it easy for shoppers to walk along adjacent streets into the mall area. This street also features the Lincoln Law Offices at one end.

The northern mall is a characteristic urban renewal area, filled with large, modern office buildings. Banks and similar establishments are located on ground floors, but the impersonal, institutional look of the street does not draw casual strollers. In addition, the north mall is further from the shopping district and borders on a declining neighborhood. Ongoing construction activities in this area also discourage pedestrians.

There are few pedestrian amenities on either mall, although there has been slightly more attention paid to

The entrance to the underground parking doubles as a raised "observation deck" in the South Plaza. Lighting is provided by modern light posts, and signs and symbols give direction and descriptions of mall activities. Musak is also provided along the mall. There are some retail shops, a restaurant, a few banks, and office space.

this on the southern one. The main attraction of either mall is, of course, the Capitol setting, and the city has chosen to rely on this. There are some benches, scattered randomly on a rectangular grid. On the southern mall, the benches are grouped with trees on one end, and on the other there is a small fountain and sculpture with a large curved bench oriented toward them. There is also a children's play area, but it is surrounded by brick walls, and regardless of the planners' protective intentions, the walls isolate the playground, and families seem afraid to use it.

IMPACT
The mall stores have benefited from their association with the Capitol area improvements. Even during construction, every business, no matter how difficult to reach, had a 10 to 30 percent increase in sales. Since completion, sales have increased about 10 percent each year. Stores are proud of their addresses and use North or South Old Capitol Plaza in their promotion and correspondence. SCADA also uses the Capitol dome in its logo, and its members, all business officials, use it in advertising. Special mall logos have been created for activities and events coordinated by SCADA, which publishes regular newsletters and annual reports.

The success of the pedestrian plazas can be partially measured in terms of the money they have brought to Springfield. During the planning and construction of the mall areas, over $7 million was spent by local merchants in remodeling and erecting new storefronts. Over the past 10 years, a total of $200 million has been invested in the downtown area.

Downtown investments, as foreseen in the master plan, have brought a wide variety of facilities into the central area. Now completed or under construction are a 30-story, multiuse complex which includes a 250-room hotel, 50 apartments, 70,000 square feet/7,000 square meters of office space, and 40,000 square feet/4,000 square meters of retail space; five office buildings equaling approximately 800,000 square feet/80,000 square meters; seven banks and loan associations, including three drive-up facilities; a 300-room Hilton Hotel with 130,000 square feet/13,000 square meters of shopping space; a convention Center with a 750-car underground parking garage; a 94,000 square foot/9,400 square meters library; a new police facility; a new $10 million medical school; a $29 million hospital extension; a new 250-apartment tower; two new Illinois Bell Telephone Company buildings; a newspaper plant; the downtown campus

of Sangamon State University; a new Attorney General's Office building; a new Bar Association building; and several parking ramps.

Many activities are planned for and staged on the malls. In 1973, there were 125 such events including concerts, rock bands, singing groups, and theater presentations. The largest art fair in the Midwest takes place on the mall. In 1974, there were over 1,000 applications to get into only 225 booths.

Downtown Springfield is certainly changing its image, although there are still deteriorating areas in the central core that need public intervention.

The restoration around Lincoln's home has been going on for years, and most of the buildings from Lincoln's period have now been restored. The area has been declared a National Park and has been cleared of all buildings not belonging to the Lincoln period. The restoration plan provides for a public open space area, within the four-block sector around the Lincoln home, and a reception area to accommodate the over 1 million yearly visitors to historic Springfield. During the tourist season, up to 15,000 people visit the Old Capitol Building daily. Both the North and South Capitol Plazas take advantage of their position as extensions of the buildings.

21

Minneapolis Minnesota

The city of Minneapolis, Minnesota, began planning for renewal of the downtown area when the first suburban shopping centers made their appearance in the 1950s. Initially, the objective of the city renewal program was simply to expand, improve, and conserve its downtown assets. However, when major companies, including General Mills, moved to the suburbs, the city realized that the issue of decline could not be ignored.

The idea of a traffic-free district for Minneapolis was an outgrowth of feasibility studies, comprehensive development plans, and renewal programs, all promoted and supported by the Downtown Council, an organization of local businesspeople. When in 1965 the Nicollet Mall project was initiated, it was the first step of an overall improvement strategy for the downtown area.

Technically a transitway, the mall allows public vehicles. But they are always subject to pedestrian priorities. Nicollet Mall has become a model carefully studied by many cities presently contemplating pedestrianization projects. Its thoughtful design and the careful attention paid to details have made it the most successful example of a pedestrian street in North America. Minneapolis is currently considering extension of the mall into new development areas and residential districts.

CITY PROFILE

Minneapolis is Minnesota's largest city. Years ago, it and St. Paul, across the Minnesota River, started to coordinate their planning policies and so dominate the entire region, which has a metropolitan area of over 600 square miles/1,550 kilometers and a population of 1.8 million. Minneapolis was chartered in 1867, and its importance grew because of its unlimited supply of water power. The city population in 1970 was 434,000 with an increase in the last decade of 10 percent.

Parallel to industrial development (mostly flour milling) was the central business district's growth as a major center for retail trade. The city employs 250,000 people of whom 83,000 work in the central business district. As in other cities of similar importance, there was a noticeable decline in retailing and property value when suburban development became competitive.

The Downtown Council of Minneapolis was formed in 1955. Initially, it financed studies to evaluate the impact of the interstate freeway system, then under construction, on downtown economy. This highway study, in turn, revealed the need for a comprehensive revitalization of the entire central area.

The Downtown Council developed a larger program, which was focused around Nicollet Avenue, the city's central commercial spine. In 1957, the Nicollet Avenue Survey Committee was created to pursue the improvement of Nicollet Avenue as the means to strengthen the entire downtown area. A comprehensive plan, which included increased office construction, designated Nicollet as a "specialized street" for prime retail uses serving the metropolitan area and region.[1]

Specific planning objectives were:

To improve pedestrian circulation in terms of efficiency (increasing the size of walking routes) and comfort (minimzing hazards and creating a more pleasing environment).

To improve access and encourage mass transportation usage by making transit more attractive, by relocating bus lines to provide more direct service to the retail area, by creating good pedestrian access to parking facilities, and by generally reducing traffic congestion.

To create new opportunities for promotion of the retail area and the central business district by building up the image of Nicollet Avenue as the prime retail center of the Upper Midwest and strengthening this identity by making the street more attractive and exciting.

To encourage private investment by creating a stable environment for retail business and other central area commercial activity.

Five alternatives for Nicollet Avenue were considered, and agreement was soon reached on a mall-transitway scheme that would incorporate all the city's planning objectives.

NICOLLET MALL

From the very beginning, the Nicollet project was highly publicized by local newspapers. The Downtown Council, through its newsletters and direct contact with merchants in the area,

Above: Nicollet Avenue in July 1966 shortly before mall construction and, opposite page, after construction.

Downtown Minneapolis: (1) Nicollet Mall, (2) Cedar Riverside, (3) Loring Park.

also circulated information about the proposed mall. This overall public information campaign was successful in minimizing opposition to the project by keeping the public up-to-date on each stage of its development.

Mall supporters had made a commitment to quality, and during the design process the city involved the best professionals it could obtain.[2] The design and materials were deemed representative of the city's image, and both the merchants and the city decided to do it right or not at all.

The famous undulating roadway and the mall itself evolved from close collaboration between merchants and planning consultants. They sought a solution to the straight tedium of many American streets, almost always designed for vehicles first and pedestrians second.

Design Features   The design of the new transitway reversed these priorities and unified the area to create a unique urban space. Nicollet's attraction is based, in part, on its sensitivity to scale in the treatment and selection of street elements, including bus shelters, kiosks, benches, paving, planters, lighting, fountains, and litter baskets. All these were meticulously selected and finished with such elegant materials as copper, bronze, or granite. Lawrence Halprin, the mall's landscape architect, calls the design a conscious effort to enhance the street's character: ''We wanted the new elements to relate, to feel as if they grew into the street in a natural way, not as a superimposed design.''[3]

The lighting system provides pools of light and relative darkness, rather than conventional uniform brilliance. Intensities are designed to make window displays prominent and to subdue distractions; lamp posts are positioned to delineate the curved roadway. Plants are located in large containers or under grates which allow for easy removal and seasonal arrangements.

Banners and exhibitions add color to the mall, which is otherwise largely monotone. Local merchants have commented that more artists should have been involved in the design process or should be asked to lend their creativity to it now. Nicollet Mall lost one piece of artwork when a Calder mobile was moved into a local museum.

Window shopping has become a

popular evening activity along the mall, so shopkeepers keep their displays interesting. Many stores have stopped advertising in the newspapers because they have learned that good promotion results in free press coverage.

Due to the severe winter climate, bus shelters on the mall have infrared heating systems. Snow-melting mats embedded in all the sidewalks provide partial relief for winter walkers.

THE SKYWAY SYSTEM
However, pedestrians on Nicollet Mall have an indoor option as well. Skyways provide an alternative for up to 18,000 people per day in downtown Minneapolis. A skyway is an elevated connection at the second floor level between buildings; it bridges the street and offers pedestrians a completely protected environment, even when climatic conditions discourage strolling on the mall itself.

The first two skyways were built in 1962, and since that time, eight additional skyways have been built. At least five more are programmed, and an additional four are in the planning stage. The skyway system has increased rental rates for space on the second level of connecting buildings so much that they nearly equal first floor rates.

The popularity of the skyways is already so great that the city is considering extending them into peripheral parking areas. City planners estimate this could more than double the number of people using the skyway system each day. If this plan is implemented, people could be protected from the moment they leave their cars, reaching their downtown destination in a way that is safe and comfortable.

The highlight of the mall and of the skyway system is Philip Johnson's Crystal Court, an enclosed galleria in the heart of Nicollet. Ten stories of cascading glass, Crystal Court contains over 20,000 square feet/2,000 square meters of indoor space that almost literally spills out onto the mall. A glassed entrance 40 feet/12 meters high makes a dramatic announcement of the mall's most glamorous social space.

IMPACT
A few merchants along the street were opposed to the idea of pedestrianization, but no legal action was

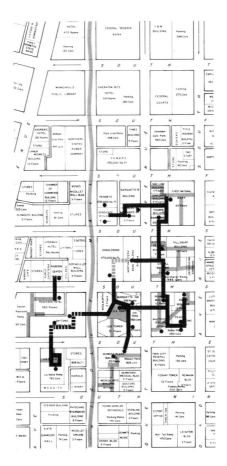

Left: Skyway system map in relation to Nicollet Mall and the downtown shopping area.

Below: The desirability of the skyway system, especially during the winter months, is evidenced by its popularity and continuing expansion.

Cedar Square West, the first of a ten-stage development, "New Town in Town," rises only a dozen blocks east of downtown Minneapolis, close to the University of Minnesota. Initiated in 1968 as a mixed-income development, Cedar-Riverside covers 340 acres/136 hectares, 240 acres/96 hectares of which are devoted to educational and medical institutions, a low-rent senior citizen housing complex, and natural riverfront parkland. The remainder of the area has been left for private housing and commercial development, half of which is available for people of low as well as moderate incomes.

taken. Now that Nicollet has proved beneficial to retail sales, new controversy has arisen over whether or not to close the roadway to traffic completely. Shop owners complain that buses and taxis continue to pollute the area with noise and fumes.

It is difficult to measure the actual impact of the mall, but some facts can be documented. Due to the increase in customer traffic, ground floor retail planning has been modified. Some stores added information booths for the convenience of new shoppers. Ground floor merchandise was expanded to include more "impulse" items popular in browsing areas.

Because of the attention focused on the mall and its many promotional campaigns, stores improved their public appearance with new fronts, windows, and plazas. The mall has led to property improvements nearby, as well as on Nicollet Avenue. In fact, Nicollet project prompted almost $225 million in new and rehabilitation projects.

Sales have risen 14 percent since the mall's completion. The smaller specialty stores have also shown remarkable gains. Vacancies occur rarely.

Despite complaints that it isn't enough, the mall has reduced noise and air pollution, traffic congestion, and pedestrian hazards. Crime has not increased, even though the number of shoppers has risen from 9,000 to 40,000 people per day.

Perhaps the most important result of the mall is the renewal of civic pride. People identify strongly with it, and the city's image relies on it. Public opinion followed that of the business community and civic leaders. Early fears that the mall could not reverse urban decay began to dissipate as its reputation grew. Reports that large crowds were again shopping on Nicollet attracted more shoppers. Downtown was once again an extremely popular place.

DOWNTOWN HOUSING OPPORTUNITIES
There are indications that Nicollet's success may even affect the residential potential of downtown Minneapolis. The downtown workforce has reached 90,000 people, many of whom would probably live downtown if housing opportunities arose.

The city has already announced intentions to increase the number of

middle- and high-income downtown dwellings, as well as replace, one by one, the lower-income residences. Although the national economy allows little hope for quick action in the housing area, the city is nonetheless planning a few major projects. These include the Loring Park Development at the end of a four-block projected extension of Nicollet Mall.

The Loring Park project is still in the preliminary phase of assembling land for the proposed development. The project will be financed by a tax increment process.[4]

Since the city's participation in the development process lowers the cost of land, the developer hopes to include features that are not otherwise feasible, such as landscaped courts and covered parking areas. Bond proceeds will also be used to construct Loring Greenway, a residential mall that will link Nicollet with the park. Nicollet would then lay claim to being part of a residential pedestrian network—one of the first in North America.[5]

This glass-enclosed galleria is part of the 57-story IDS building. The project, located in the center of Nicollet Mall, also includes a 12-story hotel, an 8-story office building, and a 2-story department store.

Sacramento California

As the capital city of California, Sacramento has an image to keep up, and it was the decline of this image that eventually led to the creation of the city's pedestrian system. The steadily deteriorating neighborhoods surrounding the State Capitol were the focus of growing concern, and in 1960, the state legislature voted $200 million for massive redevelopment.

Although a traffic-free street was not top priority in the overall plan, economic decline in the downtown area prompted the city to consider pedestrianizing part of K Street, which connects the government center and the popular and now restored Old West district of Sacramento. Planners felt that eliminating traffic from this street would strengthen community focus and renew the downtown as a center of trade.

Since both of these goals complemented the overall renewal efforts, plans for the K Street Mall proceeded. By 1970, the first phase of the project was completed.

The mall is elaborate in design, because planners wanted to give pedestrians many features to "become involved with." The result is a pedestrian thoroughfare saturated with massive forms creating fountains, landscaped plazas, pieces of sculpture, and other objects. This design has not been unanimously praised, but it has certainly focused community attention on the mall.

The K Street Mall's success in bringing new money and glamor to the downtown area has been mixed. However, the city has plans to extend it further, creating a totally traffic-free spine between the government center and the historic district. Urban renewal to the west has added three wide blocks to the mall's original length; and the city is considering the removal of some concrete structures in an effort to increase the amount of open space. As Sacramento continues to modify and expand the pedestrian area, K Street's potential as "Main Street" comes closer to being fully realized.

CITY PROFILE

Sacramento, the capital of California, is graced by a great deal of natural wealth from lumber, mineral, petroleum, water, and fertile land resources. Located about 85 miles / 145 kilometers northeast of San Francisco in the Sacramento Valley, the city is also only 75 miles / 120 kilometers from the Sierra Nevada Mountains and Lake Tahoe; the Sacramento River flows through the city.

The city grew out of the fort complex founded by John Augustus Sutter in 1839. Sutter's adobe fort was the lone frontier outpost in California's interior. The town began to boom when gold was discovered. Approximately 100,000 gold seekers came to California by wagon train and ship, most of them headed for Sacramento and Stockton. The gold rush, however, couldn't last forever.

Today, the city has a diversified economic structure, with manufacturing and aeronautics being primary industries. The state government is the major downtown employer. The 1970 census showed a city population of 257,000, which was a 34.5 percent increase over the 1960 count. Approximately 14,700 people work in the city's central business district.

PLANNING

Plans to revitalize downtown Sacramento originated in 1960 when the firm of Leo Daley of San Francisco presented a monumental study on the city's core area. At that time, the downtown's major problems were the deteriorated condition of the western part of the business district and the inadequate circulation network. The freeway system simply stopped at the Sacramento city limits.

In 1960, the city council approved funding to create the Sacramento Redevelopment Agency which started to clear away the city's slums with federal aid. The completion of Interstate 80 and an east-west freeway route through the city and the construction of a new bridge over the Sacramento River helped to alleviate the city's circulation problems.

The pedestrianization of K Street, which was one of the recommendations in the Daley report, was for a long time a low priority. However, two factors finally reawakened interest in the mall: the success of the renewal efforts and, more importantly, the increasing threat of suburban shopping centers to the dominance of downtown retail trade. Downtown merchants were losing patrons and store leases were renewed for shorter and shorter periods.

Opposite page: Aerial photograph of the downtown area, showing the Capitol building and the Capitol mall. The Old Sacramento historic district, which has just been restored, is located in the upper right corner. The K Street Mall is two blocks to the right of the Capitol.

Above and left: Water is Sacramento's central design theme. The mall provides a variety of pools, fountains, and rivulets channeled through concrete canyons and grassy areas.

Right: An electric tram winds through the hardware structures to carry customers along the pedestrian mall.

Two of the controversial design elements on Sacramento's mall—a tent for shelter and one of the concrete fountains. Citizens have asked for the removal of some of these structures.

LEGISLATION AND FINANCE

The legal basis for financing and construction of the mall was the Municipal Improvement Act of 1913 and the Mall Law of 1960, codified in the Streets and Highways Code of California.

To help finance improvements, assessment districts were formed and approved by 70 percent of the merchants. The city agreed to pay for utilities (sewers, electrical work, etc.), but when told the total cost was estimated to be $1,700,000, 80 percent of the property owners voted against the proposal.

The mayor, Walter Christensen, former president of the Merchants Association and the principal advocate of the project, regretted the merchants' vote and pushed the project further. The city council then took action to clear the way for the mall's implementation. By a vote of 8 to 0, the council overruled protests from two-thirds of the property owners affected by the assessment. The cost of the nine-block mall was $3.6 million, of which the merchants paid $2.69 million for the six blocks between 13th and 7th Streets. Federal funds made up the difference. The retail operators and property owners established a special tax district and levied an additional property tax to repay the debt incurred for construction of the mall. The tax level is maintained at a lower rate to support upkeep and promotion.

The three blocks between 7th and 4th Streets were funded with federal money through HUD. The mall cost between 5th and 7th Streets was $450,000; for the block between 4th and 5th, the cost was $465,000.

K STREET MALL

Begun in 1969, K Street Mall was completed by March 1970. Of its nine blocks, the first six were built by the city; the remaining three were built as part of the city's urban renewal program.

Construction was complicated by extensive structural work required for its foundations. Sacramento had its ground level 12 feet/4 meters at the turn of the century to avoid the ravages of regular floods from the Sacramento River; and the old retaining walls needed work.[1]

The design features grassy areas, reflecting pools, concrete fountains, a tent-like pavilion, specially designed lights, benches, trees, and flowers. There is still cross-traffic on every block except one. Special vehicles carry customers along the mall, while stores are mainly serviced from side and rear streets.

Despite the project's provocative and original look, the large fountains have drawn much local criticism, and there have been a few proposals for radical design modifications.

Since its completion, the K Street Mall has become the city's focal point and the center of its redevelopment area. Today, government employees provide the mall's most reliable patrons, especially at lunchtime.

Most merchants are happy, although the retail mix has changed, with a move away from the small, family-owned independent stores. Chain stores, discount operations, and large department store corporations have become the most prominent merchandisers. There has also been a great influx of services: restaurants and shoe, watch, and jewelry repair.

Vacancies, however, still occur and seem to last. Sacramento residents claim that the quality of the place is declining. Many shoppers are reluctant to go downtown except during midday, since Sacramento has its share of urban problems, and the amount of nighttime attractions on K Street is insufficient to draw large numbers of people.

The origin of such mixed feelings is the lack of public involvement that has characterized the project since its inception. A citizens' committee, chaired by the mayor, tried to mediate between supporters and those opposed, and it started to promote the mall to various county groups. The effort, however, was inadequate, and

criticism continued. Some people still refer to the project as "Mayor Christensen's Folly."

The local press supported the mall, and interviews with merchants have yielded favorable comments. This is hardly a universal opinion, but nonetheless valid testimony to the mall's continued vitality.

FUTURE DEVELOPMENT

The Visitors and Convention Bureau and the restoration of the Old Sacramento district are signs of renewed activities in the downtown area. The Convention Bureau, now under construction, is expected to have a strong influence on the future of the city's business district, creating a new market for tourists and conventioneers. Large, national hotel chains have taken options on land adjacent to the center, and plans call for a four-block extension of the mall to Front Street at the Sacramento River to connect downtown with the Old Sacramento historic area. Surrounded by two highways and connected by K Street to the central business district, this histroic area comprises 28 acres/11 hectares along the Sacramento River.

The California gold rush atmosphere is being recalled by restoring existing architecture and by reconstructing buildings on original sites in original styles. Two-thirds of the area is under the guidance of the Sacramento Housing and Redevelopment Agency, which started the project under a federally funded urban renewal program.

Three blocks of K Street were pedestrianized as part of an urban renewal project aimed at clearing the city's most decayed areas. Although there are large department stores on these blocks and they are similar in design to the first six blocks of the mall, they are less popular.

23

Fresno California

Fresno, California's Fulton Street Mall was created as part of a citywide renewal effort. Eliminating traffic from the central area was complementary to the city's other strategies for improving its downtown district. The goals of Fresno's program were not only commercial and economic. The city wanted to accommodate the social and transportation needs of its residents as well.

The city's traffic-free system now includes several streets that intersect Fulton, the main artery, and connect the commercial to the government sector of the city.[1]

The traffic-free district in Fresno has experienced fluctuations in patronage. When it first opened, Fulton Street attracted large numbers of people. The advent of suburban shopping centers around Fresno, however, drew people from the city. Today, the fascination with these shopping centers has worn off, and Fulton Street is regaining popularity. City planners are presently considering design modifications to the area and, more importantly, focusing on the residential potential of downtown Fresno.

CITY PROFILE
Located in the San Joaquin Valley, equidistant from Los Angeles and San Francisco, Fresno started as a small agricultural community in 1872, when the Central Pacific Railroad extended its tracks into the valley. A crude irrigation system helped Fresno grow into a farm community area, and since its incorporation in 1885, Fresno has grown steadily. By 1970, Fresno had become the eighth largest city in California and, as a county seat, is an important urban force in the valley.

The years following World War II brought rapid change to California and to Fresno. Population throughout the state burgeoned, as did industry and agriculture.

Although Fresno did not experience the serious decline that seemed to hit most American cities by the middle of the century, there were indications of eventual economic deterioration. Business continued to prosper in general during the 1950s, but the downtown core, which contained the major portion of business and governmental activities, was finding it difficult to maintain its growth rate. Since this area was also considered the metropolitan center of the region,

Fresno's prosperity had widespread implications. Retail and assessed valuations were still high, but percentages of total city sales and total city assessed valuations were decreasing rapidly. Furthermore, Fresno was not exempt from the growing domination of the automobile. Residential development had spread outside the city limits and into the suburbs, where shopping centers and industries geared themselves to the convenience of motorists.

HISTORIC PROFILE
1848 First settlement in the foothills of what is now Fresno County
1856 Legislative act established Fresno County
1872 Central Pacific Railroad establishes Fresno Station at what is now the city of Fresno, then called "Sinks of Dry Creek"
1880 County population, 9,478; city, 1,112
1885 City of Fresno incorporates as a town of fifth class
1900 County population, 37,862; city, 12,470
1950 County population, 276,515; city, 90,626
1954 Fresno leads U.S. counties in value of farm products. City streets are laid out parallel and perpendicular to railroad tracks.

PLANNING
Prior to construction of the Fulton Street Mall, a regional shopping center opened 6 miles/9.5 kilometers from Fresno's central business district, becoming the rallying point for fears about the downtown's future. The implications of the shopping center forced a shift in Fresno's planning attitudes for the future development of the city's center. And Fresno's business officials also recognized a new responsibility for maintaining downtown vitality.

Merchants, as the "Hundred Percenters" and later as the Downtown Development Association, gave initial impetus to redevelopment plans. The group decided they had to offer unique attractions to downtown shoppers or lose them altogether. The Fresno Redevelopment Agency, which had been established in November 1956, found that it had goals

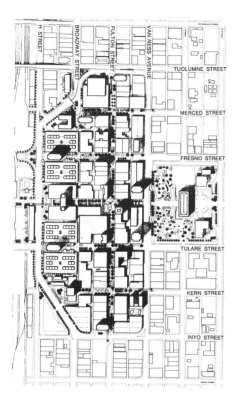

The urban renewal plan for downtown Fresno has transformed the center of the city into a core. Parking places for 4,200 cars have also been provided in the vicinity of the pedestrian area.

in common with the merchants' association. The threat of the regional shopping center was transformed into the incentive for downtown revitalization. The plan for Fresno's renewal soon evolved, with a system of pedestrian streets as its heart.

The architectural planning firm of Victor Gruen Associates handled planning for the city in general, as well as for the downtown business district and pedestrian streets. The city hired Gruen to do a master plan for the center of Fresno, covering about 2,000 acres/800 hectares. The Downtown Merchants Association retained the firm to study approximately 80 acres/32 hectares of prime downtown development. And the Fresno Redevelopment Agency worked with Gruen to define the scope of a federally assisted 36 acre/14 hectares redevelopment project. Using a single planning consultant lent continuity and consistency to the overall planning process.

The Central City Master Plan, completed in 1958, included the following recommendations:

Central Area
Strengthening of the entire city; any approach that over-emphasized the central area at the expense of the outer areas would have been self-defeating.

Programing future land and building needs for all central area uses and designating the best locations and directions for expansion of these uses.

Resolving future freeway alignments to provide optimum service for the renewed areas, while still meeting the needs of adjoining city areas.

Designing an entire street and roadway network within the central area, with related parking and the best possible service for all land uses.

Core Area
Designing separate routes for automobiles, buses, trucks, and pedestrians. The proposed mall was a vital part of this design.

Designating assets that could be retained and making arrangements for new development.

Planning adequate parking in strategic locations.

Providing links between the core and adjacent central area uses.

The Fulton Street Mall displays a number of sculptures along its length. Donated and installed by private citizens, each piece has been carefully integrated into the landscaping of the mall. A large clock tower, created by sculptor Ian de Swaart, has become the symbol and focal point of the mall, as the mall has for Fresno. Some of the more enthusiastic citizens have compared this clock tower with the church steeples of ancient cities.

The 6-block long Fulton Mall included 162
shade trees, 19,000 plants, and 25 fountains
of various sizes and configurations. Each
block is generously landscaped with green
areas, fountains, and rose beds in concrete
planters as well as different sitting arrangements and play areas. A slow-speed electric
vehicle runs the entire length of the pedestrian system.

Redevelopment Project
Defining the minimum necessary
acquisition and clearance.

Providing the analyses, justifications,
and guarantees that must accompany
any program that preempts private
ownership for the public good.

In 1963, an expanded plan, including
provisions for making the center of
the city into a "core superblock" exclusively for pedestrians, was submitted and approved by the federal
agencies.
   Planned and executed within the
total needs of the city, the elimination
of traffic from selected streets encountered virtually no opposition and
enjoyed the active participation of
public and private interests. Early in
the planning process, the mall was
presented to the public through
newspapers, radio, television, public
information meetings, luncheons,
and public hearings. In March 1964,
traffic was banned from a six-block
stretch of Fulton Street, and Fresno
had its pedestrian mall.

FULTON STREET MALL
The Fulton Street Mall was designed
to draw people downtown. Therefore,
it emphasizes not only commercial
variety, but human comfort. In fact,
Fulton Street was among the first pedestrian zones to rely heavily on
pedestrian amenities not directly
related to shopping. Its paving and
seating patterns encourage people
to make use of the entire mall area,
not just the narrow strips in front of
stores.
   Because of Fresno's warm climate,
water has been used throughout the
mall area in the form of fountains and
pools of various scale. Trellises and
shade trees shelter sitting and play
areas from the sun, and over 19,000
plants line the mall.
   In addition to the numerous places
to sit and relax, Fulton Street also has
two large playground areas, which
were donated by a department store
when the city's budget limitations
threatened their removal from the
original scheme. In terms of attractions, Fulton Street lacks nothing except, perhaps, some unadorned open
space.
   The mall has had a great impact on
the city's fortunes. Retail sales have
increased between 10 and 30 percent
along Fulton Street and the surrounding district, without sacrificing the

LEGISLATION AND FINANCE

The Municipal Improvement Act of 1913 and the Mall Law of 1960 provided the legal and financial bases for the Fresno mall project. The laws are codified in the Streets and Highways Code of California.

The Fulton Street Mall cost $1.84 million, of which about $1 million went into underground utility work invisible to shoppers or strollers. Part of the project was funded by the Redevelopment Agency and the Department of Housing and Urban Development. The merchants contributed about 38 percent ($708,000) of the total cost. Land assessments were $0.50/$100. Private contributors paid for art and other special amenities. By 1964, donations had already exceeded $200.000.

The city, through an extension of its parking authority, was responsible for providing adequate parking in the mall neighborhood. Garages were financed by taxes and revenue bonds. The Redevelopment Agency paid for construction of the mall itself, but affected merchants paid for any rehabilitation work on their own buildings. Annual maintenance costs for the mall are about $140,000, of which 70 percent are paid by special assessment.

kinds or quality of merchandise sold.

Merchants have renewed faith in downtown Fresno. They have cleaned up their stores and seem to take pride in their location on the mall. Some have painted the walls and sandblasted the fronts of their buildings.

Local leadership was strong before the mall and continues to be strong. The merchants' committee has an executive director, as well as promotional committees, activities committees, new business committees, and even committees for parking and traffic. A leading department store manager now reports that the major stores are exceeding their profit expectations.

Environmentally, the mall may have improved Fresno's downtown conditions. Although statistics are unavailable from when the area was still filled with vehicles, recent pollution measurements are promising. Air pollution averages about 0–3 ppm of carbon monoxide and never exceeds 9.9 ppm. Noise levels stay below 65 decibels. Crime and accident rates have not increased, and public opinion of the mall remains high.

From 1964 to 1967 alone, the city issued $818,000 worth of building permits for remodeling in the central area and $19.3 million for new construction. A total of $40 million has been invested in the overall business district. A convention center, office buildings, and hotels are part of new developments designed to broaden use of the core area, including the mall. Since the mall was constructed, almost $50 million in private funds has been invested in downtown construction, along with $50 million of public money.

Fresno's renewal efforts are generally regarded as highly successful, but there is still room for improvement. In the opinion of Edgardo Contini, one partner of the architectural firm that handled the project, the city must bring residents into its central area if it is to be truly revitalized.[1] This means a new effort to provide housing and better services.

Some of the different landscape arrangements along the Fulton Mall.

24

Pomona
California

Pomona's pedestrian street exemplifies the danger of traffic-free zoning outside the context of total city needs. The mall was implemented as a reaction to the success of two shopping centers on the city's outskirts, and its initial novelty as California's first traffic-free street was sufficient to increase Pomona's retail appeal. However, the mall was designed as a monument to the city, not as a center for its citizens. When Pomona's economic structure began to shift as a result of suburban competition, the mall's defects became all too evident.

Planners relied on the mere existence of the pedestrian street to draw people downtown. The spare architectural design of the place and the fact that no innovative merchandising techniques were ever put into effect have resulted in an almost complete loss of patronage. The mall itself is not to blame for the decline in Pomona's fortunes. However, if planners had broadened their perspective to include community needs in the design of the area, its present condition might not be so bleak.

Today, the city has plans to renew its downtown area, and the mall in particular, with graphic schemes and promotional activities. Planners are optimistic about their solutions, but they have learned from the past. Support for such programs is difficult to obtain at this stage. Even so, the city is continuing its effort to regain some of the vitality the mall initially brought to the area.

CITY PROFILE
The city that is "located five minutes from five freeways" lies 28 miles/45 kilometers east of Los Angeles in the Pomona Valley. The area has a Mediterranean climate, with mild, wet winters and hot, dry summers. A map of Pomona shows no center, but only a maze of highways, freeways, and scattered entertainment centers.

Originally part of a Spanish land grant, the city was the earliest settlement in the Spadra area before 1872. With the coming of the railroads, the town grew and was officially named Pomona, after the Roman goddess of fruit. The street layout developed parallel to the railroad tracks. In 1911, Pomona became a chartered city.

After the city acquired a private company's water rights and facilities and developed them into a municipal utility, agriculture became the primary industry, and citrus growing, in particular, boomed.

In the early 1950s, however, the city began to change significantly. A rapidly growing population began to make strong demands for new housing, and soon agricultural land became too valuable to remain farmland. Developers moved in, and one by one, the citrus groves fell to the bulldozer and subdivision planners. During this same period, corporate industry began to relocate in the area, and the economic base changed accordingly.

The 1970 census reported a city population of 87,384 people, a 23 percent increase over the 1960 census. Of significance for the area's social balance was the growing number of minority families moving into Pomona during the 1960s.

PLANNING
Pomona's commercial activities were historically concentrated in the downtown area along Second Street, a major retail center for the valley. As the town and its population grew, new residential areas were developed away from the downtown area.

By the early 1950s, two suburban shopping centers had been built on the outskirts of the city.[1] Their initial success led to Pomona's decision to develop a pedestrian mall downtown.[2]

In 1955, Pomona experimented with the concept by temporarily closing some public rights-of-way to vehicular traffic. The experiment was very successful, and studies were started to determine the type and location of a permanent pedestrian area. Second Street was the natural choice; the property owners were receptive and willing to assess themselves to fund the project.

During the two-year planning period which preceded construction of the mall, a small self-constituted committee of property owners met monthly with city officials and the designer to resolve problems and keep the momentum of the project going. Each member of the committee was responsible for explaining the program to other owners on his or her block. Local newspapers were also used to publicize the project.

SECOND STREET MALL
When the mall was inaugurated in 1960, it received national magazine coverage that praised it as an ex-

The Pomona Mall maintains the characteristics of a roadway, with a central lineal spine lined with trees. The electric mini-vehicle, still in operation, further contributes to the effect.

ample of urban planning strategies to come. The mall's initial success stemmed from the unifying effect it had on the downtown and the community pride it generated. It became known as the "Window on the City," and Pomona residents boasted about having the first mall in California.

There was a remarkable increase in retail sales and property values along Second Street, and the mall was nationally viewed (and erroneously assessed) as an "instant miracle" for downtown revitalization.

Design Features Unlike the pedestrian zones of later years, which were designed to cater to pedestrian comfort, Pomona's mall is stark, flat, straight, and uninteresting. During construction, the old sidewalks and streets were resurfaced with areas of pebbled and black concrete treatments. Planters and boxes were installed and stocked with trees and shrubs. A few benches, fountains, and small pieces of sculpture were rigidly arranged in a pattern calculated to achieve an overall impression of openness, but they failed to create any sense of fun, imagination, or activity. Nor were they meant to. There were no shelters, kiosks, or any other design features that could "distract" shoppers from their mission.

Two electrically driven vehicles were provided to move customers between stores or to and from parking lots. This service, however, was not enough to compensate for the greater excitement of shopping in suburban plazas.

The creation of the pedestrian street may have delayed retail decline by 3 or 4 years, but it could not stop it. Except for the attraction of one major department store and a few banks, there were no major market additions to the mall. The merchants showed little innovative merchandising. They relied on the existence of the mall itself, which soon lost its glamor.

The failure of downtown Pomona to keep pace with the rest of the market area in the late 1960s can also be attributed to its poor location in relation to the total market area. The downtown is situated in the extreme western end of the valley, while the population is growing in the eastern and central portions.

People began to leave Pomona and its mall for the suburbs. From 1960 to 1970, the population decreased by 39

Some of the few amenities along the nine blocks of the pedestrian street.

A 1968 survey of mall area shoppers and workers showed that the largest number of complaints about the mall arose from physical rather than merchandising conditions. The biggest complaint was that parking facilities were inadequate for convenient shopping in the mall. Other complaints were that stores were too far apart and that the appearance of the stores was poor. The lack of restrooms was also included, as was the lack of eating facilities. Since 1968, however, the Pomona Mall has further deteriorated and vandalism has become a major problem.

LEGISLATION AND FINANCE

Pomona's mall set the legal precedent for all California malls to follow. The legal basis for financing was the Municipal Improvement Act of 1913 and the California Mall Law of 1960, as codified in the Streets and Highways Code of California.

Prior to 1960, California had no legal mechanism for a community to establish a pedestrian mall similar to the one already operating in Kalamazoo, Michigan. The city of Pomona led the fight and urged the California legislature to adopt legislation in the form of the Pedestrian Mall Law of 1960, which indicates procedures to establish pedestrian malls in public rights-of-way without vacating or abandoning the public interest therein. Provisions are made to pay damages and abandon proceedings if a majority of property owner fronting the mall file written opposition.

percent in the city, while it increased 50 to 100 percent in the outskirts.

The mall could no longer compete with the convenience of accessibility, parking, variety, and comfort offered by the large regional shopping centers. In addition, because a series of one-stop specialty stores had been set up along the mall, customers could no longer practice comparison shopping, so typical in large suburban centers.[3]

FUTURE OUTLOOK

Now that the place is virtually deserted, its long length and lack of amenities or graphics make it seem especially empty.[4] Young people use the street for bicycle riding and as a place to stroll without disturbance. But most people avoid the area. Many stores have left, and "For Rent" signs are conspicuous. The heavy tax burden on mall merchants compared with suburban alternatives was a fur-

ther incentive to leave the mall.

Recognizing that the Second Street Mall only served to delay the decline of the area for a few years, the city of Pomona has embarked on a program to renew and enhance it. The city has set new goals for the revitalization of the downtown area with a broader perspective than ever before.[5] It plans to expand activities to attract all kinds of people both day and night. It also plans to encourage local street vendors and make design modifications that will diffuse the flat linearity of the space, with a new emphasis on urban furniture and pedestrian-oriented amenities.

Pomona is gearing up to try again, and despite its social and economic problems, its efforts to infuse mall and city life with a new sense of vitality may work. This new effort to deal with the mall in terms of total city needs is a promising start.

25

New London Connecticut

The decision to pedestrianize a section of State Street was not part of New London's original plans for downtown improvement. Once the decision was made, however, the city was determined to create a traffic-free zone that would benefit the entire downtown area.

The design of Captain's Walk capitalizes on New London's reputation as a Connecticut port town, integrating nautical themes with properly scaled pedestrian elements. The thoughtful planning of Captain's Walk combined with rational merchandising practices has resulted in a successful pedestrian street that attracts both residents and tourists into the city's business district.

CITY PROFILE

Founded in 1646, New London has remained, throughout its history, the most important city in the southeastern Connecticut region. A major whaling town and sailors' port of call, for many years the city was the third biggest port in North America after New York and Boston.

An 1847 map of New London shows that the street system of the central business district was already fully developed by that time. It has remained almost unchanged to this day. Many houses in the city's center are included in the National Register of Historic Buildings.

New London has a land area of 6.2 square miles / 16 square kilometers and a population of approximately 32,500 inhabitants. However, 225,000 people come to the city's central business district every day. The local railroad is the most active along the line connecting Boston with New York.

Only 6 percent of New London's total area is undeveloped. Although this vacant land is available, it is widely scattered and therefore does not have any real development potential. The population density of 5,200 persons per square mile indicates the relatively high intensity of development within the city limits.

PLANNING

Immediately after World War II, New London's downtown area was still thriving. Suburban development started late in the city, but when it happened, it did so quickly. By 1957, the merchants along the city's commercial route, State Street, were asking for action to reverse the city's decline.

The idea of a mall along State Street was first made public in 1969, but was not implemented for several years. Economic decay bottomed out in 1969, when major department stores left State Street for new suburban locations and when chances of a new department store opening a branch downtown became unrealistic. Shoppers' confidence was also shaken by increasing crime.

The original scheme would not have closed the street entirely to traffic, but it would have enlarged existing sidewalks and furnished them with planters and benches. However, a utility project was already planned, and it soon became evident that a full mall would be more effective if it took advantage of construction already started. To include pedestrianization of State Street in the city's renewal project, the city council's approval was necessary. Local merchants expressed their support for the project by making commitments not to move from State Street. Such examples of enthusiasm encouraged the city council, which finally approved the

---

LEGISLATION AND FINANCE

No special legislation was required to implement Captain's Walk. The city undertook the mall project within the existing legal guidelines established for municipal corporations by state statutes and local charter. The powers granted to municipalities in Connecticut are very broad, and there is no legal problem in establishing a pedestrian street as long as the right-of-way remains in public ownership and is designated as such. If the public right-of-way is abandoned, the land up to the center of the street becomes the property of abutting property owners.

In May 1974, the city council voted new regulations about pedestrian malls. These regulations affected temporary activities on the mall, the sale of goods from a stationary distribution point, and sales from movable vending sources, requiring a special permit.

The mall was developed and funded as part of an urban renewal project, which paid for the bulk of its cost and necessary improvements in circulation and parking. The total cost of the mall was $1.4 million, of which $400,000 went into surface improvements. Of this, the city contributed $50,000 out of assessments from benefited properties. The Downtown New London Association voluntarily contributed another $50,000.

Above and opposite page: Captain's Walk was designed to accommodate a variety of activities. Canopies of metal pipes and fiberglass provide shelters for art exhibits and can be expanded to house sidewalk cafes and restaurants. The area in front of city hall was left largely open to provide space for large gatherings such as festivals, speeches, and political rallies.

Raised green areas provide comfortable place to sit, while canopied structures give scale to the street.

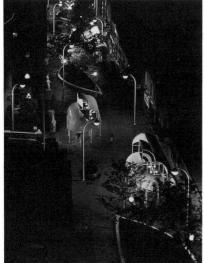

To accommodate pedestrian scale and safety, the mall has two different types of lights. Mercury vapor lamps, corrected for hue, were placed on original lamp standards and used for general lighting most nights. But for special occasions, and on those days when shops are open late, 175-watt bulbs are switched on; these are located on 10-foot/3-meter poles concealed in the grassy areas between the trees. These lights are practically invisible during the day. Similar warm light is also provided inside the canopies, adding colorful spots to the night scene. Street lighting in the downtown area has been raised to a minimum of 5 foot candles at street level.

Right: Phones are connected to a central security office, which responds to calls about accidents as well as fire and emergencies.

A winding lane for emergency vehicles has been subtly integrated into the overall design of the mall.

project in 1971. At that point the city's urban renewal agency took over.

CAPTAIN'S WALK

The design phase started in October 1972. Captain's Walk involves four of the central blocks along State Street, with the upper and lower portions treated as semimalls and the central part as a completely pedestrianized zone. The semimall areas have enlarged sidewalks and two traffic lanes. An early scheme to extend the mall two more blocks to the railroad station and riverfront had to be abandoned because closing that portion of State Street left no alternate routes.

The pedestrian area of State Street was completely redesigned to lend human scale to Captain's Walk. The street was entirely repaved in cobblestone textures, and its linearity was relieved by the staggered sequence of whale-shaped green areas for sitting. Spinnaker-shaped plastic canopies balloon over the edges of the mall, providing spatial variation as well as shelter. Almost concealed in the mall is an emergency vehicle lane designed in subtle serpentine form. Canopies, telephone booths, kiosks, mailboxes, and benches along the mall all reflect the city's nautical tradition.

The color and scale of Captain's Walk have proved a powerful attraction, and the area has drawn many new customers. Promotional activities are scheduled to keep the image of the place lively—almost one per week as an average—and local residents have responded with new interest in the future of their downtown.

Mall merchants solved the problem of suburban rivalry by avoiding direct competition. They offer a large variety of specialty goods not readily available in large shopping centers as well as a good mix of merchandise.

Captain's Walk is designed to encourage free movement from one side of the street to the other, and this too aids shopping. When the mall was constructed, the city still had a security problem and so installed emergency phones at convenient spots. However, security has improved so much that the phones are rarely used.

One portion in the center of the mall has been intentionally left open. Designed as a plaza in front of City Hall and a three-spired church, this area allows large numbers of people to congregate in comfort. Here is where public celebrations, concerts, speeches, festivals, and other performances take place, and here is where pedestrians can become an audience for community and cultural activities. The simplicity of this area adds to its effectiveness and helps to highlight the historic setting and architecture.

DOWNTOWN REVIVAL

The plans for the Winthrop Urban Renewal project included recommendations for new downtown housing. In accordance with this, a large area of slum houses within walking distance of the mall was cleared and rebuilt. This area now provides 484 new dwelling units distributed in row houses and 111 high-rise units.

The city is also undertaking several conservation and urban restoration projects. A typical example is Bank Street, which departs perpendicularly from the mall. The entire area along this street was slated for demolition, but strong opposition from the community prevented this. The existing buildings will now be restored and entertainment facilities will be encouraged to increase the night use of downtown.

The transformation of a vaudeville-period movie theater into a community center is in the planning stage, while the old and famous Union Station has been bought by a private developer and will become a transportation terminal for rail, buses, and ferries across the Long Island Sound. In addition, the new terminal will provide new office space and restaurants.

IMPACT

The project encountered very little opposition. The drive to improve the downtown area was apparently very strong. What opposition existed came from a local taxpayers' association concerned that public moneys were being used to subsidize the financial fortunes of downtown property owners and merchants. Support from the community, however, overcame these comments.

Although only a little more than a year has passed since Captain's Walk was inaugurated, its benefits are evident even in surrounding areas. The stores on the mall have redesigned or restored their facades and improved the quality of their window displays. Sales have increased and deteriorating businesses are only a memory.

There are no vacancies.

Instrumental to the mall's success were improvements to downtown traffic circulation and provision of new parking. As part of the urban renewal project, the connection between downtown and the interstate highway system was improved and two new bridges constructed. One-way streets were converted to parking garages.

A great deal of parking construction in close proximity to the mall preceded the opening of Captain's Walk. In 1970, a 406-space garage was built. Surface parking was upgraded in 1973 to provide 205 additional spaces, and in 1974 a 550-car garage was opened and linked to the pedestrian mall by a bridge. The New London parking commission controls services and rates. The merchants support a validation program providing free parking for customers. Pedestrian bridge landings in the mall are even popular gathering places.

The mall's success has also brought an influx of new investments along the pedestrian walkway. The former Crocker House Hotel in front of City Hall is being rehabilitated as an apartment building by a private developer. The same destiny is reserved for the even older Mohican Hotel, which is being readied for transformation into a residential condominium. At the same time, the city is contracting developers to build a 250-room hotel close to the mall. New London needs such accommodations because it serves a large share of Connecticut tourists. Two million visitors registered in 1974, with the mall becoming a primary tourist attraction.

26

Providence Rhode Island

From 1957 to 1961, the city administration of Providence, Rhode Island, worked on a plan to revitalize its deteriorating center, then well over 305 years old. City officials and citizens worked together closely, and the resulting plan mandated that this cooperation continue throughout implementation as well.

Westminster Mall, which opened in August 1965, was the effort's most notable achievement, and for 10 years the mall has contributed strongly to renewed prosperity in the city. Part of its strength, however, is the broad-scale planning directed at the entire downtown area. The mall, in fact, was not conceived as an isolated demonstration of urban vitality, but was carefully integrated into a citywide improvement plan that included concurrent efforts to bring new housing into the city within walking distance of the mall. Not only did the housing return people to the downtown area, but it encouraged residence by a variety of incomes and ages.

The mall, as it exists today, seems to respond to both the old and the new images of Providence. One portion of it is slightly rundown, but accepted; people seem to ignore its shabbiness, and it is usually crowded. Its design is subtle and doesn't interfere with surrounding buildings.

The second part of the mall is as slick as the former is homely. Surrounded by either new construction or barren sites awaiting new buildings, this portion remains stiff and monumental.

Providence intends to balance its traffic-free area, but the necessary funding her alterations is not readily available. Eventually, however, the city hopes to extend the mall as the unifying element for the entire business core.

CITY PROFILE
Roger Williams, a religious fugitive from the Massachusetts colony, founded Providence in 1636 and quickly established the separation of church and state. The city developed maritime trade with England and was granted legal charter from the Crown as Rhode Island and the Providence Plantations in 1664. By the beginning of the 19th century, manufacturing had become important, drawn by the city's seaport and its railway connections between New York and Boston.

In 1900, Providence became the capital of the state of Rhode Island. Modern Providence remains an active seaport, as well as a commercial and industrial center; the metropolitan area has a population of 795,311 people. The number of people living within the city limits, however, has dropped since World War II as people have left the city for the suburbs. Today, only 179,213 people live in the municipality, while before the war there were 252,981.

The central business district, with an area of 350 acres/140 hectares, is the heart of the city. It is physically defined by the Providence River on the east, the Capitol complex on the north, and highways on the south and west. These rigid human-made and natural boundaries, the advanced age of many buildings, and the still-existing original street network make this district an easily identifiable core for the entire metropolitan region.

TRANSPORTATION PLANNING

The highway system circling the downtown was completed in 1967, bringing the whole metropolitan area within 30 minutes of the downtown district. The parking system also improved, with construction of four downtown garages. A parking inventory conducted in 1974 shows that there are approximately 11,000 parking spaces in lots in the central business district. Of these, only 2,500 are short-term parking, while the remaining 8,600 spaces were used by commuters. The parking areas subtract a total of 143 acres/57 hectares from the already restricted size of Providence's central business district, but this imbalance can be solved naturally by progressively reducing car commuting and upgrading public transportation. Initial steps have been taken to improve rail and bus service. A centralized interstate bus station has opened only two blocks from the pedestrian mall, and there are plans to transform Union Station, the old railway station, into a multimode terminal.

PLANNING
Providence was not spared the blight of suburban alternatives, and as people left, it entered a period of decay. The weakened city was struck by Hurricane Carol in 1954, leaving over $20 million worth of destruction in its wake. However, Carol also left the population and merchants resolved

Opposite page: The minimal design of the Westminster Street Mall is harmonious with the austerity of the buildings that line it. Emergency vehicles have access to the mall via a 12-foot/4-meter special lane; several cross-streets are also reserved for services. The fire department and police praise the mall and its rearrangement of downtown traffic; they have discovered that fire trucks, police cars, and other emergency vehicles can move into this business section of downtown more quickly and easily than before and with virtually no traffic problems.

The mall features an orderly sequence of simple round and rectangular planters, intertwined by service areas and basic facilities.

Right: Only authorized peddlers are allowed on the Westminster Street Mall.

to upgrade their city and reverse the trends of economic and physical decay. A survey of shoppers' attitudes published in 1956 reflected the public's loss of confidence. Strong action was necessary, and it was in this context that a downtown pedestrian mall was conceived.

In 1959, the city, in collaboration with the Urban Renewal Administration, presented a master plan, Downtown Providence 1970. The three principal objectives of the plan were:

To formulate a 10-year development strategy for the downtown area

To maintain the highest degree of cooperation possible between citizens and public officials in planning as well as implementation of any improvements

To restore the core area of the city

In keeping with these goals, the master plan proposed the following: an intown residential area on Weybosset Hill, a convention center, a new bus and railway terminal, the reorganization of circulation patterns, and new parking facilities.

The plan also recommended that the major shopping avenue, Westminster Street, be pedestrianized to strengthen retailing and restore the street to its former importance. Most of the master plan has been implemented.

WESTMINSTER MALL
When the idea of closing Westminster Street to traffic was first presented, it received the strong support of the merchants. Planners sought to provide a better mixture of stores that could respond imaginatively to consumer interests. They were also challenged to redesign the old retail area to function as an up-to-date urban shopping center and still remain consistent with a conservative city image. The project would be unacceptable on any other terms.

The plan therefore reflected the need to preserve the historic retail area and avoid demolition of the old core. This approach was particularly appropriate for a street like Westminster, which has a long history of elegance and quality in its shops.

Design Features
The mall is distinguished by an orderly sequence of formal geometric design elements that enhance, not

The mall's most recent addition lacks the vitality of the older section.

overwhelm, the traditional neighborhood environment. The differences between the old architecture and new street furniture have been minimized. Nevertheless, the stark linearity of Westminster Street is now more receptive to pedestrian movement. Each block of the mall provides sitting areas located between round and rectangular planted areas. A sound system and some of the lighting fixtures are concealed in planters. Additional lights have been set into the paved areas to illuminate the trees. The need to reduce the project budget deprived the place of a square in front of Grace Episcopal Church, the focal point of the mall.

Ten years of constant use has worn down the appearance of the mall's original six blocks. However, this deterioration has not reduced patronage.

Three department stores produce some of the activity along the walkway, which is crowded from opening time in the morning to early afternoon. The peak of activity is during lunch hour, when workers take advantage of the open air to stroll and shop.

Retail deliveries are made through narrow alleys and gangways that already existed in the middle of every block. Only a few smaller shops require hand-trucked delivery.

IMPLEMENTATION

The mall did encounter opposition from a parking lot owner. The original plan extended for nine city blocks, but he objected and initiated a successful court action to prevent the mall's full implementation. Construction had already started when a court order restrained the city from blocking access to the parking lot at the corner of Westminster and Snow Streets. That injunction was soon followed by a permanent order against the city constructing a mall anywhere along Westminster Street.

Only the unanimous action of all the shop owners on the street saved the project; each merchant had to sign a waiver approving construction in front of his or her own property. The result is that the mall extends for six blocks, then is interrupted for one block, before it continues for two more. These last blocks are recent additions, planned to carry the mall into the heart of the Weybosset Hill urban renewal project.

The scale of this newer section is a

disappointment. It tries to be monumental, and the result contradicts the more sensitive texture and human scale of the older section.

The first block is lined by two new office buildings and used only by people working there. The second block is still undeveloped. The pedestrian street is envisioned as a series of platforms stepping down a hill. This block looks almost surreal, surrounded by the emptiness of surface parking lots. These lots were to have been occupied by new retail facilities and housing units. But because there are not any immediate plans for new construction, the mall now ends in a parking lot for the very cars it was intended to eliminate.

IMPACT

The first and most important impact of Westminster Mall has been a new awareness among local merchants, citizens, and administrators of the potential importance of the city's central business district on the economy of the whole metropolitan area.

Along the mall itself, over $5 million was spent in the first 4 years for new construction and renovation. A spirit of cooperation emerged as three competing department stores decided to connect their buildings with skyways to ease customers' circulation.

Most stores report that sales have

risen 15 to 20 percent since the mall opened. The mall has become the community focus for special events and civic celebrations.

Today, however, it is time for the "public sector" to resume the leading role and step up downtown progress. The pedestrian area should be extended to the entire central section of the central business district, and Union Station plans should be implemented. More parking structures are needed and so is a ring road to solve the circulation problems that would arise from full pedestrianization of the downtown district. The city planning office is already weighing federal grant opportunities.

The Weybosset Hill project, a $20 million program, brought new living accommodations to the downtown area. Three luxury apartment towers have been constructed on the west side of the mall, for a total of 440 dwelling units; a nine-story building has been constructed south of the mall, for a total of 180 dwelling units; and a YWCA hostel has been converted into a home for the elderly. All these living accommodations are only two blocks from the mall. Housing has also been constructed outside the boundaries of the Weybosset Hill project, with one high-rise building containing 200 dwelling units.

Ottawa
Ontario

The Sparks Street Mall was designed to minimize downtown traffic congestion in Canada's national capital, but it was originally initiated by business executives to increase the retail appeal of the area. Although the mall was not integrated into an overall urban development scheme nor planned as part of a citywide transport network, Sparks Street has had a very positive impact on the city's center.

The mall's contributions to downtown Ottawa have, in fact, far exceeded planners' expectations. Sparks Street marks the beginning of a new planning approach for the city. The administration has been motivated to further improve Ottawa's image by balancing the social, economic, and environmental potential of the city.

CITY PROFILE

In the years between 1841 and 1857, Canada's capital switched from Kingston to Montreal, to Toronto, to Quebec City. The choice of Ottawa came when this village was a small lumber community. From a population of about 7,700 in 1851, Ottawa became the fastest growing metropolis in eastern Canada, due largely to the presence of the federal government.

Today the fur trade and lumbering of its early years have faded away, and industry employs only a small fraction of the labor force. The federal government employs more than 75,000 workers in nearly 150 buildings. As the national capital. Ottawa also attracts many commercial and financial associations from around the country, as well as embassies, trade associations, and the like. Together, they contribute significantly to the city's multilingual, cultural, and cosmopolitan atmosphere.

Since the beginning of this century, urban planning has concerned Ottawa, and in 1913, the Ottawa Improvement Commission was established. A National Capital Region, including territories in Quebec as well as Ontario, began to shape up. In 1927, a newly formed Federal District Commission replaced the former one, and by 1958, this was replaced by the present National Capital Commission.

With the collaboration of the French planner Jacques Greber, the redevelopment of the National Capital District has made Ottawa one of the most beautiful of Canadian cities.

PLANNING

Ottawa's dual role as the primary seat of government and retail center of its metropolitan area gives the city great strength and vitality and assures remarkably stable employment. Although government is the principal business, it does not dominate the city's trade and culture, which have grown almost as fast as the population.

By the year 2000, the National Capitol Region will support a population of more than 1.2 million, about double the present figure. There were indications of this trend as early as 1950, when Ottawa adopted a master plan to prevent the consequences of uncontrolled development. The plan, which was based on the concept of "open space therapy," recommended the establishment of a green belt around the city, the development of a parks system, and the relocation of downtown railroad yards. These recommendations were carried out under a large-scale program of land acquisition and expropriation by the federal government. Public ownership also allowed the National Capital Commission to provide sites for housing and government buildings.

The 1950 master plan has been substantially implemented, and a new planning concept for the next 25 years is now emerging. Objectives include a more balanced distribution of population and economic opportunities between the two provinces (Ontario and Quebec) and creation within the city core of residential areas. Ottawa is planning a number of major redevelopment projects, and great emphasis has been placed on pedestrian space due to the success of the Sparks Street experiment.

SPARKS STREET MALL

Contrary to malls that start in the minds of city administrators who must then combat local business people, Sparks Street Mall had the enthusiastic and determined support of local merchants from the start. The merchants had to convince the city administrators that the mall was a good idea.

Legend has it that the mall was born during a lunchtime walk by the late architect Watson Balharrie. He began to see trees, benches, and planters along Sparks Street. Balharrie was almost run over by passing traffic before he returned to the real world and

Ottawa's "Green Belt," a unique planning feature for the North American continent, was recommended in the 1950 Greber's Plan for the National Capital and implemented through the years by land use controls and governmental land acquisition policies. The green belt contributes to control ribbon developments and urban sprawls within its boundaries as well as provides a reserve of sites for all kinds of public uses and protection of local agricultural activities.

Above: Sheltered sitting areas are provided in each service module.

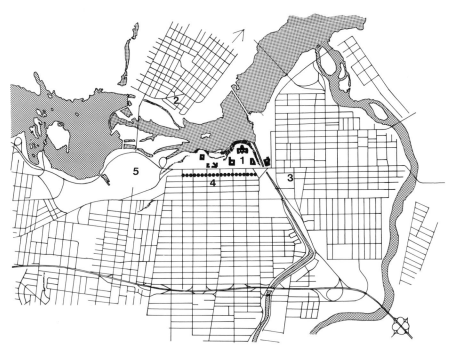

Left: Key to the plan: (1) Parliament Hill, (2) Downtown Hull, (3) Rideau Street, (4) Sparks Street Mall, (5) Le Breton Flats.

went back to the drawing board. He sent a sketch of his ideas, along with a photo of Sparks Street as it was, to the local newspaper, and he got full-page coverage.

A group of business officials responded immediately. They wanted to revitalize the central city area, which was losing out to newer suburban shopping centers, and they found the sketch inspiring. The Sparks Street Development Association (SSDA) was then formed to promote the idea.

The pedestrian project started in 1959 with a series of six "summer malls" before the SSDA and the city agreed to become partners and construct a permanent mall. In 1965, a three-block mall was finally completed, and in 1972, an additional block was added to the projected six-block mall in the capital city central business district.

Design Features The changeover from temporary to permanent pedestrian blocks required repaving the sidewalks across the street's width. A pattern was created by using 8-foot square/2.4-meter square exposed aggregate panels. The experimental malls had led the city to assemble some street furniture, but not enough. Movable benches of stained cedar on steel and precast concrete bases were added to the mall area. Two steel canopied service modules stand on each block, replete with store directories, public phones, water fountains, and seating. Trees and shrubs grow in precast concrete tubs, and flower bases and fountains double as seating. Landscaping highlights Canadian plant species. National pride is expressed in a central court of small boulders representing each of the ten provinces and two territories.

The mall has a wide variety of features designed for pedestrian comfort and amusement. These include open-air restaurants, steel and glass exhibition kiosks, an information booth, a speaker's platform, and a clock tower.

Mall Management The city created the Sparks Street Mall for the benefit and enjoyment of its citizens and has strictly enforced a ban on what it considers "disruptive" activities. This means that even fund raising is forbidden, whether it is panhandling or collecting on behalf of the Red Cross. Vendors are carefully screened and then are given single-block permits;

LEGISLATION AND FINANCE

When the city of Ottawa applied to the Ontario provincial legislature for mall legislation, property owners inserted an amendment stating that a majority of owners representing one-half of the assessment involved would have to consent to any permanent mall plans.

The Mall Authority contacted the owners and managed to get 90 percent to agree to pay two-thirds of the capital construction cost and all the maintenance costs. The assessment was based on a front-footage basis rather than on the total value of the property.

The assessment figure was $7.28 per front foot to amortize the mall's capital cost over 20 years at 6 percent, plus $1.00 per front foot for maintenance.

Following the consensus of the owners in June 1966, the city received final approval to proceed and the mall officially opened on June 28, 1967, just 48 hours before the celebration of Canada's 100th birthday.

Top: A central court features stones from each of Canada's provinces and emphasizes Ottawa's role as the national capital.

Middle: Sparks Street's fourth pedestrian block includes a major hotel and two movie theaters. In the background the new Bank of Canada's headquarters building is being completed on a fifth pedestrian block.

Bottom: Public phones and water fountains are part of the stell-canopied service modules.

Opposite page: Sparks Street's first three pedestrian blocks.

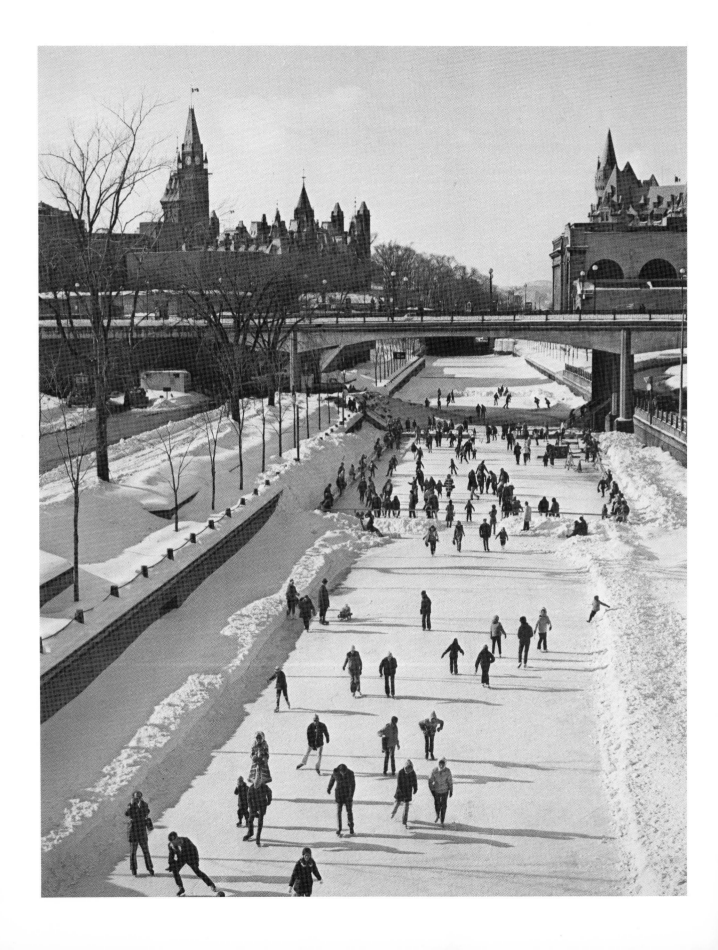

they may only sell fresh fruit, flowers, or ice cream. Stores and restaurants may not extend serving areas onto the mall unless designed and approved for that. Drunks and so-called undesirables are not excluded, but they are carefully monitored. Soliciting people's attention or distributing leaflets and posters is also banned. Although enforcement of such a rigid code might affect the mall's social openness and vitality, the place remains pleasant, and people truly consider it the nicest spot in town to meet, stroll, and relax.

This success is largely that of Ottawa's Mall Authority, an independently operated council which has been responsible for all phases of the Sparks Street Mall project. The authority was created in 1965, during the fifth provisional mall. At that time, the permanent mall plans were jeopardized by people who considered malls only a summertime attraction.

The Mall Authority successfully handled both design and construction. Construction was done in two separate phases to minimize business disruptions. The authority also handles the administration and promotion of Sparks Street.

NEW DEVELOPMENTS
Since its completion, Sparks Street Mall has provided a major incentive to renovate and develop the entire central business district. Electrical wires have been placed underground, signs removed, and stores and buildings remodeled. A number of multimillion dollar developments have been completed, among which is Place de Ville, three 25-story mixed use buildings, located on Sparks Street's fourth pedestrian block. The complex includes a major hotel and two movie theaters. Place de Ville was developed in conjunction with construction on abutting property. The Bank of Canada is building its new headquarters on the fifth block, and the government is putting up additional office buildings. A further extension one block west is also being considered to link the mall with the Garden of Provinces and eventually to the proposed residential community of Le Breton Flats.

In the meantime, the Mall Authority has been asked by the Bank Street merchants and property owners to manage a five-block semimall along their street. Assessments for this proj-

ect have already been collected, and a number of environmental improvements are under way.[1]

Sparks Street Mall has been so successful, in both social and economic terms, that the areas competing with Ottawa's central business district have declined rapidly. The National Capital Commission is now renewing Central Hull and the Rideau Street-Byward Market area in an attempt to achieve an overall balance in the city.

DEVELOPMENT POLES

There are three major development poles of the national capital's core: the area south of Parliament Hill, downtown Hull, and Rideau Street.

The area south of Parliament Hill, where Sparks Street Mall is located, monopolized the hotel, commercial, and federal office market. This area has grown quickly and may be further improved by the completion of the eight-block mall and development of a residential community at LeBreton Flats (over 150 acres/60 hectares of government-owned land) located west of the mall, less than 1 mile/1.6 kilometers from the Parliament.

Since 1969, downtown Hull has become the second major mixed-use center for the capital core area. The government purchased over 15 acres/6 hectares of Hull's center and has started a massive redevelopment program. The program will provide more than 3 million square feet/300,000 square meters of office and commercial space, a major hotel, urban housing, and department stores. By 1976, Place du Portege, the first federal government building complex, accommodated 11,000 public servants as well as 1,600 employees of the stores and other businesses occupying street-level floors. Place du Centre, another planned development, will provide another 7,000 jobs in the center of Hull.

East of Parliament Hill and the Rideau Canal, Ottawa's oldest commercial area is the forerunner of a third dimension of the capital core: Rideau Center. The principal features proposed are a three-block enclosed pedestrian galleria on Rideau Street between Waller and Sussex Streets; a regional bus station; a 200,000 square-foot/20,000 square meters department store and supplementary shops in a galleria directly connected to the Byward Market; a 650-room hotel; 1.2 million feet/120,000 square meters of federal office accommodations; and a large terrace, which will include services, over the east bank of the Rideau Canal.

The present year-round use of the Rideau Canal is further incentive for viewing Ottawa as a model of innovative planning strategies for low-cost urban improvements.

Taking advantage of the winter climate and central location, 5 miles/8 kilometers of the Rideau Canal have been equipped to serve each winter as the world's longest and most effective skating rink, connecting downtown Ottawa with Carlton University. Up to 50,000 people a day have been counted using the canal as a transportation medium. The skating system is fully equipped with adequate lighting, parking and service facilities, music, and guards.

During the summer months, the canal is filled with all types of pleasure boats, from yachts and luxurious cruisers to rowboats and canoes. The banks of the waterway are equipped with bikepaths, which are part of a 40-mile/65-kilometer city bikeway system.

Furthermore, the National Capital Commission (NCC) has been laying out hiking trails and skiing trails in Gatineau Park, through the Greenbelt, and along the major river courses. The NCC is also renting out over 4,000 garden plots ($10 per year) to city gardeners, and many people, especially senior citizens, have signed a waiting list for additional plots.

Quebec City
Quebec

The St. Roche Mall in Quebec City is the first and only street in North America that has been covered, climatized, and restored as a shopping arcade. Such a canopied street is a significant technical achievement, but it also entails a serious financial commitment that other cities have avoided.

The St. Roche neighborhood was once the primary commercial center for its entire metropolitan region, but by the mid-1960s pedestrianization area had deteriorated to the point that large numbers of retail establishments were closing down. The pedestrainization of five blocks of St. Joseph Street was the first phase of a major rehabilitation program for the whole neighborhood.

Over $4.5 million was spent on the St. Roche Mall, and even so it is far from attractive in the conventional sense. There is no street furniture, nor any landscaping. However, it is heavily patronized and sales have risen up to 25 percent. Furthermore, vacancies have disappeared and the majority of stores have been upgraded.

CITY PROFILE

Quebec City, the capital of Canada's eastern province, is an important government and economic center, hosting the National Assembly and serving as the main commercial gateway for the eastern Quebec region. The French founded Quebec City in 1608 at the mouth of the Saint-Laurent River, and the city was originally a fortified settlement at the top of a rocky prow-shaped promontory, controlling water access as far as the Great Lakes. For two and a half centuries, this city served as Canada's unique terminal for ocean traffic and as the gateway for the colonization of the North American territory.

Quebec City has a well-preserved historic urban pattern and architectural heritage, together with a deeply rooted sense of culture and tradition that has made it an international tourist center. Tourism is an important financial resource, but until 1880, fur, fish, seal and beluga oil, lumber, and shipbuilding were the major sources of income. Then the city benefited from small industries suited to local skills: leather, shoes, clothing, furniture, cooperage, and metal works.

The city eventually expanded the original high land settlements, which were dedicated to administrative and defense functions, to include a lower town for commerce and trade. This split-level urban structure has survived, and today the main poles of activity are the Old Town, the Parliamentary City, and the Youville Square in the high city area, and the St. Roche area in the lower city.

PLANNING

Following World War II, the St. Roche neighborhood, because of its location and accessibility, was the most active development area for administration and commerce. This trend toward concentration suddenly ended in the late 1950s, when large segments of the city population shifted to the suburbs. At the same time, new regional expressways and suburban shopping centers drew even more people out of the area, resulting in a tremendous decline of St. Roche's commercial appeal.

The revival of Quebec's high city in the mid-1960s made St. Roche's deterioration even more evident. The resident population of the neighborhood had dropped from 15,000 to 5,000, and many businesses began to close.

At this stage, the city formulated a general strategy to overcome the development gap between the upper and lower city. The plan called for improved access to the lower neighborhood and improved mobility within the area; the expansion and upgrading of commercial facilities in the direction of the upper city; elimination of railroad tracks and incompatible industries; and the rezoning of land for residential dwellings and facilities intended to bring the population back up to 10,000.

In 1960, this rehabilitation program was presented to the public without arousing any opposition, which cleared the way for legal action. The city began to develop financing and construction strategies, and the St. Roche Mall became the key element for the area's economic revitalization.

St. Joseph Street, the major commercial thoroughfare of the St. Roche neighborhood, was experimentally closed to traffic in 1967. The temporary closing arrested retail decline and convinced the merchants that further street improvements would benefit their businesses.

Enclosing the 2,000-foot/600-meter pedestrian street was a strategy intended to provide the downtown

Key to the map, main activity modes:
(1) Old town, (2) Parliamentary City, (3) Youville Square, (4) St. Roche Mall.

LEGISLATION AND FINANCE

The St. Roche Mall, conceived as part of an urban renewal proposal by the city of Quebec, was authorized by existing province legislation. This legal tool and the public support for the project led the city to apply to the province for power to implement the mall and finance part of its construction by selling bonds. Following approval, the city closed St. Joseph Street to traffic and established an independent body, the St. Roche Mall Corporation, to develop and administer the project.

The only serious issue was how to balance the cost with potential revenues—in short, how to make the project self-financing. The financial plan follows:

Infrastructural expenses, including drainage sewers, electrical cables, water and gas pipes (about $800,000) were met through Federal and Provincial Government Grants (75 percent) matched by the city (25 percent). Construction cost ($3.5 million) plus technicians' fees and other expenses ($300,000) were met through a subsidy of the Ministry for Regional Economic Development ($400,000), the sale of city bonds ($2.2 million), and a low-interest loan ($1.2 million). The mall revenues were to come from the rental of boutiques and kiosks along the center of the mall on the basis of the market price (about $300,000 per year) and a special tax burdening only the merchants facing the mall for about $0.50 every $100 of assessed business value (for a total of about $100,000 per year). This money would balance the yearly operating costs and the repayment of loans and interest.

The self-financing premise of the project has worked quite well, even if the mall's yearly operating expenses reach $750,000 and revenues only $400,000. The $750,000 includes not only the repayment of the mortgage and interest, plus administration, publicity, and promotion expenses, but also $380,000 for maintenance. The gap between costs and revenues will be matched by the city, which has benefited from the additional taxes resulting from increased business volume and higher real estate assessments.

neighborhood with a mall similar to suburban shopping centers. By 1970, both merchants and the city had agreed to create a roofed pedestrian street.

ST. ROCHE MALL
The mall was designed, and construction started the following year. The mall provides an enclosed, patrolled, lighted environment for 24 hours a day, 7 days a week. After stores close, the mall as any city street, remains open to visitors and strollers.

Police and ambulance vehicles are allowed to enter the enclosure in cases of emergency, and small trucks may serve the boutiques located in the center of the passageway. Serving most shops, however, is easily accomplished from the side and rear streets. Because of service limitations for firetrucks, sprinklers had to be installed at merchant expense in the buildings facing the mall.

The project was not dedicated until October 31, 1974, and it is still too early to evaluate the impact of the mall on the St. Roche neighborhood. The first year of operation, however, has significantly increased business, and a major hotel has been built at the west entrance of the mall.

The fact that the space is far from beautiful to start with is made even more regrettable due to the lack of street amenities, its crude design, and the artificial environment. The west wing of the mall has a more sophisticated range of stores, and it is certainly the most attractive. Large department stores are being solicited to locate by the eastern entrance, and plans for providing furniture and landscaping will soon be approved.

FUTURE DEVELOPMENT
Completion of St. Joseph Street is the most significant urban renewal event so far, but other projects may soon complement it. The north-south branch of the expressway bordering the neighborhood is now under construction, but the east-west connection has generated serious criticism and may soon be dropped. Such a decision, far from decreasing the area's accessibility, may actually benefit it because the expressway would have created a barrier between the lower and upper city, requiring a complex system of passageways to bridge the highway.

The criticism of the urban express-

way reflects an increased social and environmental awareness that has caused people to reevaluate the role of the automobile and encourages development of alternate public transportation systems. The highway was conceived when building roads was still an acceptable use of taxpayer's funds.

These reordered priorities, however, cannot change the city's basic reliance on automobile transportation. Although many citizens oppose the portion of the highway that would divide the upper and lower cities, especially now that there are plans to consolidate the two neighborhoods, there is public support for other improvements to the area's road system, including a bridge across the St. Charles River.

As part of this riverfront improvement, planners are now studying the feasibility of a waterfront housing project, which would also include recreational park areas. This housing, along with a program that would allow the city to finance restoration of dilapidated houses in the St. Roche neighborhood, would improve the ambience and economics of that area, making it an attractive place for people to live and work, and would add to the pedestrian mall in its revitalization of Quebec's central area.

Opposite page and below:
The mall roof is an independent structure made of prefabricated concrete elements supported by columns following a modular pattern of 25 by 22 feet / 7.5 by 6.6 meters. It was considered impractical to hang a roof along building facades lining the street because these buildings are obsolete and provide poor structural conditions. Plexiglas domes run along the center and sides of the passageway. These skylights, together with occasional windows on side streets and open spaces along the mall, allow for sun and natural light to penetrate the mall and increase its visual appeal. During the winter months, a roof heating system melts an average of 6 inches / 15 centimeters of snow every 24 hours.

Afterword

The open spaces that a mall provides in an otherwise constricted landscape have important behavioral and psychological implications for all the people for whom walking restores a sense of scale and community involvement. By reversing the city dweller's reliance on the automobile and improving the physical, social, and economic conditions of daily life, pedestrian malls are a crucial step in helping restore urban centers to their traditional roles as the axes of civilizations, providing unique opportunities for human communication, growth, and a depth and range of experiences.

We hope that this book will supply the information and incentive needed for cities to muster their resources in support of pedestrian malls for commercial, historic, and residential districts. The commercial mall is the most familiar version, but a growing awareness of neighborhood recycling and preservation, plus recent disillusionment with the automobile, are making residential malls an idea pertinent to the times. The European experience has demonstrated that even with limited funds, a coalition of citizens and government agencies can play important advocacy roles in the pedestrian process. In the United States, promised atmospheric standards from the Environmental Protection Agency may provide added stimulus by forcing cities to eliminate vehicular access in polluted zones.

It is, in fact, the union of government and citizen action that is crucial to the future of cities generally and to pedestrian malls specifically. The federal government's jurisdiction includes policy and money. If it would enact a National Pedestrian Planning Policy, similar to the 1955 Federal Highway Act, which would give priority and funding support to cities contemplating a pedestrian mall, the future of pedestrianization would be assured.

At the local level, citizens and municipal officials can participate in making their cities more attractive and humane; it is here that the real leadership for pedestrian spaces must occur, from design and construction to support of the final project. Ultimately, it is by and for people that malls exist and cities prosper.

San Francisco, California. Two ways of dealing with the city: more highways or more places for people?

Appendix: Compendium of American Urban Malls

This book provides an easily understandable and comparative overview of a majority of North American pedestrianization experiments through the presentation of vital statistics and visual representations of 70 urban malls. Ever since Kalamazoo, Michigan, constructed the first downtown pedestrian zone in 1959, every city considering a traffic-free area for its central business district has looked to existing examples for guidance. This flow of information among cities has been largely responsible for the increasing number of pedestrian zones. And, perhaps more importantly, as cities learn from each other, the potential of traffic-free zoning comes closer to being fully realized.

As of June 1976, every North American city with an operational pedestrian zone was invited to provide information for this Compendium. A series of questionnaires were sent to each city, which was also asked to provide a photograph and descriptive mate-rial that would best represent its mall.

The data received were condensed into the following categories: statistics on the city, including population, modal split of home-to-work trips, and the number of available parking spaces in the central business district; statistics on the mall itself, including physical dimensions and methods of operation; information relating to the implementation of the project, including population, modal split of home-to-work trips, and the number of available parking spaces in the central business district; statistics on the mall itself, including physical dimensions and methods of operation; information relating to the implementation of the project, including legislation and finance; and, finally, the name of the person or agency to contact for further data on each mall.

The purpose of the Compendium is not to provide a comprehensive picture of every pedestrian zone in North America. Rather, it illustrates the fundamental framework of traffic-free experiments of varying size and scope. As such, it is a reference that can serve as a guide to planners and urban advocates contemplating traffic bans for their cities.

CONTENTS

KEY

 Accessibility refers to the modes of transportation people use to travel to the central business district.

 Parking refers to the number of available parking spaces within the boundaries of the central business district: on-street, surface lot, and garage spaces.

 Dimensions refers to the linear measurement (in feet) of the pedestrian district. The number of blocks covered is also indicated.

 Mobility refers to the kinds of vehicles allowed on the mall and methods of delivery. If delivery vehicles have access to the mall, time restrictions are indicated.

 Legislation indicates what, if any, legal devices were necessary for implementation of the mall. Distinction has been made between state and local levels.

 Cost/Finance provides the total cost of the mall and gives a breakdown of funding sources for its construction and maintenance.*

 Information provides the name, address, and telephone of the person or agency to contact for further data on each mall.

*Federal funding sources cover a wide range of programs, including the following: Federal-Aid Urban System Transportation Funds, Urban Mass Transportation Funds, Federal Revenue Sharing, Housing and Community Development Act, 1974, Community Development Block Grant Program. Malls constructed with Urban Renewal monies, however, have been specified, since this program was the principal source of federal funds for mall construction in the 1950s and 1960s. Providence, Minneapolis, Fresno, Salisbury, Eugene, New London, and Atchison were among the cities that took advantage of this program. In 1973, the Department of Housing and Urban Development halted the renewal program and replaced it with the Community Development Block Grant Program.

EXPLANATION OF SYMBOLS

 Automobile

 Bus

 Taxi

 Railway

 Bicycle

 Foot

 People-Mover

 Delivery

 Emergency

Kalamazoo, Mich.
Kalamazoo Mall, 1959
85,000

Inaugurated in 1959, the Kalamazoo Mall was the first pedestrian street in the United States. The two original blocks have since been extended to four. In 1970, the entire mall was renovated, with a combination of brick, concrete, and green areas giving the mall a new look. Overhead structures were installed to provide protection for shoppers and special attractions were constructed: a clock tower in the north block, a specially designed postal station in the center area, and a Japanese garden in the south block. Other design elements include new light fixtures, flower planters, benches, and playgrounds. The shopping atmosphere is very lively and the mall is crowded during most of the day. The new Kalamazoo Convention Center, recently added to the mall's fourth block, includes a hotel, restaurant, and new shopping facilities, bringing even more activity to downtown Kalamazoo.

Miami Beach, Fla.
Lincoln Road Mall, 1960
87,072

Miami's tropical climate led the designers of Lincoln Road Mall to provide shade with exotic trees down the middle of the street and canopies and covered arcades along the sides. During the day, and on some evenings, a mini-bus moves shoppers from one end of the mall to the other. The Lincoln Road Mall was created to accommodate the increasing number of tourists who are the city's principal customers. The architecture plays a major role in the street scenario, since most of the buildings along Lincoln Road were constructed in the 1920s and are well-preserved examples of Miami's resort glamor of that period.

Knoxville, Tenn.
Market Square Mall, 1961
174,587

Knoxville's mall stands on the site of the pre-Civil War "Market House," which was destroyed by fire. An open-air market, where farmers sell their own products, plants, and flowers, stands at the north end of the mall. Pedestrian amenities include pastel colored sidewalks and a continuous canopy to protect shoppers from inclement weather. The central area of Market Square features grass, trees, a fountain, and a raised platform for public events. There are no empty stores along the mall, and Market Square has become a focal point for community activities, including concerts and festivals.

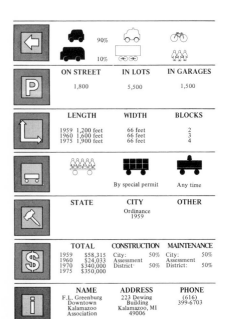

	ON STREET	IN LOTS	IN GARAGES
	1,800	5,500	1,500

	LENGTH	WIDTH	BLOCKS
1959	1,200 feet	66 feet	2
1960	1,600 feet	66 feet	3
1975	1,900 feet	66 feet	4

		By special permit	Any time

	STATE	CITY	OTHER
		Ordinance 1959	

	TOTAL	CONSTRUCTION	MAINTENANCE
1959	$58,315	City: 50%	City: 50%
1960	$24,033	Assessment	Assessment
1970	$340,000	District 50%	District: 50%
1975	$350,000		

	NAME	ADDRESS	PHONE
	F.L. Greenburg Downtown Kalamazoo Association	223 Dewing Building Kalamazoo, MI 49006	(616) 399-6703

90%
10%

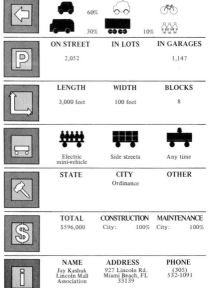

	ON STREET	IN LOTS	IN GARAGES
	2,052		1,147

	LENGTH	WIDTH	BLOCKS
	3,000 feet	100 feet	8

	Electric mini-vehicle	Side streets	Any time

	STATE	CITY	OTHER
		Ordinance	

	TOTAL	CONSTRUCTION	MAINTENANCE
	$596,000	City: 100%	City: 100%

	NAME	ADDRESS	PHONE
	Jay Kashuk Lincoln Mall Association	927 Lincoln Rd. Miami Beach, FL 33139	(305) 532-1091

60%
30%
10%

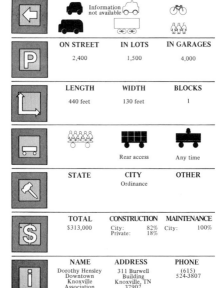

Information not available

	ON STREET	IN LOTS	IN GARAGES
	2,400	1,500	4,000

	LENGTH	WIDTH	BLOCKS
	440 feet	130 feet	1

		Rear access	Any time

	STATE	CITY	OTHER
		Ordinance	

	TOTAL	CONSTRUCTION	MAINTENANCE
	$313,000	City: 82% Private: 18%	City: 100%

	NAME	ADDRESS	PHONE
	Dorothy Hensley Downtown Knoxville Association	311 Burwell Building Knoxville, TN 37902	(615) 524-3807

Pomona, Calif.
Pomona Mall, 1963
87,384

Pomona Mall was a great success when it was built in the early 1960s. It was dubbed "the window of the city" and received a great amount of national publicity. It was also the first in a long series of pedestrian streets built under the California Mall Law of 1960. In recent years, however, the mall has deteriorated. Many stores have left as a result of general economic decline in the city and a shift in population mix. The mall lacks pedestrian-oriented facilities and provides very few attractions or surprises along its seemingly endless length. A mini-bus carries customers along the mall's nine blocks.

Fresno, Calif.
Fulton Mall, 1964
165,972

Fresno's pedestrian system is the heart of large-scale renewal efforts throughout the city. Almost baroque in its extravagant design, Fulton Mall incorporates amenities that entertain as well as attract pedestrians. Its six blocks are filled with fountains, sitting and play areas, trellises and shade trees of varied scale and configuration. In fact, the mall lacks nothing except, perhaps, unadorned open space. A large clock tower has become the symbol and focal point of the mall, as the mall has for Fresno. The Fulton pedestrian district has had a positive effect on both downtown economics and the image of the city.

Jackson, Miss.
Progress Place, 1964
45,484

Numerous trees, shrubs, and flowers in raised planter boxes have been placed throughout Jackson's Progress Place, creating a leisurely, pleasant atmosphere for shopping. The mall's innovations were designed around already-existing utility openings and were constructed on the street surface, greatly reducing construction costs. A unique feature of Jackson's mall is the incorporation of parking bays at the end of each block. The creation of Progress Place has stimulated new development plans, including the construction of pedestrian walkways to connect the mall area to side street parking and an extension of the mall itself.

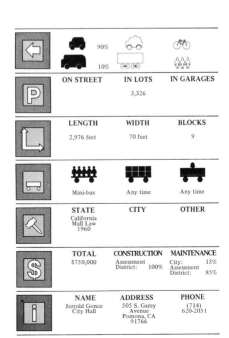

	90% / 10%		
	ON STREET	**IN LOTS**	**IN GARAGES**
		3,326	
	LENGTH	**WIDTH**	**BLOCKS**
	2,976 feet	70 feet	9
	Mini-bus	Any time	Any time
	STATE California Mall Law 1960	**CITY**	**OTHER**
	TOTAL $750,000	**CONSTRUCTION** Assessment District: 100%	**MAINTENANCE** City: 15% Assessment District: 85%
	NAME Jerrold Gonce City Hall	**ADDRESS** 505 S. Garey Avenue Pomona, CA 91766	**PHONE** (714) 620-2051

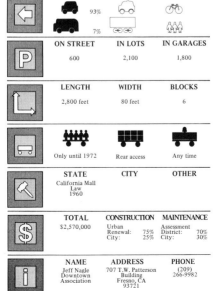

	93% / 7%		
	ON STREET	**IN LOTS**	**IN GARAGES**
	600	2,100	1,800
	LENGTH	**WIDTH**	**BLOCKS**
	2,800 feet	80 feet	6
	Only until 1972	Rear access	Any time
	STATE California Mall Law 1960	**CITY**	**OTHER**
	TOTAL $2,570,000	**CONSTRUCTION** Urban Renewal: 75% City: 25%	**MAINTENANCE** Assessment District: 70% City: 30%
	NAME Jeff Nagle Downtown Association	**ADDRESS** 707 T.W. Patterson Building Fresno, CA 93721	**PHONE** (209) 266-9982

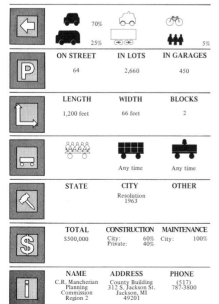

	70% / 25% / 5%		
	ON STREET	**IN LOTS**	**IN GARAGES**
	64	2,660	450
	LENGTH	**WIDTH**	**BLOCKS**
	1,200 feet	66 feet	2
		Any time	Any time
	STATE	**CITY** Resolution 1963	**OTHER**
	TOTAL $500,000	**CONSTRUCTION** City: 60% Private: 40%	**MAINTENANCE** City: 100%
	NAME C.R. Mancherian Planning Commission Region 2	**ADDRESS** County Building 312 S. Jackson St. Jackson, MI 49201	**PHONE** (517) 787-3800

Atchison, Kans.
Atchison Mall, 1965
13,556

Landscaped with trees, large lawn areas, and flowers, the Atchison Mall provides many features to attract people downtown. Each of the mall's three sections contains a pool and an elaborate fountain enhanced by colored lighting for nighttime strollers. Parking lots surround the mall and entrances to businesses from these lots give shoppers easy access to the mall itself. Playground equipment has been installed for children. A permanent free-standing canopy protects shoppers from the weather and provides a unifying effect for the entire area.

Dallas, Tex.
Stoneplace Mall, 1965
844,401

Although Stoneplace Mall is located in the very heart of Dallas's central business district, its creation was not related to downtown retailing. When the municipal government abandoned this short street to improve vehicular circulation, it was transformed into a pedestrian walkway, connecting two major avenues. Stoneplace Mall serves as a mini-park for downtown office workers, providing a safe and attractive pedestrian-oriented environment in the midst of the automobile-oriented central business district.

Providence, R.I.
Westminster Mall, 1965
179,116

Westminster Mall was built as part of a broad strategy to improve the downtown area. Because of opposition from a parking lot owner on the street, the mall was constructed in two sections separated by a block where traffic is still allowed. One section is characterized by an orderly sequence of design elements that have been successfully integrated into the old, austere architecture of the neighborhood, while the newer portion looks monumental and is less popular. The overall impact of the project has benefited both the merchants and the city, and plans are in progress to bring new housing downtown within walking distance of the mall.

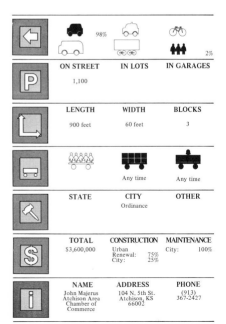

	ON STREET	IN LOTS	IN GARAGES
	1,100		

	LENGTH	WIDTH	BLOCKS
	900 feet	60 feet	3

		Any time	Any time

	STATE	CITY	OTHER
		Ordinance	

	TOTAL	CONSTRUCTION	MAINTENANCE
	$3,600,000	Urban Renewal: 75% City: 25%	City: 100%

	NAME	ADDRESS	PHONE
	John Majerus Atchison Area Chamber of Commerce	104 N. 5th St. Atchison, KS 66002	(913) 367-2427

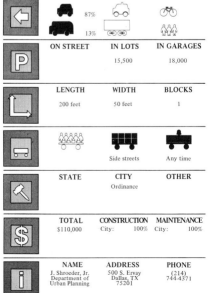

	ON STREET	IN LOTS	IN GARAGES
		15,500	18,000

	LENGTH	WIDTH	BLOCKS
	200 feet	50 feet	1

		Side streets	Any time

	STATE	CITY	OTHER
		Ordinance	

	TOTAL	CONSTRUCTION	MAINTENANCE
	$110,000	City: 100%	City: 100%

	NAME	ADDRESS	PHONE
	J. Shroeder, Jr. Department of Urban Planning	500 S. Ervay Dallas, TX 75201	(214) 744-4371

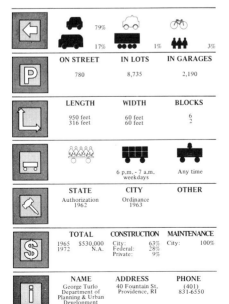

	ON STREET	IN LOTS	IN GARAGES
	780	8,735	2,190

	LENGTH	WIDTH	BLOCKS
	950 feet 316 feet	60 feet 60 feet	6 2

		6 p.m. - 7 a.m. weekdays	Any time

	STATE	CITY	OTHER
	Authorization 1962	Ordinance 1963	

	TOTAL	CONSTRUCTION	MAINTENANCE
	1965 $530,000 1972 N.A.	City: 63% Federal: 28% Private: 9%	City: 100%

	NAME	ADDRESS	PHONE
	George Turlo Department of Planning & Urban Development	40 Fountain St, Providence, RI	(401) 831-6550

Santa Monica, Calif.
Santa Monica Mall, 1965
88,289

Even with heavy competition from the Santa Monica Pier, a beachfront park, and the beach itself, the Santa Monica Mall is a popular place for strollers as well as shoppers. There are over 100 retail establishments along the mall, in addition to restaurants, movie theaters, and professional offices. Design features include a variety of trees and shrubs, reflecting pools, and a sculptured octagonal fountain donated by eight Santa Monica families. Lighting fixtures have been specially designed to enclose a sound system for music and public announcements.

Riverside, Calif.
Downtown Mall, 1966
154,500

Riverside's Downtown Mall is filled with palms and other exotic trees, and has been generously endowed with fountains, ponds, rivulets, playgrounds, and seating areas for both intimate and large gatherings. The mall's character is now shifting from a retail center to a mini-park for governmental buildings. A new City Hall has been built at one end of the mall, and a cultural center is planned for the other end.

Burbank, Calif.
Golden Mall, 1967
88,871

The Golden Mall is designed as a linear park with variegated spaces that contrast with the linearity of the street. The mall features large, hexagonal patterns in its landscaping, paving, and architectural details. Woven into these patterns are sitting areas, small cafes, fountains, and pools; two central pavilions provide restrooms, refreshments, and a focus for community and promotional activities. Although retail sales have increased since the mall was completed and vacancies are the lowest since 1939, most people in Burbank feel that the mall did not attract the private dollars and large department stores that were hoped for. The city is now planning a new strategy for the revitalization of the downtown area, with the Golden Mall as its main element.

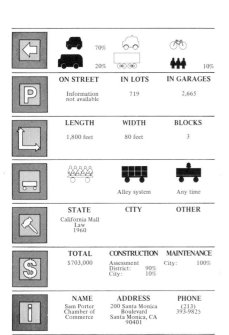

	ON STREET	IN LOTS	IN GARAGES
70% / 20% / 10%	Information not available	719	2,665

	LENGTH	WIDTH	BLOCKS
	1,800 feet	80 feet	3

		Alley system	Any time

	STATE	CITY	OTHER
	California Mall Law 1960		

	TOTAL	CONSTRUCTION	MAINTENANCE
	$703,000	Assessment District: 90% City: 10%	City: 100%

	NAME	ADDRESS	PHONE
	Sam Porter Chamber of Commerce	200 Santa Monica Boulevard Santa Monica, CA 90401	(213) 393-9825

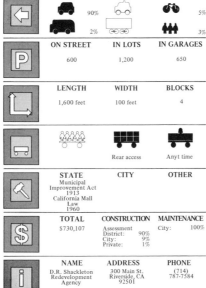

	ON STREET	IN LOTS	IN GARAGES
90% / 2% / 5% / 3%	600	1,200	650

	LENGTH	WIDTH	BLOCKS
	1,600 feet	100 feet	4

		Rear access	Anyt time

	STATE	CITY	OTHER
	Municipal Improvement Act 1913 California Mall Law 1960		

	TOTAL	CONSTRUCTION	MAINTENANCE
	$730,107	Assessment District: 90% City: 9% Private: 1%	City: 100%

	NAME	ADDRESS	PHONE
	D.R. Shackleton Redevelopment Agency	300 Main St. Riverside, CA 92501	(714) 787-7584

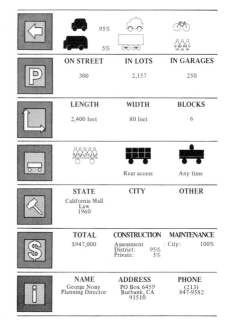

	ON STREET	IN LOTS	IN GARAGES
95% / 5%	300	2,157	250

	LENGTH	WIDTH	BLOCKS
	2,400 feet	80 feet	6

		Rear access	Any time

	STATE	CITY	OTHER
	California Mall Law 1960		

	TOTAL	CONSTRUCTION	MAINTENANCE
	$947,000	Assessment District: 95% Private: 5%	City: 100%

	NAME	ADDRESS	PHONE
	George Nony Planning Director	PO Box 6459 Burbank, CA 91510	(213) 847-9582

Danville, Ill.
Vermilion Park Mall, 1967
42,570

A wide variety of trees, shrubs, and grassy areas, two fountains, and a number of stone benches make Vermilion Mall a popular place to shop and relax. Features such as children's play areas and a speaker system for public events provide community focus to the mall. Wide walk areas along storefronts and curved sidewalks across the middle of the mall allow access for emergency vehicles. The project has stimulated further remodeling efforts and retail expansions, including "gaslight era" specialty shops, which were constructed in an alley adjacent to the mall.

Minneapolis, Minn.
Nicollet Mall, 1967
434,500

Nine years after its dedication, Nicollet Mall is considered an outstanding example of a mall that works. Although it has not banned motor traffic completely, the Nicollet "transitway" has subjected buses and mini-buses to pedestrian priorities. Since its completion, the mall has prompted more than $220 million in rehabilitation and new projects. Sales have increased dramatically and a strong sense of civic pride has emerged. The mall's success is due, in part, to its sensitivity to scale and the selection of prestigious materials such as copper, bronze, and granite for the elements along it. Perhaps one of the most important features of Nicollet Mall is its three-dimensional movement pattern. Pedestrians can walk on or over the mall—either along its pavement or on skyway bridges between the upper levels of buildings.

Ottawa, Ontario
Sparks Street Mall, 1967
619,000

Located in the heart of Ottawa, Sparks Street Mall is an elegant and lively area, featuring a wide variety of stores and businesses, open-air restaurants, movie theaters, and a major hotel. With the mall's implementation, overhead wires were removed and storefronts were remodeled. Functional street furniture was provided, including service modules complete with store directories, public phones, water fountains, and seating. Native Canadian plants enhance the mall, and a central court features a large rock from each of Canada's ten provinces and two territories. Originally three blocks long, the Sparks Street Mall has already expanded to a fourth block, and the completion of two more blocks is expected shortly.

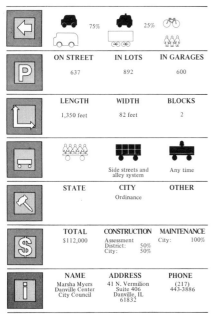

	ON STREET	IN LOTS	IN GARAGES
	637	892	600
	LENGTH	WIDTH	BLOCKS
	1,350 feet	82 feet	2
		Side streets and alley system	Any time
	STATE	CITY	OTHER
		Ordinance	
	TOTAL	CONSTRUCTION	MAINTENANCE
	$112,000	Assessment District: 50% City: 50%	City: 100%
	NAME	ADDRESS	PHONE
	Marsha Myers Danville Center City Council	41 N. Vermilion Suite 406 Danville, IL 61832	(217) 443-3886

Auto 75% Bus 25%

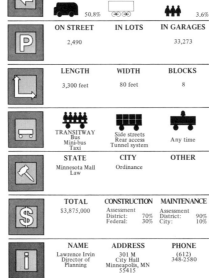

	ON STREET	IN LOTS	IN GARAGES
	2,490		33,273
	LENGTH	WIDTH	BLOCKS
	3,300 feet	80 feet	8
TRANSITWAY Bus Mini-bus Taxi		Side streets Rear access Tunnel system	Any time
	STATE	CITY	OTHER
	Minnesota Mall Law	Ordinance	
	TOTAL	CONSTRUCTION	MAINTENANCE
	$3,875,000	Assessment District: 70% Federal: 30%	Assessment District: 90% City: 10%
	NAME	ADDRESS	PHONE
	Lawrence Irvin Director of Planning	301 M City Hall Minneapolis, MN 55415	(612) 348-2580

42.6% 50.8% 3% 3.6%

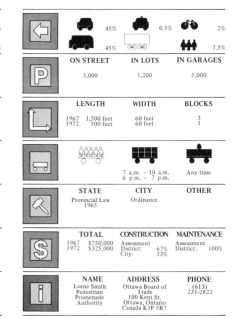

	ON STREET	IN LOTS	IN GARAGES
	3,000	1,200	5,000
	LENGTH	WIDTH	BLOCKS
1967	1,500 feet	60 feet	3
1972	500 feet	60 feet	1
		7 a.m. - 10 a.m. 6 p.m. - 7 p.m.	Any time
	STATE	CITY	OTHER
	Provincial Law 1965	Ordinance	
	TOTAL	CONSTRUCTION	MAINTENANCE
1967	$750,000	Assessment District: 67% City: 33%	Assessment District: 100%
1972	$325,000		
	NAME	ADDRESS	PHONE
	Lorne Smith Pedestrian Promenade Authority	Ottawa Board of Trade 100 Kent St. Ottawa, Ontario Canada K1P 5R7	(613) 231-2822

45% 45% 0.5% 2% 7.5%

Freeport, Ill.
Downtown Plaza, 1968
27,736

It took less than 90 days to transform Stephenson Street from a traffic artery to a lively and popular pedestrian plaza. Financed entirely by the Downtown Freeport Association, the plaza has renewed the city's center by creating a comfortable and attractive atmosphere for shopping. Trees, grass, ornamental shrubbery, flowers, fountains, and pools enhance the plaza. There are benches, a children's playground, and a centrally located kiosk, which is available to nonprofit organizations to promote or display their projects. Downtown Plaza has even stimulated efforts to renew downtown housing.

Michigan City, Ind.
Franklin Square Mall, 1968
39,369

Franklin Square creates a parklike atmosphere in the center of Michigan City and provides a garden and picnic area for downtown employees. Each block has its own fountain and pool system and the entire 40,000-square-foot/4,000-square-meter area is landscaped with grass and over 500 mature trees. The openness of Franklin Square contrasts dramatically with the dense development of Michigan City's central business district.

Salisbury, Md.
Downtown Plaza, 1968
15,252

Salisbury's Downtown Plaza runs along a main street that is comfortably narrow and human in scale. Gradual turns and changes in slope make the walkway inherently interesting. Many buildings along the mall have been either rehabilitated or modernized. Side streets provide nice vistas and easy walks to parking areas. The overall design treatment is simple and modest in scale, with the bulk of expenditures being literally sunk into the street, creating varied and attractive walkways throughout the mall's length. The old cast-iron gas lamp posts that line the mall have been outfitted with 200-watt bulbs and hurricane globes. Additional lighting, planting, benches, kiosks, and small structures fill out the scene.

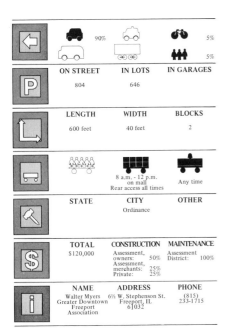

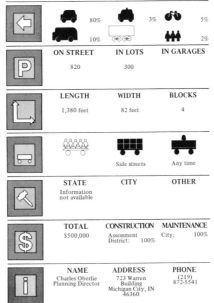

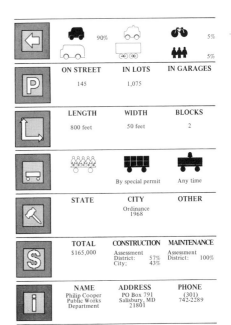

Freeport, Ill.

| | 90% | | 5% |
| | | | 5% |

	ON STREET	IN LOTS	IN GARAGES
P	804	646	

	LENGTH	WIDTH	BLOCKS
	600 feet	40 feet	2

		8 a.m. - 12 p.m. on mall Rear access all times	Any time

	STATE	CITY	OTHER
		Ordinance	

	TOTAL	CONSTRUCTION	MAINTENANCE
$	$120,000	Assessment, owners: 50% Assessment, merchants: 25% Private: 25%	Assessment District: 100%

	NAME	ADDRESS	PHONE
i	Walter Myers Greater Downtown Freeport Association	6½ W. Stephenson St. Freeport, IL 61032	(815) 233-1715

Michigan City, Ind.

| | 80% | 3% | 5% |
| | 10% | | 2% |

	ON STREET	IN LOTS	IN GARAGES
P	820	300	

	LENGTH	WIDTH	BLOCKS
	1,380 feet	82 feet	4

		Side streets	Any time

	STATE	CITY	OTHER
	Information not available		

	TOTAL	CONSTRUCTION	MAINTENANCE
$	$500,000	Assessment District: 100%	City: 100%

	NAME	ADDRESS	PHONE
i	Charles Oberlie Planning Director	723 Warren Building Michigan City, IN 46360	(219) 872-5541

Salisbury, Md.

| | 90% | | 5% |
| | | | 5% |

	ON STREET	IN LOTS	IN GARAGES
P	145	1,075	

	LENGTH	WIDTH	BLOCKS
	800 feet	50 feet	2

		By special permit	Any time

	STATE	CITY	OTHER
		Ordinance 1968	

	TOTAL	CONSTRUCTION	MAINTENANCE
$	$165,000	Assessment District: 57% City: 43%	Assessment District: 100%

	NAME	ADDRESS	PHONE
i	Philip Cooper Public Works Department	PO Box 791 Salisbury, MD 21801	(301) 742-2289

Coos Bay, Oreg.
City Center Mall, 1969
14,130

Honolulu, Hawaii
Fort Street Mall, 1969
324,871

Oxnard, Calif.
Plaza Park Mall, 1969
85,104

The City Center Mall has stimulated an overall renewal effort in Coos Bay. The mall itself is a full pedestrian thoroughfare, landscaped with many trees and flowers, and featuring wooden sidewalk canopies. Utility lines have been buried and the road surface, curbs, gutters, and sidewalks have been improved. A new street lighting system was designed and new parking facilities have been constructed to improve access to the mall, and many of the old buildings along it have been renovated. There are virtually no vacancies in the downtown area, due to the drawing power of the mall.

Paved in brick and cement, Honolulu's Fort Street Mall is densely landscaped with a great variety of vegetation. Exotic coco-palms, monkey-pod and coral trees, and numerous tropical flowers create an atmosphere harmonious with the city itself. Architectural features include two fountains, a waterfall, a children's sandbox, and four large cement arcades designed in the form of trellises. These archways support flowering vines and conceal indirect lighting fixtures. A pedestrian underpass constructed at the busy King Street intersection provides pedestrian continuity. Even the underpass has a special attraction—a 70 by 9 foot / 22 by 3 meter mural that simulates ancient Hawaiian rock carvings.

Multicolored concrete walkways, grass, shrubbery and trees make Oxnard's Plaza Park Mall an inviting place to the city's residents. With the mall's implementation, all overhead wires were removed, new buildings constructed, and ornamental lamps with piped music systems were installed. A variety of retail stores, restaurants, and businesses provide diverse attractions. Design elements include covered stage areas, a large fountain in each block, playgrounds, and numerous benches.

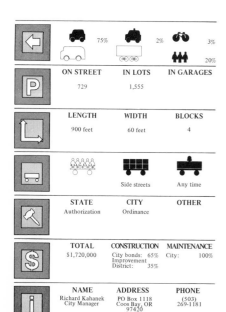

75%	2%	3%
		20%

ON STREET	IN LOTS	IN GARAGES
729	1,555	

LENGTH	WIDTH	BLOCKS
900 feet	60 feet	4

	Side streets	Any time

STATE	CITY	OTHER
Authorization	Ordinance	

TOTAL	CONSTRUCTION	MAINTENANCE
$1,720,000	City bonds: 65% Improvement District: 35%	City: 100%

NAME	ADDRESS	PHONE
Richard Kahanek City Manager	PO Box 1118 Coos Bay, OR 97420	(503) 269-1181

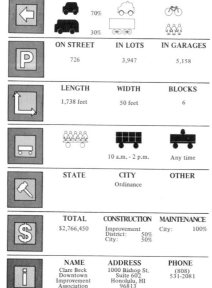

70%		
30%		

ON STREET	IN LOTS	IN GARAGES
726	3,947	5,158

LENGTH	WIDTH	BLOCKS
1,738 feet	50 feet	6

	10 a.m. - 2 p.m.	Any time

STATE	CITY	OTHER
	Ordinance	

TOTAL	CONSTRUCTION	MAINTENANCE
$2,766,450	Improvement District: 50% City: 50%	City: 100%

NAME	ADDRESS	PHONE
Clare Beck Downtown Improvement Association	1000 Bishop St. Suite 602 Honolulu, HI 96813	(808) 531-2081

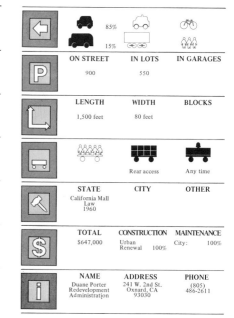

85%		
15%		

ON STREET	IN LOTS	IN GARAGES
900	550	

LENGTH	WIDTH	BLOCKS
1,500 feet	80 feet	

	Rear access	Any time

STATE	CITY	OTHER
California Mall Law 1960		

TOTAL	CONSTRUCTION	MAINTENANCE
$647,000	Urban Renewal 100%	City: 100%

NAME	ADDRESS	PHONE
Duane Porter Redevelopment Administration	241 W. 2nd St. Oxnard, CA 93030	(805) 486-2611

Pittsburgh, Pa.
East Liberty Mall, 1969
525,275

Pittsburgh's East Liberty Mall is actually a system of interconnected transitways along the streets. Covering a total of 14 blocks, the mall accommodates buses, mini-buses, and taxicabs; there is also a lane for private traffic along the Highland section to make up for the lack of rear access along that street. However, the overall design emphasizes pedestrian comfort. The mall is landscaped with a variety of trees and shrubbery in round planters. There are numerous benches and shelters, which also serve as display units. Globe lighting fixtures have been installed, and paving has been laid in various patterns.

Sacramento, Calif.
Downtown Mall, 1969
264,000

Sacramento's Downtown Plaza was implemented as part of a redevelopment project designed to improve the core of California's capital city. The contemporary design of the mall has caused controversy, but to judge from users' response, the balance of grass, concrete, and water work together to create an urbane and attractive place. Three blocks have been added to the mall's original length, and there are plans to extend the pedestrian street to the river, where the Old Sacramento District is presently under restoration.

Centralia, Ill.
Downtown Mall, 1970
15,217

The design of Centralia's Downtown Mall emphasizes greenery, creating a comfortable pedestrian space downtown. The mall is landscaped with numerous trees, and a grassy area with shrubbery runs down the center. Benches and lamp posts provide variety of scale. The mall has generated physical improvements to the stores and businesses along it, as well as the construction of a new parking lot for shoppers' convenience. Streets adjacent to the Downtown Mall have been influenced by the plaza concept and have installed several new design elements, including new lighting, landscaping, and street furniture.

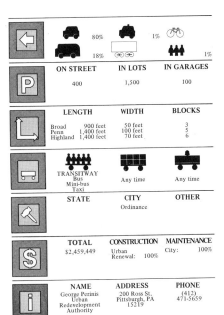

	ON STREET	IN LOTS	IN GARAGES
	400	1,500	100

	LENGTH	WIDTH	BLOCKS
Broad	900 feet	50 feet	3
Penn	1,400 feet	100 feet	5
Highland	1,400 feet	70 feet	6

TRANSITWAY Bus Mini-bus Taxi	Any time	Any time

STATE	CITY	OTHER
	Ordinance	

TOTAL	CONSTRUCTION	MAINTENANCE
$2,459,449	Urban Renewal: 100%	City: 100%

NAME	ADDRESS	PHONE
George Perinis Urban Redevelopment Authority	200 Ross St. Pittsburgh, PA 15219	(412) 471-5659

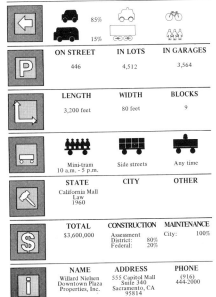

	ON STREET	IN LOTS	IN GARAGES
	446	4,512	3,564

	LENGTH	WIDTH	BLOCKS
	3,200 feet	80 feet	9

Mini-tram 10 a.m. - 5 p.m.	Side streets	Any time

STATE	CITY	OTHER
California Mall Law 1960		

TOTAL	CONSTRUCTION	MAINTENANCE
$3,600,000	Assessment District: 80% Federal: 20%	City: 100%

NAME	ADDRESS	PHONE
Willard Nielsen Downtown Plaza Properties, Inc.	555 Capitol Mall Suite 340 Sacramento, CA 95814	(916) 444-2000

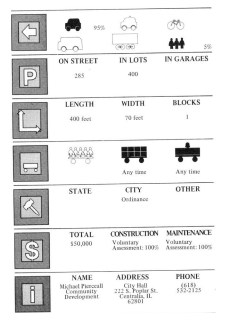

	ON STREET	IN LOTS	IN GARAGES
	285	400	

	LENGTH	WIDTH	BLOCKS
	400 feet	70 feet	1

	Any time	Any time

STATE	CITY	OTHER
	Ordinance	

TOTAL	CONSTRUCTION	MAINTENANCE
$50,000	Voluntary Assessment: 100%	Voluntary Assessment: 100%

NAME	ADDRESS	PHONE
Michael Pierceall Community Development	City Hall 222 S. Poplar St. Centralia, IL 62801	(618) 532-2125

Decatur, Ill.
Landmark Mall, 1970
90,397

Only the two inner blocks of the Landmark Mall are fully pedestrianized, while the two outer ones allow restricted vehicular movements. Brick paving surfaces the entire space, including the intersections where curbs have been eliminated and the vehicular planting areas with trees and shrubs, benches, and sculptures on which children can climb. Lighting is sensibly designed for pedestrian scale.

East Lansing, Mich.
East Lansing Alley, 1970
47,450

The East Lansing Alley Improvement project provides pedestrians with an alternate travel route through the city center. The alley, running parallel to the city's main shopping and traffic thoroughfare, was converted to pedestrian use, offering a viable and comfortable alternative apart from major vehicular activity. Improvements to the alley include landscaping, street furniture, and repaving. As a result of positive public response to the project, a number of store owners have upgraded the appearance of their rear entrances, adding further to the attraction of the alley.

Lake Charles, La.
Downtown Mall, 1970
77,998

The Downtown Mall was originally planned as part of an overall traffic-control policy for downtown Lake Charles. The merchants, however, supported only the pedestrianization of Ryan Street, and the rest of the plan was pushed aside. This caused a serious handicap to the mall itself. As it looks now, the mall has a split personality: one part is full of vacancies and shows signs of physical deterioration; the other part is clean and modern in the suburban way. The architectural elements of the project are uniform in size, materials, and appearance. Although they provide a number of amenities, there is little sensitivity to pedestrian needs, as evidenced by such details as sloped footings that tend to keep people away from planters and fountains.

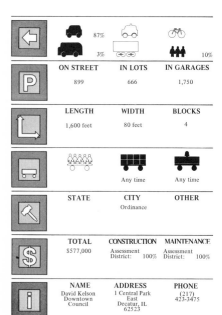

	ON STREET	IN LOTS	IN GARAGES
	899	666	1,750
	LENGTH	WIDTH	BLOCKS
	1,600 feet	80 feet	4
		Any time	Any time
	STATE	CITY	OTHER
		Ordinance	
	TOTAL	CONSTRUCTION	MAINTENANCE
	$577,000	Assessment District: 100%	Assessment District: 100%
	NAME	ADDRESS	PHONE
	David Kelson Downtown Council	1 Central Park East Decatur, IL 62523	(217) 423-3475

87% / 3% / 10%

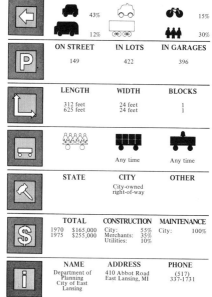

	ON STREET	IN LOTS	IN GARAGES
	149	422	396
	LENGTH	WIDTH	BLOCKS
	312 feet / 625 feet	24 feet / 24 feet	1 / 1
		Any time	Any time
	STATE	CITY	OTHER
		City-owned right-of-way	
	TOTAL	CONSTRUCTION	MAINTENANCE
	1970 $165,000 / 1975 $255,000	City: 55% / Merchants: 35% / Utilities: 10%	City: 100%
	NAME	ADDRESS	PHONE
	Department of Planning City of East Lansing	410 Abbot Road East Lansing, MI	(517) 337-1731

43% / 12% / 15% / 30%

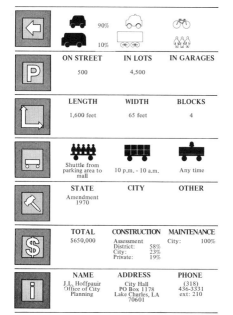

	ON STREET	IN LOTS	IN GARAGES
	500	4,500	
	LENGTH	WIDTH	BLOCKS
	1,600 feet	65 feet	4
	Shuttle from parking area to mall	10 p.m. - 10 a.m.	Any time
	STATE	CITY	OTHER
	Amendment 1970		
	TOTAL	CONSTRUCTION	MAINTENANCE
	$650,000	Assessment District: 58% / City: 23% / Private: 19%	City: 100%
	NAME	ADDRESS	PHONE
	J.L. Hoffpauir Office of City Planning	City Hall PO Box 1178 Lake Charles, LA 70601	(318) 436-3331 ext: 210

90% / 10%

Lebanon, N.H.
Downtown Mall, 1970
9,725

Lebanon's Downtown Mall provides an atmosphere conducive to shopping as well as all types of community activities. The road surface has been repaved with brick and concrete in attractive patterns, and tree-shaded benches and globe lighting fixtures have been installed. In response to the new look of the mall, property owners in the district have painted all exterior woodwork and erected new signs. Further upgrading of older structures is now being planned. The Downtown Mall has been successful in drawing people back downtown, a fact attested to by the crowded parking lots that surround the central business district.

Eugene, Oreg.
Eugene Mall, 1971
94,000

Eugene's Mall emerged from many years of urban renewal. It combines the old and new of the city, and both seem to prosper as a result. The mall caters to a diverse population, including merchants, the elderly, university students, and people from the surrounding farm and lumbering regions. Consequently, the mall has something for everyone, including craft, art, and clothing boutiques; large department stores; and traditional specialty shops. The buildings are a mix of 19th-century storefronts, 1950s modern, and contemporary buildings of architectural distinction that have won the city many awards. The mall has charm and coherence, despite its diversity, and Eugene is firmly committed to extending pedestrian zoning throughout the heart of its downtown, inviting both day and nighttime activites.

Evansville, Ind.
Main Street Walkway, 1971
138,764

The Main Street Walkway is a seven-block serpentine pedestrian thoroughfare that has been landscaped with hundreds of trees, shrubs, and flowers. The lighting system consists of white acrylic globes mounted on black poles, and there are coordinated sidewalk canopies protecting store entrances. Two shoppers' directories located on each block also serve as bulletin boards for public announcements. Graphic murals have been painted on the sides of several buildings. Two mini-parks and five fountains add further to the agreeable atmosphere that pervades the mall.

Lebanon, N.H.

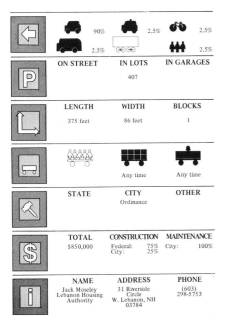

Transportation modes: 90% / 2.5% / 2.5% / 2.5% / 2.5%

ON STREET	IN LOTS	IN GARAGES
	407	

LENGTH	WIDTH	BLOCKS
375 feet	86 feet	1

	Any time	Any time

STATE	CITY	OTHER
	Ordinance	

TOTAL	CONSTRUCTION	MAINTENANCE
$850,000	Federal: 75% City: 25%	City: 100%

NAME	ADDRESS	PHONE
Jack Moseley Lebanon Housing Authority	31 Riverside Circle W. Lebanon, NH 03784	(603) 298-5753

Eugene, Oreg.

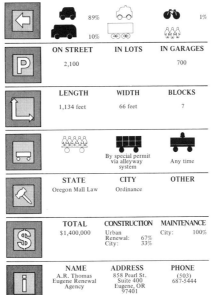

Transportation modes: 89% / 10% / 1%

ON STREET	IN LOTS	IN GARAGES
2,100		700

LENGTH	WIDTH	BLOCKS
1,134 feet	66 feet	7

	By special permit via alleyway system	Any time

STATE	CITY	OTHER
Oregon Mall Law	Ordinance	

TOTAL	CONSTRUCTION	MAINTENANCE
$1,400,000	Urban Renewal: 67% City: 33%	City: 100%

NAME	ADDRESS	PHONE
A.R. Thomas Eugene Renewal Agency	858 Pearl St. Suite 400 Eugene, OR 97401	(503) 687-5444

Evansville, Ind.

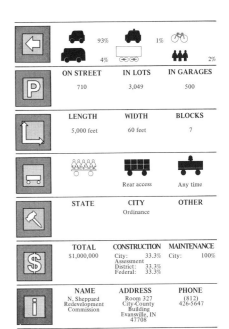

Transportation modes: 93% / 4% / 1% / 2%

ON STREET	IN LOTS	IN GARAGES
710	3,049	500

LENGTH	WIDTH	BLOCKS
5,000 feet	60 feet	7

	Rear access	Any time

STATE	CITY	OTHER
	Ordinance	

TOTAL	CONSTRUCTION	MAINTENANCE
$1,000,000	City: 33.3% Assessment District: 33.3% Federal: 33.3%	City: 100%

NAME	ADDRESS	PHONE
N. Sheppard Redevelopment Commission	Room 327 City-County Building Evansville, IN 47708	(812) 426-5647

Parsons, Kans.
Parsons Plaza, 1971
13,015

The focal point of Parsons Plaza is its central Pavilion, which is used for summer evening entertainment, such as band concerts and community gatherings. The four-block plaza incorporates standard pedestrian amenities, including benches, trees, shrubbery, and specially designed lighting fixtures. Canopies have been constructed to shelter walkway areas around buildings. The open plaza space is often utilized by merchants for promotional functions, such as sidewalk sales and trade shows.

Springfield, Ill.
Old Capitol Plaza
91,753

Springfield's pedestrian district is the result of a significant restoration project focused around the Old Capitol Building, which was dismantled stone by stone and rebuilt according to the original plan. The two pedestrian streets are parallel, bordering the Capitol lawns, but they are quite different in character. One is a rather comfortable commercial street and the other is a more austere environment, dominated by large, new office buildings. The commercial mall is more interesting and therefore more popular, but the Capitol grandeur overrides the image of both streets, and the entire area is filled with people, residents, and tourists alike. There are some scattered benches, trees, and sculptures. There is also a children's play area, but it is surrounded by brick walls that tend to isolate it. Many events are staged on the mall, and the entrances to a large parking garage, built under the Capitol, double as observation decks.

Galveston, Tex.
Central Plaza, 1972
61,109

The atmosphere on Central Plaza is simple and relaxed. The design is straightforward with flat, grassy areas (but few benches) for rest and conversation. Bulletin board kiosks announce the beginning and end of the plaza and can be used by anyone. Structures tend to be wood, brick, or concrete. There is a walkway down the mall's center and a large open space in the middle, with grassy areas on either side. The short length of this project contributes to the plaza effect, creating a small green oasis in the indiscriminate city grid. The mall is only two blocks from the Strand, an area featuring the finest concentration of historic commercial structures in the country. The Strand is presently being restored, and plans are in progess to link this area to Central Plaza.

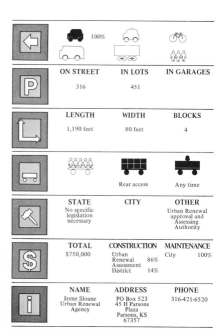

	100%		
	ON STREET	IN LOTS	IN GARAGES
	316	451	
	LENGTH	WIDTH	BLOCKS
	1,190 feet	80 feet	4
		Rear access	Any time
	STATE	CITY	OTHER
	No specific legislation necessary		Urban Renewal approval and Assessing Authority
	TOTAL	CONSTRUCTION	MAINTENANCE
	$750,000	Urban Renewal 86% Assessment District 14%	City 100%
	NAME	ADDRESS	PHONE
	Irene Sloane Urban Renewal Agency	PO Box 523 45 H Parsons Plaza Parsons, KS 67357	316-421-6520

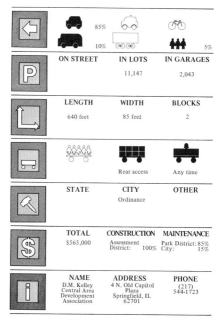

	85% 10%		5%
	ON STREET	IN LOTS	IN GARAGES
		11,147	2,043
	LENGTH	WIDTH	BLOCKS
	640 feet	85 feet	2
		Rear access	Any time
	STATE	CITY	OTHER
		Ordinance	
	TOTAL	CONSTRUCTION	MAINTENANCE
	$565,000	Assessment District: 100%	Park District: 85% City: 15%
	NAME	ADDRESS	PHONE
	D.M. Kelley Central Area Development Association	4 N. Old Capitol Plaza Springfield, IL 62701	(217) 544-1723

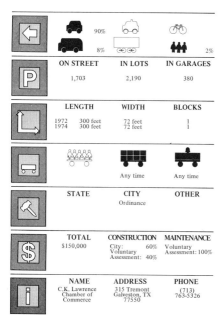

	90% 8%		2%
	ON STREET	IN LOTS	IN GARAGES
	1,703	2,190	380
	LENGTH	WIDTH	BLOCKS
	1972 300 feet 1974 300 feet	72 feet 72 feet	1 1
		Any time	Any time
	STATE	CITY	OTHER
		Ordinance	
	TOTAL	CONSTRUCTION	MAINTENANCE
	$150,000	City: 60% Voluntary Assessment: 40%	Voluntary Assessment: 100%
	NAME	ADDRESS	PHONE
	C.K. Lawrence Chamber of Commerce	315 Tremont Galveston, TX 77550	(713) 763-5326

Las Cruces, N. Mex.
Downtown Mall, 1972
37,857

Fully canopied and extending seven blocks, the Las Cruces Downtown Mall provides a relaxing atmosphere complete with benches, fountains, planters, playground equipment, and a serpentine yellow brick pedestrian path. On Saturday and Wednesday mornings, people are especially drawn to the Farmers' Market, which features a variety of goods from local producers. The significant number of still-vacant lots and storefronts provide evidence, however, that entrepeneur and consumer confidence has not yet been fully developed since the mall's completion in 1972.

Redding, Calif.
Redding Mall, 1972
16,659

Located in the heart of the central business district, the Redding Mall is unique in that it is a free-standing structure enclosed by the new and preexisting buildings it serves. Small areas of plants and shrubbery, some trees, and the columns supporting the structure work together to create the effect of an interior courtyard.

Richmond, Ind.
The Promenade, 1972
43,399

Richmond's Promenade is filled with features to attract pedestrians downtown. New street lighting, benches, planters, four large fountains, trees, flowers, and evergreens have been placed throughout the mall's four blocks. Sidewalk canopies and eight information centers have been constructed, along with a piped music system. The street surface has been repaved in a number of brick patterns delineating walkways, and new sidewalks have been installed. Service drives running parallel to the mall permit rear access to shops. The mall has stimulated new construction in the downtown area, including a library, large department store, and a multilevel parking garage.

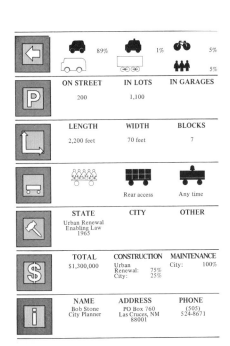

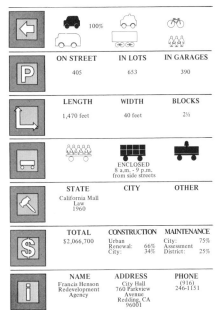

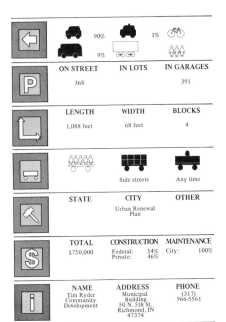

	ON STREET	IN LOTS	IN GARAGES
	200	1,100	
	LENGTH	**WIDTH**	**BLOCKS**
	2,200 feet	70 feet	7
		Rear access	Any time
	STATE	**CITY**	**OTHER**
	Urban Renewal Enabling Law 1965		
	TOTAL	**CONSTRUCTION**	**MAINTENANCE**
	$1,300,000	Urban Renewal: 75% City: 25%	City: 100%
	NAME	**ADDRESS**	**PHONE**
	Bob Stone City Planner	PO Box 760 Las Cruces, NM 88001	(505) 524-8671

	ON STREET	IN LOTS	IN GARAGES
	405	653	390
	LENGTH	**WIDTH**	**BLOCKS**
	1,470 feet	40 feet	2½
		ENCLOSED 8 a.m. - 9 p.m. from side streets	
	STATE	**CITY**	**OTHER**
	California Mall Law 1960		
	TOTAL	**CONSTRUCTION**	**MAINTENANCE**
	$2,066,700	Urban Renewal: 66% City: 34%	City: 75% Assessment District: 25%
	NAME	**ADDRESS**	**PHONE**
	Francis Henson Redevelopment Agency	City Hall 760 Parkview Avenue Redding, CA 96001	(916) 246-1151

	ON STREET	IN LOTS	IN GARAGES
	368		391
	LENGTH	**WIDTH**	**BLOCKS**
	1,088 feet	68 feet	4
		Side streets	Any time
	STATE	**CITY**	**OTHER**
		Urban Renewal Plan	
	TOTAL	**CONSTRUCTION**	**MAINTENANCE**
	$750,000	Federal: 54% Private: 46%	City: 100%
	NAME	**ADDRESS**	**PHONE**
	Tim Ryder Community Development	Municipal Building 50 N. 5th St. Richmond, IN 47374	(317) 966-5561

Atlantic City, N.J.
Gordon's Alley, 1973
47,859

Gordon's Alley is unique among pedestrian malls in that it was developed and financed by a private family in an effort to further develop its retail market. The Alley was initially a narrow street connecting two major avenues. The Gordon family repaved the street with cobblestones, planted shade trees, and added new design elements such as lights and benches. Old structures along the alley were renovated and transformed into fashionable specialty shops.

Lansing, Mich.
Washington Square, 1973
131,546

The three-block Washington Square is the focal point of an extensive urban renewal project in Lansing. The plaza features a sunken pool, formal sculpture, display kiosks, a play area for children, and an exhibition space with a reflecting pool. Wooden benches, trees and planting, varied paving patterns, and new lighting complete the mall's design.

Louisville, Ky.
River City Mall, 1973
361,472

River City Mall features a variety of seating areas and hundreds of trees and ground cover plants. New paving was installed, with brick areas integrated into the mall's surface. There are large shelters located on each of the mall's three blocks. The roof of each shelter is constructed of bronze-tinted plexiglas, allowing light to pass through, but filtering harsh sunrays. Lighting along the mall is uniform, at pedestrian level, to ensure safety.

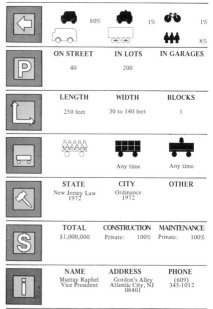

	80%	1%	1%
			8%

ON STREET	IN LOTS	IN GARAGES
40	200	

LENGTH	WIDTH	BLOCKS
250 feet	30 to 140 feet	1

	Any time	Any time

STATE	CITY	OTHER
New Jersey Law 1972	Ordinance 1972	

TOTAL	CONSTRUCTION	MAINTENANCE
$1,000,000	Private: 100%	Private: 100%

NAME	ADDRESS	PHONE
Murray Raphel Vice President	Gordon's Alley Atlantic City, NJ 08401	(609) 345-1012

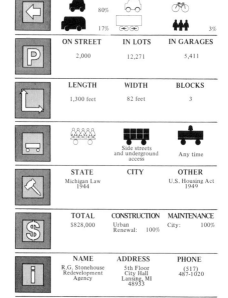

	80%		
	17%		3%

ON STREET	IN LOTS	IN GARAGES
2,000	12,271	5,411

LENGTH	WIDTH	BLOCKS
1,300 feet	82 feet	3

	Side streets and underground access	Any time

STATE	CITY	OTHER
Michigan Law 1944		U.S. Housing Act 1949

TOTAL	CONSTRUCTION	MAINTENANCE
$828,000	Urban Renewal: 100%	City: 100%

NAME	ADDRESS	PHONE
R.G. Stonehouse Redevelopment Agency	5th Floor City Hall Lansing, MI 48933	(517) 487-1020

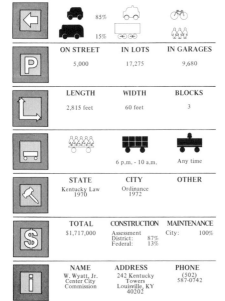

	85%		
	15%		

ON STREET	IN LOTS	IN GARAGES
5,000	17,275	9,680

LENGTH	WIDTH	BLOCKS
2,815 feet	60 feet	3

	6 p.m. - 10 a.m.	Any time

STATE	CITY	OTHER
Kentucky Law 1970	Ordinance 1972	

TOTAL	CONSTRUCTION	MAINTENANCE
$1,717,000	Assessment District: 87% Federal: 13%	City: 100%

NAME	ADDRESS	PHONE
W. Wyatt, Jr. Center City Commission	242 Kentucky Towers Louisville, KY 40202	(502) 587-0742

Monroe, N.C.
Courthouse Plaza, 1973
13,000

Courthouse Plaza, created as part of an urban renewal effort, functions as a pedestrian area for the governmental center of Monroe. People working in the City Hall, the Post Office, the Courthouse, and surrounding offices benefit directly from the vehicle-free plaza. Paving stones have been laid down in a distinctive pattern, and large, circular planters contain a variety of trees. The planters also provide seating on the plaza.

New London, Conn.
Captain's Walk, 1973
31,360

Captain's Walk, part of a large urban renewal effort to revitalize the downtown area, occupies four blocks along State Street, with the upper and lower portions treated as semi-malls. The street was repaved with cobblestone textures, and its linearity relieved by a staggered sequence of "whale-shaped" green areas. Spinnaker-shaped canopies balloon over the edges of the mall, providing visual variation as well as shelter. An emergency vehicle lane, designed in a subtle serpentine form, runs almost invisibly through the mall. The entire area is pervaded with a nautical atmosphere, leaving no doubt as to New London's maritime heritage. The design of canopies, telephone booths, mailboxes, and benches reflect this theme.

Poughkeepsie, N.Y.
Main Street Mall, 1973
32,029

There are over seventy establishments lining Poughkeepsie's Main Mall, offering a wide variety of goods and services. In addition to over one hundred trees, numerous benches, and six fountains, the mall features a bandstand, a pavilion, and playground equipment, all combining to give the space a sense of community. Bricks, concrete, and granite have replaced the original street surface, new lighting has been installed, and bus shelters erected. The mall is at its busiest during midday, when the lunchtime crowd uses it as a place to gather and relax.

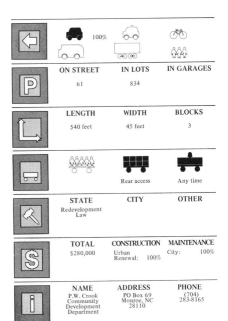

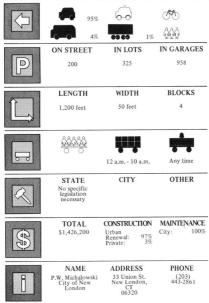

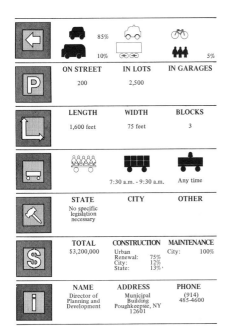

	Monroe	New London	Poughkeepsie
Vehicle %	100%	95% / 4% / 1%	85% / 10% / 5%
Parking	ON STREET 61 / IN LOTS 834 / IN GARAGES	ON STREET 200 / IN LOTS 325 / IN GARAGES 958	ON STREET 200 / IN LOTS 2,500 / IN GARAGES
Dimensions	LENGTH 540 feet / WIDTH 45 feet / BLOCKS 3	LENGTH 1,200 feet / WIDTH 50 feet / BLOCKS 4	LENGTH 1,600 feet / WIDTH 75 feet / BLOCKS 3
Access	Rear access / Any time	12 a.m. - 10 a.m. / Any time	7:30 a.m. - 9:30 a.m. / Any time
Legislation	STATE Redevelopment Law / CITY / OTHER	STATE No specific legislation necessary / CITY / OTHER	STATE No specific legislation necessary / CITY / OTHER
Cost	TOTAL $280,000 / CONSTRUCTION Urban Renewal: 100% / MAINTENANCE City: 100%	TOTAL $1,426,200 / CONSTRUCTION Urban Renewal: 97% Private: 3% / MAINTENANCE City: 100%	TOTAL $3,200,000 / CONSTRUCTION Urban Renewal: 75% City: 12% State: 13% / MAINTENANCE City: 100%
Contact	NAME P.W. Crook Community Development Department / ADDRESS PO Box 69 Monroe, NC 28110 / PHONE (704) 283-8165	NAME P.W. Michalowski City of New London / ADDRESS 33 Union St. New London, CT 06320 / PHONE (203) 443-2861	NAME Director of Planning and Development / ADDRESS Municipal Building Poughkeepsie, NY 12601 / PHONE (914) 485-4600

Seattle, Wash.
Occidental Mall, 1973
550,000

The Occidental Mall is located in the center of Seattle's Pioneer Square Historic District. Together with the adjacent Occidental Square, the mall provides a generous space for outdoor activites. During the warm months, the mall is filled with vendor carts and art exhibits. Open-air concerts are popular and frequent. Overhead wiring has been removed and street furniture added to the area. Historic globe fixtures provide lighting. Occidental Mall also serves as the main pedestrian thoroughfare for special events taking place in the domed stadium to the south.

Toccoa, Ga.
Downtown Mall, 1973
8,000

Toccoa's Downtown Mall features a 12-foot/4-meter wide, free standing canopy along both sides of the street, with the exception of a short stretch in front of the Courthouse. Four covered crosswalks in the mall area allow shoppers to move easily across the space, even in bad weather. Trees and shrubbery have been set into raised planters, and the street has been resurfaced in brick. The mall often hosts outdoor art exhibits, and open-air stands are frequently set up, adding color and activity to the area.

Winston-Salem, N.C.
Downtown Walkway, 1973
133,683

Winston-Salem's pedestrian system covers eight blocks, with the main traffic-free spine running down Trade Street. Smaller pedestrian walkways connect Trade Street to two parallel arteries. A parking deck and a garage, located at the entrances of these walkways, are linked to the mall level by stairways. In addition to the usual pedestrian amenities, such as repaving, seating, landscaping, sheltered areas, and new lighting, the mall also connects directly to a number of public facilities, among them an indoor ice skating rink. The lower end of Trade Street turns into a pedestrian bridge that links the mall to a plaza area.

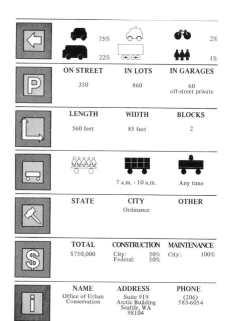

	75%		2%
	22%		1%

ON STREET	IN LOTS	IN GARAGES
350	860	60 off-street private

LENGTH	WIDTH	BLOCKS
560 feet	85 feet	2

	7 a.m. - 10 a.m.	Any time

STATE	CITY	OTHER
	Ordinance	

TOTAL	CONSTRUCTION	MAINTENANCE
$750,000	City: 50% Federal: 50%	City: 100%

NAME	ADDRESS	PHONE
Office of Urban Conservation	Suite 919 Arctic Building Seattle, WA 98104	(206) 583-6054

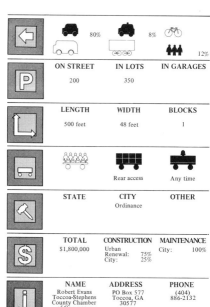

	80%		8%		
					12%

ON STREET	IN LOTS	IN GARAGES
200	350	

LENGTH	WIDTH	BLOCKS
500 feet	48 feet	1

	Rear access	Any time

STATE	CITY	OTHER
	Ordinance	

TOTAL	CONSTRUCTION	MAINTENANCE
$1,800,000	Urban Renewal: 75% City: 25%	City: 100%

NAME	ADDRESS	PHONE
Robert Evans Toccoa-Stephens County Chamber of Commerce	PO Box 577 Toccoa, GA 30577	(404) 886-2132

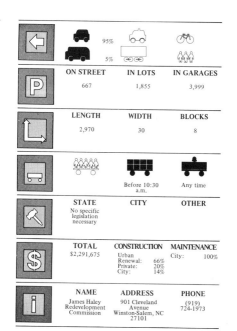

	95%			
	5%			

ON STREET	IN LOTS	IN GARAGES
667	1,855	3,999

LENGTH	WIDTH	BLOCKS
2,970	30	8

	Before 10:30 a.m.	Any time

STATE	CITY	OTHER
No specific legislation necessary		

TOTAL	CONSTRUCTION	MAINTENANCE
$2,291,675	Urban Renewal: 66% Private: 20% City: 14%	City: 100%

NAME	ADDRESS	PHONE
James Haley Redevelopment Commission	901 Cleveland Avenue Winston-Salem, NC 27101	(919) 724-1973

Baltimore, Md.
Lexington Mall, 1974
905,759

Lexington Mall, lined with a variety of stores on both sides, provides a vital pedestrian link between the office district to the east and the department stores to the west in Baltimore's downtown area. The mall has been improved with new paving, pedestrian lighting, landscaping, and benches. Extension of the mall for at least another block to the west is planned, in order to connect directly to a proposed subway entrance in the retail district.

Frankfort, Ky.
St. Clair Mall, 1974
23,000

Frankfort's many historic buildings have been carefully preserved and continue to function as office and commercial structures. The city built the St. Clair Mall in its central business district as part of a Twelve Point Program for revitalization of the core area. The design of the mall reinforces the historic image, with landscaping, lighting, and signage chosen to highlight the old structures along the street. Frankfort now plans to extend the traffic-free concept with a series of pedestrianways that will connect the major downtown activity areas.

Helena, Mont.
Last Chance Mall, 1974
24,651

Helena's Last Chance Gulch was perfectly suited for pedestrianization. The street is narrow and crooked and is lined with buildings of architectural significance, some of which. date back to the Gold Rush Days. The design of the mall, with its landscaped areas, new pavement, and lighting, lends coherence to the street. Seating areas and an imaginative fountain have also been installed. New parking has been provided around the perimeter of the central business district so that residents will find downtown shopping as convenient as that in suburban shopping centers. The mall is part of a $16 million renewal program centered around the restoration and recycling of Helena's historic architecture.

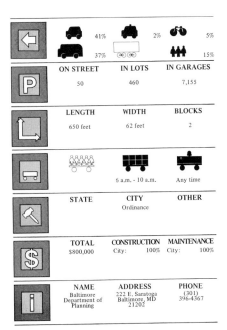

41%	2%	5%
37%		15%

ON STREET	IN LOTS	IN GARAGES
50	460	7,155

LENGTH	WIDTH	BLOCKS
650 feet	62 feet	2

6 a.m. - 10 a.m.		Any time

STATE	CITY	OTHER
	Ordinance	

TOTAL	CONSTRUCTION	MAINTENANCE
$800,000	City: 100%	City: 100%

NAME	ADDRESS	PHONE
Baltimore Department of Planning	222 E. Saratoga Baltimore, MD 21202	(301) 396-4367

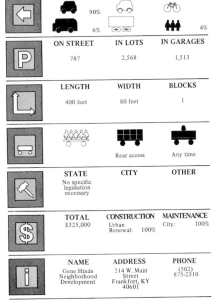

90%		
6%		4%

ON STREET	IN LOTS	IN GARAGES
787	2,568	1,513

LENGTH	WIDTH	BLOCKS
400 feet	80 feet	1

	Rear access	Any time

STATE	CITY	OTHER
No specific legislation necessary		

TOTAL	CONSTRUCTION	MAINTENANCE
$325,000	Urban Renewal: 100%	City: 100%

NAME	ADDRESS	PHONE
Gene Hinds Neighborhood Development	214 W. Main Street Frankfort, KY 40601	(502) 875-2310

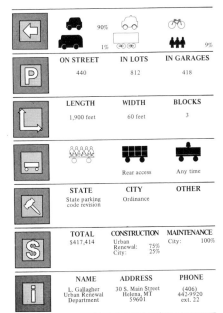

90%		
1%		9%

ON STREET	IN LOTS	IN GARAGES
440	812	418

LENGTH	WIDTH	BLOCKS
1,900 feet	60 feet	3

	Rear access	Any time

STATE	CITY	OTHER
State parking code revision	Ordinance	

TOTAL	CONSTRUCTION	MAINTENANCE
$417,414	Urban Renewal: 75% City: 25%	City: 100%

NAME	ADDRESS	PHONE
L. Gallagher Urban Renewal Department	30 S. Main Street Helena, MT 59601	(406) 442-9920 ext. 22

Napa, Calif.
Parkway Mall, 1974
35,978

Parkway Mall, located in the center of Napa's downtown commercial area, is a large plaza with partially covered walkways running along the storefronts which face the mall. The most outstanding design aspects are a 72-foot/22-meter timber clock with the world's largest illuminated face and a sculptured sunken pool with a waterfall. Two more outdoor sculptures, winners of a national competition, have recently been added to the mall. Trees, plants, trellises, and an outdoor forum for public events are among the pedestrian amenities along Parkway Mall. There are plans to extend the mall.

New Bedford, Mass.
Downtown Mall, 1974
101,777

The Downtown Mall stands on what was formerly New Bedford's busy main street. The pedestrian space now contains trees, colorful planters, and a centrally located lighted fountain. Benches, new lighting, kiosks, and a music broadcast system contribute to the comfortable atmosphere along the mall, attracting shoppers and visitors. The emergency driving lane alternates sides on each of the mall's three blocks, reducing, as far as possible, the appearance of a conventional city street.

Oak Park, Ill.
Oak Park Village Mall, 1974
62,511

The two sections of Oak Park's mall intersect, offering an alternative to the usual linear structure of traffic-free zones. Design elements are simple and scaled to pedestrian needs. Landscaping has been introduced in the form of islands with grass, trees, and shrubbery, surrounded by benches. All curbs have been eliminated and the street surface repaved in a brick texture. The mall's separate features combine to form a spacious and comfortable area in the village center.

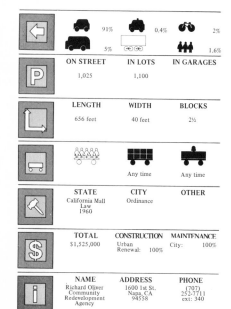

	91%	0.4%	2%
	5%		1.6%

ON STREET	IN LOTS	IN GARAGES
1,025	1,100	

LENGTH	WIDTH	BLOCKS
656 feet	40 feet	2½

	Any time	Any time

STATE	CITY	OTHER
California Mall Law 1960	Ordinance	

TOTAL	CONSTRUCTION	MAINTENANCE
$1,525,000	Urban Renewal: 100%	City: 100%

NAME	ADDRESS	PHONE
Richard Oliver Community Redevelopment Agency	1600 1st St., Napa, CA 94558	(707) 252-7711 ext: 340

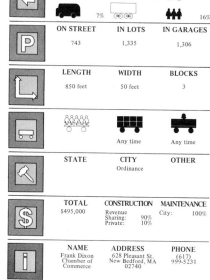

	75%	2%
	7%	16%

ON STREET	IN LOTS	IN GARAGES
743	1,335	1,306

LENGTH	WIDTH	BLOCKS
850 feet	50 feet	3

	Any time	Any time

STATE	CITY	OTHER
	Ordinance	

TOTAL	CONSTRUCTION	MAINTENANCE
$495,000	Revenue Sharing: 90% Private: 10%	City: 100%

NAME	ADDRESS	PHONE
Frank Dixon Chamber of Commerce	628 Pleasant St. New Bedford, MA 02740	(617) 999-5231

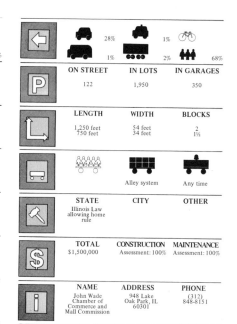

	28%	1%	1%
	1%	2%	68%

ON STREET	IN LOTS	IN GARAGES
122	1,950	350

LENGTH	WIDTH	BLOCKS
1,250 feet 750 feet	54 feet 34 feet	2 1½

	Alley system	Any time

STATE	CITY	OTHER
Illinois Law allowing home rule		

TOTAL	CONSTRUCTION	MAINTENANCE
$1,500,000	Assessment: 100%	Assessment: 100%

NAME	ADDRESS	PHONE
John Wade Chamber of Commerce and Mall Commission	948 Lake Oak Park, IL 60301	(312) 848-8151

Spartanburg, S.C.
Main Street Mall, 1974
44,456

Two blocks of downtown Spartanburg have been totally repaved and landscaped, creating a comfortable scaled pedestrian district. Green areas, with trees and plants, run the length of the mall, on either side of a central walkway, which is lined with hanging globe lighting fixtures. Low wooden benches provide seating, and a centrally located pool and fountain serve as the focal point of the pedestrian area.

Tacoma, Wash.
Broadway Plaza, 1974
154,581

Tacoma's Broadway Plaza is the nucleus of the central business district. Street furniture, fountains, trees, shrubbery, and grass create a downtown park for office workers and shoppers alike. Product shows, displays, and a farmers' market are often located beneath the several covered areas along the mall, bringing additional activity into the area. Other pedestrian-oriented amenities include playground equipment and a stage for formal concerts and other performances. The mall's primarily modern design incorporates some details of earlier periods, and the buildings along the plaza are a mix of historic and newly built structures, further heightening the eclectic look of the space. An extension of the mall's original four blocks is now being planned.

Tampa, Fla.
Franklin Mall, 1974
292,109

In addition to functioning as a retail center, Franklin Mall is frequently the scene of special entertainment, from symphony orchestra concerts to art shows and craft fairs. With construction of the mall, all overhead wiring was buried and a special sound system was installed to broadcast events. Planters and seating have been placed throughout the area, encouraging shoppers and downtown employees to use the mall as a place to relax and soak up the Florida sun.

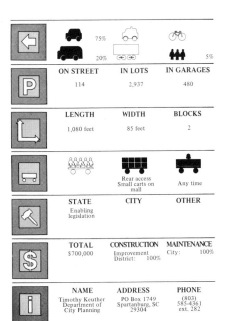

		75%				5%
		20%				

	ON STREET	IN LOTS	IN GARAGES
	114	2,937	480

	LENGTH	WIDTH	BLOCKS
	1,080 feet	85 feet	2

		Rear access Small carts on mall	Any time

	STATE	CITY	OTHER
	Enabling legislation		

	TOTAL	CONSTRUCTION	MAINTENANCE
	$700,000	Improvement District: 100%	City: 100%

	NAME	ADDRESS	PHONE
	Timothy Keuther Department of City Planning	PO Box 1749 Spartanburg, SC 29304	(803) 585-4361 ext. 282

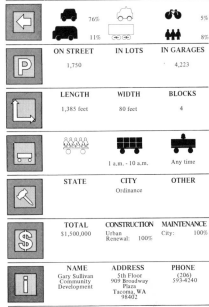

		76%			5%
		11%			8%

	ON STREET	IN LOTS	IN GARAGES
	1,750		4,223

	LENGTH	WIDTH	BLOCKS
	1,385 feet	80 feet	4

		1 a.m. - 10 a.m.	Any time

	STATE	CITY	OTHER
		Ordinance	

	TOTAL	CONSTRUCTION	MAINTENANCE
	$1,500,000	Urban Renewal: 100%	City: 100%

	NAME	ADDRESS	PHONE
	Gary Sullivan Community Development	5th Floor 909 Broadway Plaza Tacoma, WA 98402	(206) 593-4240

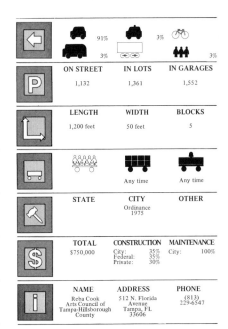

		91%	3%		3%
		3%			3%

	ON STREET	IN LOTS	IN GARAGES
	1,132	1,361	1,552

	LENGTH	WIDTH	BLOCKS
	1,200 feet	50 feet	5

		Any time	Any time

	STATE	CITY	OTHER
		Ordinance 1975	

	TOTAL	CONSTRUCTION	MAINTENANCE
	$750,000	City: 35% Federal: 35% Private: 30%	City: 100%

	NAME	ADDRESS	PHONE
	Reba Cook Arts Council of Tampa-Hillsborough County	512 N. Florida Avenue Tampa, FL 33606	(813) 229-6547

Trenton, N.J.
The Commons, 1974
104,638

The Trenton Commons returns two blocks of State Street to pedestrians. Sidewalks have been eliminated and the street has been resurfaced in brick textures. The mall's original design incorporated several large canopied areas with merchandising and sitting space situated beneath them. These have recently been removed, and flowering trees have been planted in the same spots. A specially designed newsstand and bus stop is located where Broad Street intersects the mall. The city plans to extend the pedestrian thoroughfare to connect with the State Capitol and City Hall.

Vancouver, B.C.
Granville Mall, 1974
426,520

Shade trees line the "street" that runs down the center of Vancouver's Granville Mall. Although the mall is a pedestrian thoroughfare, a traffic lane has been included in the design scheme to allow buses, emergency vehicles, and taxis (for pick-ups and deliveries only) along the mall. Sidewalks, curbs, and the street surface have all been improved, and new lighting and utilities have been installed.

Wilmington, Del.
Market Street Mall, 1974
80,000

The construction of Wilmington's Main Street Mall was part of a major revitalization effort for the entire downtown area. Not only has the Main Street Mall renewed residents' confidence in the downtown, but it has reversed a 20-year decline of the area as a regional shopping center. The Grand Opera House, Delaware's Center for the Performing Arts with its $5.2 million restoration, is located at the north end of the mall. Plans are now in progress to relocate six of the city's historically significant houses onto the southern portion of the mall. This area is intended to serve as a center for civic activity and displays.

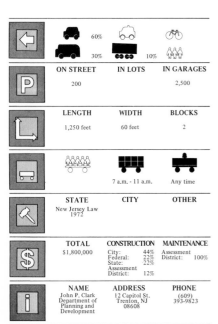

	ON STREET	IN LOTS	IN GARAGES
	200		2,500

	LENGTH	WIDTH	BLOCKS
	1,250 feet	60 feet	2

	7 a.m. - 11 a.m.		Any time

	STATE	CITY	OTHER
	New Jersey Law 1972		

	TOTAL	CONSTRUCTION	MAINTENANCE
	$1,800,000	City: 44% / Federal: 22% / State: 22% / Assessment District: 12%	Assessment District: 100%

	NAME	ADDRESS	PHONE
	John P. Clark Department of Planning and Development	12 Capitol St. Trenton, NJ 08608	(609) 393-9823

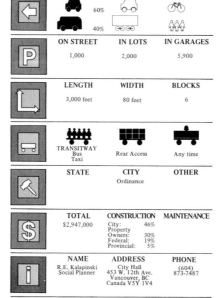

	ON STREET	IN LOTS	IN GARAGES
	1,000	2,000	5,900

	LENGTH	WIDTH	BLOCKS
	3,000 feet	80 feet	6

	TRANSITWAY Bus Taxi	Rear Access	Any time

	STATE	CITY	OTHER
		Ordinance	

	TOTAL	CONSTRUCTION	MAINTENANCE
	$2,947,000	City: 46% / Property Owners: 30% / Federal: 19% / Provincial: 5%	

	NAME	ADDRESS	PHONE
	R.E. Kalapinski Social Planner	City Hall 453 W. 12th Ave. Vancouver, BC Canada V5Y 1V4	(604) 873-7487

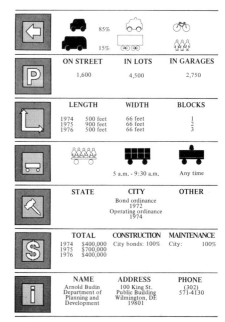

	ON STREET	IN LOTS	IN GARAGES
	1,600	4,500	2,750

	LENGTH	WIDTH	BLOCKS
1974	500 feet	66 feet	1
1975	900 feet	66 feet	2
1976	500 feet	66 feet	3

	5 a.m. - 9:30 a.m.		Any time

	STATE	CITY	OTHER
		Bond ordinance 1972 Operating ordinance 1974	

	TOTAL	CONSTRUCTION	MAINTENANCE
1974	$400,000	City bonds: 100%	City: 100%
1975	$700,000		
1976	$400,000		

	NAME	ADDRESS	PHONE
	Arnold Budin Department of Planning and Development	100 King St. Public Building Wilmington, DE 19801	(302) 571-4130

Winchester, Va.
Loudon Street, 1974
19,429

Located in Winchester's historic central business district, the Loudon Street Mall has ensured the continued vitality of the city's major shopping area. A wide variety of retail stores and restaurants attract people downtown, and nearby parking garages and municipal parking lots provide easy access to the mall itself. The amenities along Loudon Street Mall are primarily made of wood, preserving the comfortable atmosphere of the downtown area. Wooden planters and benches have been interspersed with trees, and street lighting has been redesigned in the form of old lamp posts mounted on wooden poles. Overhead wires and curbs have been eliminated, and the entire street surface has been repaved.

Youngstown, Ohio
Federal Plaza, 1974
140,909

Youngstown's Federal Plaza represents the conversion of a three-block section of the downtown area into a pedestrian-oriented plaza with curvilinear walkways, twin decorative fountains, information kiosks, and street furnishings. Trees rising to a height of 40 feet / 13 meters are accented by flowering planters, creating a park-like setting in the heart of the city. A sunken plaza large enough for concerts and outdoor exhibits is a special feature of the eastern end of the plaza. Lighting fixtures have been designed in globe clusters mounted on poles. Ramps located throughout the plaza provide easy access for the handicapped.

Quebec City, Quebec
St. Roch Mall, 1974
187,833

Quebec City has developed the first totally enclosed pedestrian mall in North America. Traffic was eliminated from a 2,000-foot / 600-meter stretch of a main commercial street; the street was repaved, and a roof, with a number of skylights, was constructed to cover the whole length of the mall. A climate-control system was then installed. A peculiarity of this project is that the enclosure does not depend on any of the structures beneath it for support. It is totally free-standing.

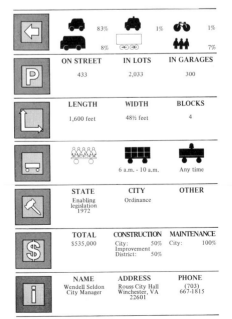

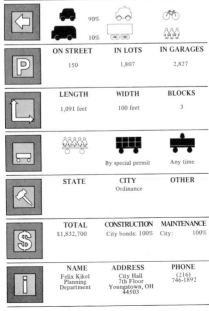

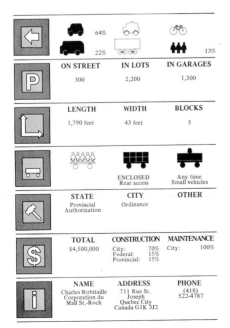

Winchester, Va.

	83%		1%		1%
	8%				7%

ON STREET	IN LOTS	IN GARAGES
433	2,033	300

LENGTH	WIDTH	BLOCKS
1,600 feet	48½ feet	4

	6 a.m. - 10 a.m.	Any time

STATE	CITY	OTHER
Enabling legislation 1972	Ordinance	

TOTAL	CONSTRUCTION	MAINTENANCE
$535,000	City: 50% Improvement District: 50%	City: 100%

NAME	ADDRESS	PHONE
Wendell Seldon City Manager	Rouss City Hall Winchester, VA 22601	(703) 667-1815

Youngstown, Ohio

	90%		
	10%		

ON STREET	IN LOTS	IN GARAGES
150	1,807	2,827

LENGTH	WIDTH	BLOCKS
1,091 feet	100 feet	3

	By special permit	Any time

STATE	CITY	OTHER
	Ordinance	

TOTAL	CONSTRUCTION	MAINTENANCE
$1,832,700	City bonds: 100%	City: 100%

NAME	ADDRESS	PHONE
Felix Kikel Planning Department	City Hall 7th Floor Youngstown, OH 44503	(216) 746-1892

Quebec City, Quebec

	64%			13%
	22%			

ON STREET	IN LOTS	IN GARAGES
300	2,200	1,300

LENGTH	WIDTH	BLOCKS
1,790 feet	43 feet	5

	ENCLOSED Rear access	Any time Small vehicles

STATE	CITY	OTHER
Provincial Authorization	Ordinance	

TOTAL	CONSTRUCTION	MAINTENANCE
$4,500,000	City: 70% Federal: 15% Provincial: 15%	City: 100%

NAME	ADDRESS	PHONE
Charles Robitaille Corporation du Mall St.-Roch	711 Rue St. Joseph Quebec City Canada G1K 3J2	(418) 522-4787

Battle Creek, Mich.
Michigan Mall, 1975
38,931

Michigan Mall is located in the heart of Battle Creek's downtown shopping district. The two outer blocks of the mall are technically "promenades," allowing for traffic flow in conjunction with pedestrian movement along widened sidewalks. The two central blocks, however, are free of all vehicular traffic. This section of the mall is landscaped with trees, plants, and fountains and features outdoor art objects donated by private citizens. All utility wires have been buried, and a specially designed public address system also provides background music for shoppers along the entire four blocks. Sodium-vapor lights provide high-intensity yet warm and glowing illumination during evening hours.

Greenville, S.C.
Coffee Street Mall, 1975
61,208

The Coffee Street Mall has transformed two blocks of Greenville's central business district into a plazalike space for downtown workers and shoppers. The mall's design features a large pool and fountain. Raised areas and steps relieve the flatness of the space, and movable planters containing flowering trees allow for alternative landscaping patterns. A covered patio is located in the center of the mall, offering shelter in inclement weather and serving as a focus for community events. Greenville plans to extend its pedestrian area and reorient adjacent businesses so that they can take direct advantage of their proximity to the mall.

Ithaca, N.Y.
Ithaca Commons, 1975
26,226

Over fifty business establishments are located directly on the three-block Ithaca Commons, which has been the backbone of the city's renewal efforts. Design features include a small amphitheater, a fountain, and a large play structure for children. Four pavilions provide sheltered space for exhibits and street vendors. Over 70 trees and hundreds of shrubs and flowers have been placed throughout the mall. Raised planters also provide seating.

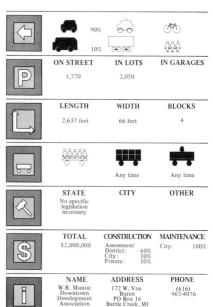

	90%			
	10%			

ON STREET	IN LOTS	IN GARAGES
1,770	2,050	

LENGTH	WIDTH	BLOCKS
2,637 feet	66 feet	4

	Any time	Any time

STATE	CITY	OTHER
No specific legislation necessary		

TOTAL	CONSTRUCTION	MAINTENANCE
$2,000,000	Assessment District: 60% City: 30% Private: 10%	City: 100%

NAME	ADDRESS	PHONE
W.R. Munoz Downtown Development Association	172 W. Van Buren PO Box 16 Battle Creek, MI 49016	(616) 962-4076

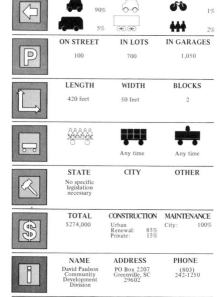

	90%			1%
	5%			2%

ON STREET	IN LOTS	IN GARAGES
100	700	1,050

LENGTH	WIDTH	BLOCKS
420 feet	50 feet	2

	Any time	Any time

STATE	CITY	OTHER
No specific legislation necessary		

TOTAL	CONSTRUCTION	MAINTENANCE
$274,000	Urban Renewal: 85% Private: 15%	City: 100%

NAME	ADDRESS	PHONE
David Paulson Community Development Division	PO Box 2207 Greenville, SC 29602	(803) 242-1250

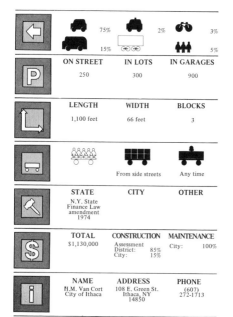

	75%		2%			3%
	15%					5%

ON STREET	IN LOTS	IN GARAGES
250	300	900

LENGTH	WIDTH	BLOCKS
1,100 feet	66 feet	3

	From side streets	Any time

STATE	CITY	OTHER
N.Y. State Finance Law amendment 1974		

TOTAL	CONSTRUCTION	MAINTENANCE
$1,130,000	Assessment District: 85% City: 15%	City: 100%

NAME	ADDRESS	PHONE
H.M. Van Cort City of Ithaca	108 E. Green St. Ithaca, NY 14850	(607) 272-1713

Muncie, Ind.
Walnut Plaza, 1975
69,082

Muncie's four-block Walnut Plaza is lined with over fifty commercial establishments. The simple design of the traffic-free area was chosen to harmonize with the city's turn-of-the-century architecture. The street surface has been repaved in alternating patterns of brick and concrete slabs, and there are landscaped areas in the middle of each block. The focal point of the pedestrian zone is a Cyrus E. Dallin statue entitled ''The Passing of the Buffalo,'' which was purchased especially for the mall.

Paterson, N.J.
Main Street, Mall, 1975
144,824

The first phase of a comprehensive pedestrian project for Paterson's Lower Main Street has been completed. Fair Street has been converted into a 300-foot/90-meter long pedestrian domain, with a galleria, a mini-park, and covered arcades in front of all the shops. Old gas lamp standards have been redesigned to provide light, and groupings of stationary chairs have been arranged beneath trees, creating pleasant spots to relax. The program of landscaping, graphics, and multicolored canopies has been integrated with existing buildings, forming a lively and unique pedestrian space.

Philadelphia, Pa.
Chestnut Street Transitway, 1975
1,950,089

Philadelphia chose to implement a transitway rather than a fully pedestrianized street along twelve blocks of its finest shopping street. Buses are allowed to travel both ways along Chestnut Street, but the area has been redesigned according to pedestrian priorities. Sidewalks have been widened and paved in brick, and sections of curbing have been eliminated at intersections and midblock crossings to accommodate the handicapped. Trees and plantings, ornamental lighting fixtures, information columns, benches, and new bus shelters have been installed along the entire length of the project. Specially designed newsstands are located at each intersection. Even the telephone booths, trash receptacles, and midblock pedestrian/traffic signals have been designed to emphasize the pedestrian scale of the area.

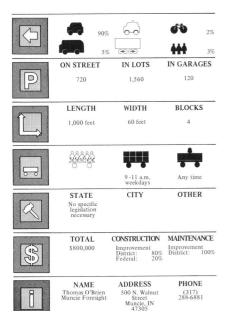

	90% / 5%		2% / 3%
ON STREET	**IN LOTS**	**IN GARAGES**	
720	1,560	120	
LENGTH	**WIDTH**	**BLOCKS**	
1,000 feet	60 feet	4	
	9-11 a.m. weekdays	Any time	
STATE	**CITY**	**OTHER**	
No specific legislation necessary			
TOTAL	**CONSTRUCTION**	**MAINTENANCE**	
$800,000	Improvement District: 80% Federal: 20%	Improvement District: 100%	
NAME	**ADDRESS**	**PHONE**	
Thomas O'Brien Muncie Foresight	500 N. Walnut Street Muncie, IN 47305	(317) 288-6881	

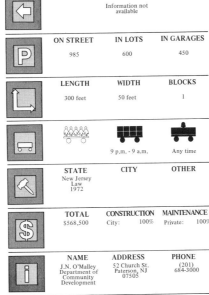

Information not available		
ON STREET	**IN LOTS**	**IN GARAGES**
985	600	450
LENGTH	**WIDTH**	**BLOCKS**
300 feet	50 feet	1
	9 p.m. - 9 a.m.	Any time
STATE	**CITY**	**OTHER**
New Jersey Law 1972		
TOTAL	**CONSTRUCTION**	**MAINTENANCE**
$568,500	City: 100%	Private: 100%
NAME	**ADDRESS**	**PHONE**
J.N. O'Malley Department of Community Development	52 Church St. Paterson, NJ 07505	(201) 684-3000

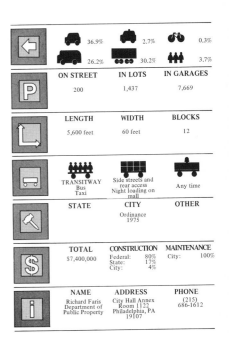

	36.9% / 26.2%	2.7% / 30.2%	0.3% / 3.7%
ON STREET	**IN LOTS**	**IN GARAGES**	
200	1,437	7,669	
LENGTH	**WIDTH**	**BLOCKS**	
5,600 feet	60 feet	12	
TRANSITWAY Bus Taxi	Side streets and rear access Night loading on mall	Any time	
STATE	**CITY**	**OTHER**	
	Ordinance 1975		
TOTAL	**CONSTRUCTION**	**MAINTENANCE**	
$7,400,000	Federal: 80% State: 17% City: 4%	City: 100%	
NAME	**ADDRESS**	**PHONE**	
Richard Faris Department of Public Property	City Hall Annex Room 1122 Philadelphia, PA 19107	(215) 686-1612	

Portland, Maine
Maine Way Mall, 1975
65,116

Portland's planners felt that a traffic-free area should serve as a background for pedestrian activities, rather than be a central attraction in itself. Accordingly, the design of the city's Main Way is very simple. The large plaza effect of the area is unified by an orderly sequence of large shade trees and wooden benches. Groups of round planters and different paving textures provide variety in the mall's appearance without diminishing its openness. The design of Main Way encourages activites as art shows, open-air sales booths, and civic events, all of which draw more people into Portland's downtown area.

Reading, Pa.
Penn Square, 1975
87,643

Penn Square, half of which is a semimall allowing motor vehicles on restricted traffic lanes, is the focal point of downtown activity in Reading. Over 100,000 square feet / 10,000 square meters of new pedestrian pavement has been set down, and hundreds of trees, shrubs, and flowers have been placed throughout the mall area. Two fountains have been set into terraced areas, providing variety in the street level. The streets surrounding these fountains also serve as places to sit and relax. A number of ramps were incorporated into the mall's design to ensure that all public facilities would be available to the handicapped. A variety of lighting fixtures, including landscape lights, add to the mall's appeal.

Rockford, Ill.
State Street Mall, 1975
147,370

As a result of sound planning and design policies, Rockford's State Street Mall has drawn enough people downtown to increase business volume by 10 percent. In addition to standard pedestrian design elements, such as new paving, lighting, and landscaping, a large public square has been incorporated into the central section of the mall. The square, which includes a raised platform, serves as a focus for numerous civic events. The success of the State Street Mall has generated approximately $42 million worth of new construction in the downtown area.

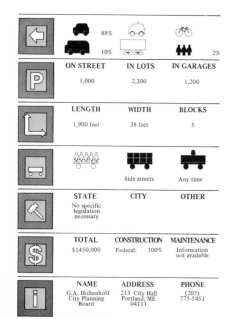

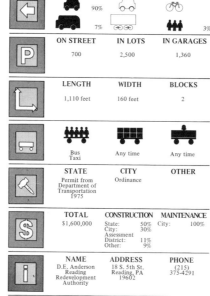

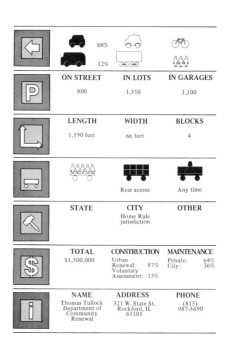

Portland, Maine

	88%		
	10%		2%

ON STREET	IN LOTS	IN GARAGES
1,000	2,300	1,200

LENGTH	WIDTH	BLOCKS
1,900 feet	38 feet	5

	Side streets	Any time

STATE	CITY	OTHER
No specific legislation necessary		

TOTAL	CONSTRUCTION	MAINTENANCE
$1450,000	Federal: 100%	Information not available

NAME	ADDRESS	PHONE
G.A. Holtenhoff City Planning Board	213 City Hall Portland, ME 04111	(207) 775-5451

Reading, Pa.

	90%		
	7%		3%

ON STREET	IN LOTS	IN GARAGES
700	2,500	1,360

LENGTH	WIDTH	BLOCKS
1,110 feet	160 feet	2

Bus Taxi	Any time	Any time

STATE	CITY	OTHER
Permit from Department of Transportation 1975	Ordinance	

TOTAL	CONSTRUCTION	MAINTENANCE
$1,600,000	State: 50% City: 30% Assessment District: 11% Other: 9%	City: 100%

NAME	ADDRESS	PHONE
D.E. Anderson Reading Redevelopment Authority	18 S. 5th St. Reading, PA 19602	(215) 375-4291

Rockford, Ill.

	88%		
	12%		

ON STREET	IN LOTS	IN GARAGES
800	1,350	1,100

LENGTH	WIDTH	BLOCKS
1,190 feet	66 feet	4

	Rear access	Any time

STATE	CITY	OTHER
	Home Rule jurisdiction	

TOTAL	CONSTRUCTION	MAINTENANCE
$1,500,000	Urban Renewal: 87% Voluntary Assessment: 13%	Private: 64% City: 36%

NAME	ADDRESS	PHONE
Thomas Tullock Department of Community Renewal	321 W. State St. Rockford, IL 61101	(815) 987-5690

Baltimore, Md.
Old Town Mall, 1976
905,759

Baltimore's Old Town Mall is the heart of one of the city's neighborhood commercial districts. More than $1 million has been invested by merchants along the mall's two blocks in an effort to rehabilitate stores. Formerly vacant commercial establishments are now occupied, and the mall has become a focal point for community activities. The street has been repaved in brick, and landscaping and new lighting fixtures have been installed. There are several fountains, a stage, and facilities for neighborhood entertainment.

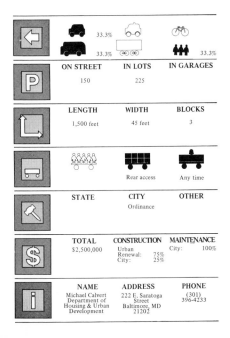

	33.3%		
	33.3%		33.3%
	ON STREET	IN LOTS	IN GARAGES
	150	225	

	LENGTH	WIDTH	BLOCKS
	1,500 feet	45 feet	3

		Rear access	Any time

	STATE	CITY	OTHER
		Ordinance	

	TOTAL	CONSTRUCTION	MAINTENANCE
	$2,500,000	Urban Renewal: 75% City: 25%	City: 100%

	NAME	ADDRESS	PHONE
	Michael Calvert Department of Housing & Urban Development	222 E. Saratoga Street Baltimore, MD 21202	(301) 396-4233

Photography Credits

All photographs and drawings are the property of the Institute for Environmental Action, Inc., with the exception of the following that are identified by page number:

Cover: The City of Essen, Germany.

11: B. Tobey; © 1975, The *New Yorker* Magazine, Inc.

16, right: Swedish Information Center.

17, top: Van Ginkel Associates, Montreal, Canada.

19: Danish Information Office.

23: Renato Bazzoni, Milan, Italy.

24: Renato Bazzoni, Milan, Italy.

26: Rockefeller Center, Inc., New York.

38: OLMD, Office of Lower Manhattan Development, New York.

46–47: The City of Norwich, England.

51, right, middle: "Group M," Vienna, Austria.

52, bottom: Vignelli Associates, New York.

55, right/154, left: Monica A. Wolff, New London, Connecticut.

57, right: Swedish Information Service.

61, bottom: Danish Information Office.

64: The City of Rotterdam, Holland.

67, top and bottom/70: Swedish Information Service.

74, top/75: German Information Center.

79/81/82, top: Danish Information Office.

86/87, top: Consulate General of the Netherlands.

91, bottom: Italian Government Travel Office.

93: The City of Bologna, Italy.

94: Italian Cultural Institute.

97, left and right: Atelier d'Urbanisme, Rouen, France.

100/102, top, left and bottom, right/103: The City of Norwich, England.

105, left/106/107: The City of Essen, Germany.

109, top: *Architecture Plus*.

109, bottom: The City of Munich, Germany.

110/112, top and bottom/113, top and bottom: E. Glesmann, Munich, Germany

115, top: Austrian National Tourist Office.

116, top: The City of Vienna, Austria. Drawing by Wolfgang & Traude Windbrechtinger.

116, bottom/117, middle: Austrian National Tourist Office.

117, bottom: The City of Vienna, Austria.

124: Downtown Kalamazoo Association, Kalamazoo, Michigan.

126, bottom: ELS associates.

130/133, top, left: Downtown Council of Minneapolis, Minnesota.

135: Cedar-Riverside Associates, Inc.

137: The City of Sacramento, California.

142, left: *Architecture Plus*.

162/166: Canada National Capital Commission, Ottawa, Canada.

165, top: The City of Ottawa, Canada.

Notes

Chapter 1: Traffic Management

1. Boris S. Pushkarev and Jeffrey M. Zupan, *Urban Space for Pedestrians* (Cambridge, Mass.: MIT Press, 1975), p. 133.

2. Emanuel Berk et al., *Downtown Improvement Manual* (Springfield, Ill.: Office of Research and Planning, 1975).

Chapter 2: Economic Revitalization

1. Emanuel Berk et al., *Downtown Improvement Manual* (Springfield, Ill.: Office of Research and Planning, 1975), chap. 21, p. 3.

2. Ibid.

3. Greater London Council, *Pedestrian Streets* (London: Greater London Council, 1973).

Chapter 3: Environmental Improvement

1. *New York City Metropolitan Area Air Quality Implementation Plan Transportation Controls* (New York: New York State Department of Environmental Conservation, 1973), chap. 1, p. 2.

2. Ibid., Chap. 7, p. 26.

3. Kai Lemberg, "Copenhagen," in *Streets for People* (Paris: OECD, 1974).

4. A. A. Wood, *The Creation of a Foot Street* (Norwich: Norwich Corporation, 1969).

Chapter 4: Social Benefits

1. Boris S. Pushkarev with Jeffrey M. Zupan, *Urban Space for Pedestrians* (Cambridge, Mass.: MIT Press, 1974), p. 60.

2. Jörg Kühnemann and Robert Witherspoon, *Streets for People* (Paris: OECD, 1974).

3. Kai Lemberg, "Copenhagen," in *Streets for People* (Paris: OECD, 1974).

Chapter 6: Legislation and Finance

1. Legal controls regulate private development by establishing land use patterns for particular urban areas. Methods such as zoning and subdivision controls are based on the role of government in protecting the welfare and amenities of the citizens it serves. Legal devices and their applications vary from country to country, and their degree of success in providing public control over development patterns has been mixed.

2. City of New York, *New Life for Plazas* (New York: City Planning Commission, 1975).

3. This new method of financing has been recently introduced in the state of Illinois through efforts of the village of Oak Park, which created a special tax district in its downtown. Such a tax district can either pay for mall construction directly or can retire bonds sold to cover construction and maintenance costs. The planning and administration of Oak Park's mall has been financed out of general village revenues while the construction cost and some parking improvements have been met through general obligation bonds sold to Chicago-area banks. These bonds will be retired through a special service tax levied in the project area. For additional reference, see Arthur C. Thorpe, "A New Approach to Financing of Public Improvements," *Illinois Municipal Review*, January 1974.

4. Of the 75 cities contacted, more than 40 demonstrated a strong interest in the Auto Restricted Zone Project. The cities finally selected for the demonstration project were Boston, Massachusetts; Burlington, Vermont; Memphis, Tennessee; Providence, Rhode Island; and Tucson, Arizona. American cities wishing to implement auto-restricted zones can apply for matching funds from the Urban Mass Transit Administration's operating and capital assistance program, as well as from the Federal Highway Administration's urban systems program.

Chapter 7: Designing Public Spaces

1. Jan Gehl, "Mannesker til Fods," *Arkitekten*, no. 20, 1968.

2. Ibid. Individuals on the street walked faster than groups. Fastest among single walkers were men (record: 48 sec/100 m), followed by teenagers and women. The slowest walkers were found to be patroling police officers (137 sec/100 m average).

3. Ibid. When the temperature reached 16–17° C, all available seats were occupied. These figures apply to seats not receiving sunshine. Seats in the sun were used even when the temperature was around zero and there was no wind.

4. Edward T. Hall, *The Hidden Dimension* (Garden City, N.Y.: Doubleday & Co., Inc., 1966).

Chapter 8: Managing Implementation

1. *Downtown Malls: Feasibility and Development* (New York: Downtown Research and Development Center, 1974).

Chapter 9: Stockholm

1. Edward H. Homes, *Report to the International Road Federation* (Washington, D.C., 1972).

2. Department of Planning and Building Control, *Traffic Planning in Stockholm* (Stockholm, 1972).

3. In addition, two north-to-south and east-to-west roads tangential to the central business district are planned as part of this traffic scheme.

4. People are entitled to housing on the basis of family size, mix, and condition of their present residence. As new housing is put on the market, it is offered to the highest person on the waiting list. If the location is unsuitable, he or she can refuse it without penalty and remain in the same place on the waiting list.

5. The policy on redistribution of population seems to have succeeded outside Stockholm because the severe housing shortages during the 1950s and 1960s no longer exist. Vacancy rates in a city like Gothenburg, the second largest in Sweden,

are as high as 40 percent in some areas.

6. The Greater Stockholm City Council initiated a land acquisition policy more than 70 years ago, and some of the land being developed today was acquired as early as 1912. The council also owns the mass transportation system.

Chapter 10: Cologne

1. Cologne's prewar population of 768,000 was reduced to 489,000 by 1945 after 262 air raids. Once 239,000 people inhabited the inner city before the war, but today only 86,000 people live in the reconstructed district.

2. The inner road is 1 mile / 1.6 kilometers, the middle ring is 1.8 miles / 2.9 kilometers and the outer ring is 2.5 miles / 4 kilometers from the center of Cologne. Radial roads converging on Cologne tie into the national *autobahn* or highway, which, at that point, is part of the outer ring. From the outer road, traffic filters through the middle and inner rings into the central business district.

3. Deliveries for the stores on both streets are made at the rear buildings. Cäcilienstrasse serves the Schildergasse, and Burgerstrasse plays the same role for Hohe Strasse. Delivery trucks are permitted on Schildergasse and Hohe Strasse between 5 and 10 A.M. Emergency vehicles are permitted at any time.

Chapter 12: Amsterdam

1. Five thousand dwellings were destroyed in the war, and new construction has been very slow since it takes 2 years to create land on which to construct housing. The housing shortage became more acute because of the drop in the occupancy rate from 3.4 to below 3 people per unit due to changes in the family structure.

2. The Compulsory Purchase Act, which dates back to 1851, allows Dutch municipalities to expropriate land needed for approved new land use. Expropriated land value is computed by subtracting the cost of soil preparation from the land's value once it has been developed. Though compulsory purchase can be contested in court, as a rule this is done only in relationship to the amount of indemnity offered by the municipality. The city administration of Amsterdam is equipped with an excellent tool for renewal, but how it can be used for urban conservation and restoration remains an open question.

3. Owners can be subsidized for up to 40 percent of the restoration costs. However, a weak point in the legislation is that owners cannot be forced to restore or maintain their property, so that after a few years of neglect, many buildings are demolished in the interest of public safety. So far, over 200 buildings were restored in Amsterdam during 1973. But even with a city budget of f10,025,000 ($3,712,962) for 1974, it will take 35 years to restore all the buildings in Amsterdam at the 1973 rate.

4. Between 1957 and 1965, the number of cars in Amsterdam increased from 53,000 to 131,000. Though traffic restrictions have been imposed, provision of alternate means of transportation remains incomplete.

Chapter 13: Bologna

1. During the 12th and 13th centuries, thousands of students came to study Roman law under celebrated scholars. At that time, the university did not have its own buildings, and lectures were given in halls, monasteries, and convents throughout the city. Today, the university remains a major attraction of the city. It had a student population of 35,000 in 1970.

2. Today, Bologna has 500,000 inhabitants, and the city administration plans for an optimum population of 600,000. Eighty-nine thousand people live in the historic center, which covers some 1,125 acres; some 40,000 people work there.

Chapter 14: Rouen

1. In the 1960s the economic capacity and population of the lower Seine region were expected to double by the end of the century. Moreover, electrification of the Paris–Le Havre rail line and completion of the A-13 superhighway put Rouen within 1 hour of Paris. These factors caused the city planners and administrators to fear that the city would be reduced to a suburb of the French capital.

2. The city planners decided to move the wholesale and industrial functions of Rouen to the Saint-Sever district on the left bank of the Seine where the new government headquarters and civic center were being constructed. Converting the center from commercial to business activities drew strong opposition. Moreover, merchants in the central area were suspicious of the proposed major changes in the city.

3. Engineers, architects, and town planners traveled to Sweden and Great Britain to visit new shopping centers which were designed around an inner pedestrian concourse. They became convinced that they must not only prohibit vehicles from the central district, but also eliminate sidewalks.

4. Most of the merchants approved of the parking policy and were enthusiastic about installing parking meters, but they remained unconvinced about creation of a pedestrian street.

5. Police, fire, and ambulance vehicles can still circulate during emergencies. Store deliveries are permitted between 6 and 11 A.M.

6. Future plans call for an additional 10,000 feet / 3 kilometers of pedestrian streets on the left bank. If the pedestrian system is extended to the left bank, a similar hierarchy of traffic patterns and types of transportation will be used. In addition, there will have to be connectors from the highways

leading into the central area and adequate parking facilities created near pedestrian streets.

Chapter 15: Norwich

1. Since 1900, the city's population has remained relatively stable, increasing about 5 percent per year. In 1971, Norwich had a population of 170,000. However, it serves as the economic and commercial center for a region containing 350,000. Of the 98,000 people who work in Norwich, 38,000 do so in the central area. Its major industries are footwear, building construction, food and drink processing, engineering, printing, retailing, banking, and insurance.

2. Police and other emergency vehicles as well as service trucks and hearses are allowed to enter the street.

3. Dove Street is only partially closed to allow for delivery to the local brewery.

4. In 1968, the British Parliament empowered municipalities to close streets to vehicular traffic under the Town and Country Planning and Transportation Acts. The London Street experiment in Norwich was, without doubt, influential in pushing the legislation through Parliament.

Chapter 16: Essen

1. Service and deliveries to the shops and office buildings on Limbecker and Kettwiger are handled from parallel streets. Where rear servicing is impossible, deliveries are permitted on streets between 7 P.M. and 10 A.M.

2. Presently, there are plans to introduce pedestrian streets into nearby Borbeck and Steels, as well as convert existing shopping streets in the Ruttenschild, Holsterhausen, Heisinger, and Kuferdreh districts of Essen.

Chapter 17: Munich

1. The population increase, due in large part to foreign workers, has slackened recently because of the European recession. However, Munich still draws on the surrounding region's 1,800,000 people as well as tourists to maintain its strong economy.

2. Completed in 1965, the study stressed that Kaufingerstrasse and Neuhauserstrasse, as well as Wein and Theatinerstrasse, were mainly dependent on pedestrian customers who were attracted to the high concentration of shops in the area. Most cars in the area were those of commuters, not shoppers, and they presented a hazard to pedestrians, a fact which was emphasized in the report.

3. Before the mall was created, about 72,000 people used Kaufingerstrasse and Neuhauserstrasse between 7 A.M. and 7 P.M. daily. After conversion to a pedestrian mall, the number of people in the same time period jumped to 120,000.

4. Ministries at the federal level can and will

give only indirect support through existing legislation. However, within the framework of federal support for public housing programs and urban renewal projects, car-free zones can be given a greater amount of consideration. For instance, in Munich's Perla housing development, a pedestrian mall was created for the community's 80,000 residents.

5. Emergency vehicles are allowed in the mall areas without special permission. However, deliveries are permitted in the Frauenplatz only between 10:30 P.M. and 12:45 A.M. throughout the week. Delivery trucks must maintain pedestrian speed while in the mall and cannot make U-turns. Some of the major department stores are served by delivery facilities that can be entered from new underground garages.

6. Some 10 miles/16 kilometers of the subway or U-Bahn were completed in time for the 1972 Olympic Games. Of the remaining 46.3 miles/74 kilometers in the system, 25/40 are expected to be complete by 1990. The S-Bahn, a 2.6-mile/4.1-kilometer subway connection to the federal railroad lines, links the new city subway with 430 miles/688 kilometers of municipal surface rail lines. Timetables for the subway and surface lines are coordinated; and a unified ticketing system is used throughout Munich and the surrounding region.

Chapter 18: Vienna

1. Despite the decline in population and wealth from the Imperial era, Vienna employs 800,000 people, and more than 130,000 of them work in the inner city defined by the Ringstrasse. In addition, about 80,000 people visit the city daily, which gives the inner city a population of 235,000 people on any given day.

Chapter 19: Kalamazoo

1. A 45-foot/14-meter deep excavation right under the Old Capitol now holds the two-story subterranean State Historic Library and a bilevel 450-car garage.

Chapter 21: Minneapolis

1. The origin of shoppers was about 15 percent regional, 20 percent metropolitan, 30 percent walk-in daytime population, and 35 percent neighborhood.

2. The success of Nicollet Mall is largely due to the collaboration among City Planning Director Larry Irvin, planners Barton-Aschman Associates, and Lawrence Halprin Associates, which was responsible for the mall's landscape design.

3. "New Street Scene," *Architectural Forum*, January–February 1969.

4. The city of Minneapolis will sell general obligation bonds to acquire existing properties within the district, relocate the present occupants, demolish existing structures, and administer the project.

5. Minneapolis already has one residential project that is fully developed. Cedar-Riverside, the first HUD-designated "new town in town," rises only a dozen blocks east of downtown Minneapolis, close to the University of Minnesota. Initiated in 1968 as a mixed-income development, Cedar-Riverside covers 340 acres/136 hectares, 240 acres/96 hectares of which are education and medical institutions, a low-rent senior citizen housing complex, and natural riverfront parkland. The remainder of the area has been left for private housing and commercial development, half of which is available for people of low, as well as moderate, incomes.

Chapter 22: Sacramento

1. The city raised the ground level, retaining walls were built, and the first floors became basements. The sidewalks existing before the mall became slabs stretching from the building to the old retaining walls. A considerable amount of money was spent repairing structural systems along the mall.

Chapter 23: Fresno

1. From correspondence with the authors.

Chapter 24: Pomona

1. The two shopping centers are the Pomona Valley Center, 1½ miles/2.4 kilometers from downtown, and the Eastland Shopping Center, 8 miles/13 kilometers away.

2. While Pomona planned its traffic-free street, it also improved downtown parking. When the mall was completed, there were 1,154 public off-street parking places available in 16 lots. In the immediate vicinity of the mall the number of spaces available was close to 1,000. By 1964, the figure of public off-street parking had doubled, with a total of 2,211 spaces in 21 lots, and the number reached 3,326 spaces by the end of 1967. Most of the parking spaces were located near the four central blocks of Second Street.

3. By August 1966, there were 90 businesses established along the mall, doing $18 million in gross sales. The Montclair Shopping Center, that same year, had 25 stores doing a sales volume of $17 million. The sales per square foot of floor area along the mall were $30. The sales per square foot of floor area in the shopping center were $76. Since then, the situation on the mall has continued to decline.

4. As deserted as Pomona's mall appears, there has recently been a slight gain in retail sales, although apparently not enough to stem the tide of desertion. Taxable retail sales in Pomona increased 68 percent from 1962 to 1971, compared with a composite growth rate of 85 percent for all areas in the vicinity.

5. The city of Pomona, under direction of the local Community Redevelopment Agency, hired the architectural firm of Lawrence Halprin & Associates to design a new plan for the mall area.

Chapter 27: Ottawa

1. Bank Street, one of the older major shopping streets in central Ottawa, is being redesigned to reduce traffic and improve pedestrian amenities. The width of the right-of-way has been reduced to one lane in each direction; sidewalks have been widened and provided with new lighting, furniture, and plantings. The next phase of improvements includes installation of a sidewalk canopy and modernization of storefronts along five blocks of the street's length.

Selected Bibliography

General Readings

Ardrey, R. *The Territorial Imperative.* New York: Atheneum, 1966.

Brambilla, Roberto, ed. *More Streets for People.* New York: Italian Art & Landscape Foundation, 1973.

Breines, Simon, and William J. Dean. *The Pedestrian Revolution: Streets without Cars.* New York: Vintage Books, 1975.

Caldwell, William A., ed. *How to Save Urban America.* New York: Regional Plan Association, 1973.

Churchill, Henry S. *The City Is the People.* New York: Reynal & Hitchcock, 1945.

Gans, Herbert. *People and Plans.* Cambridge, Mass.: MIT Press, 1970.

———. *The Urban Villagers.* New York: The Free Press, 1962.

Glazer, Nathan, and Daniel P. Moynihan. *Beyond the Melting Pot.* Cambridge, Mass.: MIT Press, 1963.

Gruen, Victor. *The Heart of Our Cities.* London: Thames & Hudson, 1965.

Hall, E. T. *The Hidden Dimension.* New York: Doubleday & Company, 1966.

Jacobs, Jane. *The Death and Life of Great American Cities.* New York: Random House, 1961.

Lynch, Kevin. *The Image of the City.* Cambridge, Mass.: M.I.T. Press, 1960.

Ministry of Transport. *Traffic in Towns.* London: Her Majesty's Stationery Office, 1965.

Mumford, Lewis. *The City in History.* New York: Harcourt, Brace, & World, 1961; Harbinger Book, 1961.

———. *The Highway and the City.* New York: Harcourt, Brace & World, 1958.

Napier, John. "The Antiquity of Human Walking. *Scientific American,* April 1967.

Robertson, Jaquelin T. "Rediscovering the Street." *Architectural Forum,* November 1973.

Rorig, Frits. *The Medieval Town.* Berkeley: University of California Press, 1967.

Rothschild, Emma. *Paradise Lost: The Decline of the Auto-Industrial Age.* New York: Random House, 1973.

Rudofsky, Bernard. *Streets for People: A Primer for Americans.* Garden City, N.Y.: Doubleday & Company, 1969.

Strunsky, Simeon. *No Mean City.* New York: Dutton, 1944.

Sussman, Aaron, and Ruth Goode. *The Magic of Walking.* New York: Simon & Schuster, 1967.

Wilson, James Q., ed. *Urban Renewal: The Record and the Controversy.* Cambridge, Mass.: MIT Press, 1966.

Traffic Managment

Benepe, B. "The Pedestrian in the City." *Traffic Quarterly* 19, no. 1 (January 1965).

Blachuicki, H., and E. Browne. "Over-Under-: A Survey of Problems of Pedestrian-Vehicle Segregation." *Architectural Review,* May 1961.

Carstens, R. L., and S. L. Ring. "Pedestrian Capacities of Shelter Entrances." *Traffic Engineering,* December 1970.

Greater London Council. *Pedestrian Streets.* London: Greater London Council, 1973.

Hankin, B. D., and R. A. Wright. "Passenger Flow in Subways." *Operation Research Quarterly* (Great Britain), 1958.

Hoel, L. A. "Pedestrian Travel Rates in Central Business Districts," *Traffic Engineering,* January 1968.

Lautso, Kari and Peutti Murola. "A Study of Pedestrian Traffic in Helsinki," in *Traffic Engineering and Control.* Helsinki, 1974.

Navin, P. D., and R. J. Wheeler. "Pedestrian Flow Characteristics." *Traffic Engineering,* June 1969.

Older, S. J. "Movement of Pedestrians on Footways in Shopping Streets." Road Research Laboratory, Ministry of Transport, Traffic Engineering and Control, August 1968.

"Research on Road Traffic." Road Research Laboratory, Her Majesty's Stationery Office, 1965.

Rispoli, Caniglia. *Spazio Pubblico per la Città: Problemi Mobilità Pedonale. Napoli,* 1970.

World Bank Sector Policy Paper. *Urban Transport.* Washington: World Bank, May 1975.

Economics

Adde, Leo. *Nine Cities: The Anatomy of Downtown Renewal.* Washington, D.C.: Urban Land Institute, 1969.

Group on the Urban Environment. *Low-Cost Improvement of the Outdoor Environment of Urban Areas.* Paris: OECD, 1976.

Gruen, Victor, and Larry Smith. *Shopping Towns U.S.A.* New York: Reinhold Publishing Corporation, 1960.

Jacobs, Jane. *The Economy of Cities.* New York: Random House, 1970.

Tafuri, Manfredo. *La Città Americana.* Bari: Laterza, 1973.

Environment

Appleyard, D., and M. Lintell. "Environmental Quality of City Streets." Berkeley: Center of Planning and Development Research, University of California at Berkeley, Working Paper no. 142, December 1970.

Citizen's Policy Guide to Environmental Priorities for New York City, 1974–1984: An Interim Report. New York: Council on the Environment of New York City, 1973.

Dober, Richard P. *Environmental Design.* New York: Van Nostrand Reinhold Co., 1969.

Haskell, Douglas. "Unity and Harmony at Rockefeller Center." *Architectural Forum,* January-February, 1966.

Insall, Donald. *The Care of Old Buildings Today: A Practical Guide.* New York: Whitney Library of Design, 1974.

Moore, G., ed. "Emerging Methods in Environmental Design and Planning: Proceedings International Conference." Cambridge, Mass.: MIT Press, June 1968.

New York City Metropolitan Area Air Quality Implementation Plan Transportation Controls. New York: New York State Department of Environmental Conservation, 1973.

New York City Streets: A Guide to Making Your Block More Livable. New York: The Council on the Environment of New York City, 1973.

Robinette, Gary O. *Plants, People and Environmental Quality,* Washington, D.C.: U.S. Government Printing Office, 1972.

Strauss, Anselm L. *Images of the American City.* New York: Free Press of Glencoe, 1961.

Tandy, Cliff. *Handbook of Urban Landscape.* London: The Architectural Press, 1972.

Ziegler, Arthur P., Jr. *Historic Preservation in Inner City Areas: A Manual of Practice.* Pittsburgh: Allegheny Press, 1971.

Pedestrian Safety and Behavior

Bekker, M. G. *Theory of Land Locomotion.* Ann Arbor, Mich.: University of Michigan Press, 1956.

Biehl, B. M. *Pedestrian Safety.* Paris: OECD. 1970.

Broer, M. R. *Efficiency of Human Movements.* 2nd ed. New York: W. B. Saunders Company, 1966, pp. 107–141.

Cavagna, G. A., et al. "Mechanics of Walking." *Journal of Applied Physiology* 21, no. 1 (1966), pp. 271–278.

Freedman, Jonathan L. *Crowding and Behavior.* New York: Viking Press, 1975.

Horowitz, M. S., et al. "The Body Buffer Zone: An Exploration of Personal Space," *Archives General Psychiatry* 11 (1964), pp. 651–656.

Lommer, Robert. *Personal Space: The Behavioral Basis of Design.* Englewood Cliffs, N.J.: Prentice-Hall, 1969.

"Manual on Pedestrian Safety." Washington, D.C.: American Automobile Association, 1964.

Newman, Oscar. *Defensible Space: Crime Prevention through Urban Design.* New York: Macmillan Company, 1972.

"Pedestrians." Highway Users Foundation for Safety and Mobility, 1970.

"Pedestrian Safety," Road Research Laboratory, October 1969.

Williams, M., and H. Lissner. *Biomechanics of Human Motion.* New York: W. B. Saunders Company, 1926.

Legal Aspects

Adrian, Charles R. *Governing Urban America.* New York: McGraw-Hill Book Company, 1961.

Barnett, Jonathan. *Urban Design as Public Policy.* New York: Architectural Record Books, 1974.

"Examples of Local and State Financing of Property Rehabilitation." *Community Planning and Development Guide No. 1.* Washington, D.C.: U.S. Department of Housing and Urban Development, 1974.

Executive Office of the President, Office of Management and Budget. *The 1975 Catalogue of Federal Domestic Assistance.* Washington, D.C.: U.S. Government Printing Office, 1975.

Haar, Charles M., ed. *Law & Land, Anglo-American Planning Practice.* Cambridge, Mass.: Harvard University Press, 1964.

The President's Council on Environmental Quality. *5th Annual Report.* Washington, D.C.: U.S. Government Printing Office, 1974.

Searles, Sidney Z. *A Practical Guide to the Legal and Appraisal Aspects of Condemnation.* Philadelphia: American Land Institute, 1970.

Starr, Roger. "Vacant Land Management: A Challenge to New York City." *Fordham Law Review* 29, April 1961.

Urban Land Policies and Land Use Control Measures, vol. 7, *Global Review.* United Nations: Department of Economic and Social Affairs, 1975.

Planning and Design

"Aerial Walkways: Big Plans for the Future." *Business Week,* Dec. 26, 1970.

Alden Self Transit Systems Corp. "Starrcar: System Description and Application Notes."

American Society of Planning Officials. "The Pedestrian Count." Report no. 199, June 1965.

Baerwald, Edward J. *Traffic Engineering Handbook.* Washington, D.C.: Institute of Traffic Engineers, 1965.

Brooks, Mary. "Bonus Provisions in Central City Areas." American Society of Planning Officials.

"Building Standards for the Handicapped, 1965." Supplement no. 7, The National Building Code of Canada.

Caplan, Basil. "New Ways of Moving People." *Mechanical Handling,* September 1968.

Central Council for the Disabled. *Planning for Disabled People in the Urban Environment.* London, 1966.

"City Malls: Fresh Life for Downtown." *U.S. News and World Report,* Jan. 11, 1971.

Design for All Americans: A Report for the National Commission on Architectural Barriers. Washington, D.C.: U.S. Government Printing Office.

"The Development and Demonstration of a Family of Practical Moving-Way." Columbus, Ohio: Transport Systems for Pedestrians, PB 178 255, Battelle Memorial Institute, October 1967.

Drew, D. R. *Traffic Flow Theory and Control.* New York: McGraw-Hill Book Company, 1968.

Ewald, W. R. *Street Graphics.* McLean, Va.: American Society of Landscape Architects Foundation, 1971.

Federal Highway Administration, U.S. Department of Transportation. *A Manual for Planning Pedestrian Facilities.* Washington, D.C.: U.S. Government Printing Office, 1974.

Fruin, John J. "Designing for Pedestrians: A Level-of-Service Concept." Dissertation, Polytechnic Institute of Brooklyn, June 1970.

Garbrecht, Dietrich. "The Binomial Model of Pedestrian Flows: Implications and Experiments." *Traffic Quarterly,* July 1969.

———. "Distributions of Pedestrians in a Rectangular Grid." *Journal of Transport Economics and Policy,* January 1970.

The Goodyear Tire and Rubber Co. *"The Carveyor: Solution to City Traffic Snarls."*

Gusrea, G. "Moving Sidewalks." *Architectural Record,* June 1956.

Hilleary, James. "Buildings for All to Use: The Goal of Barrier—Free Architecture." *AIA Journal,* March 1969.

Illuminating Engineering Society. *Recommended Levels of Illumination.* New York. Report no. RP-15, 1966.

Lessieu, E. "Pedestrian Circulation Systems." Transportation Research Forum.

Malt, Harold L. *Furnishing the City.* New York: McGraw-Hill Book Company, 1970.

Metropolitan Association of Urban Designers and Environmental Planners. *Proceedings of the Seminar on Bicycle / Pedestrian Planning and Design.* New York: American Society of Civil Engineers, 1974.

Moon, I. A., and F. A. Everest. "Time Lapse Cinematography." *Journal of the Society of Motion Picture & Television Engineers* 76, February 1967.

Morris, R. L., and S. F. Zisman. "The Pedestrian, Downtown, and the Planner." *Journal of the American Institute of Planners* 28, no. 37 (August 1962).

Moving in Cities. Boulder, Colorado: Westview Press, 1976.

Murray, M. P., et al. "Comparison of Free and Fast Speed Walking Patterns of Normal Men." *American Journal of Physical Medicine* 45, no. 1, 1966.

Ness, M. D., J. F. Morall, and B. G. Hutchinson. "An Analysis of Central Business District Pedestrian Circulation Patterns." *Highway Research Record,* no. 283.

Noakes, E. H. "Transit for the Handicapped." *Nation's Cities,* March 1967.

The Port of New York Authority. *"Cameras Aloft: Project Sky Count."* Operations Services Department, Operations Standards Division, 1968.

———. *"Staggered Work Hours Project in Lower Manhattan."* Internal report.

Public Street and Highway Safety Lighting Bureau. "Design and Application of Roadway Lighting." New York.

Pushkarev, Boris S., and Joffrey M. Zupan. *Urban Space for Pedestrians.* Cambridge, Mass.: MIT Press, 1975.

Richards, Brian. *New Movement in Cities.* New York: Reinhold, 1966.

Schreiber, T. J. "General Purpose Simulation System / 360 Introductory Concepts and Case Studies." Preliminary edition. Ann Arbor, Mich.: University of Michigan, September 1968.

Stuart, D. G. "Planning for Pedestrians." *Journal of the American Institute of Planners,* January 1968.

"Transportation Needs of the Handicapped: Travel Barriers." Cambridge, Mass.: ABT Associates, Inc., August 1969.

Westphal, Joachim. *Unterdachugen von Fussgaengerbewegungen auf Bahnhoefen mit starkem Nahverkehr.* Hanover, Germany: Technische Universitaet, 1971.

Whyte, William H. "Please, Just a Nice Place to Sit." *More Streets for People.* New York: Italian Art & Landscape Foundation, 1973.

Wood, A. A. *The Creation of a Foot Street.* Norwich, England: Norwich Corporation, 1969.

Index

Edited by Susan Braybrooke and Susan Davis
Designed by James Craig
Set in 9 point Vega by Publishers Graphics, Inc.
Printed by Halliday Lithograph Corp.
Bound by A. Horowitz & Son